ARUM AND KING

ARUM AND KING

SIX DECADES OF BOXING GOLD

Marty Corwin

ROWMAN & LITTLEFIELD
Lanham • Boulder • New York • London

Published by Rowman & Littlefield
An imprint of The Rowman & Littlefield Publishing Group, Inc.
4501 Forbes Boulevard, Suite 200, Lanham, Maryland 20706
www.rowman.com

86-90 Paul Street, London EC2A 4NE, United Kingdom

British Library Cataloguing in Publication Information Available

Library of Congress Cataloging-in-Publication Data

Names: Corwin, Marty, 1958– author.
Title: Arum and King : six decades of boxing gold / Marty Corwin.
Description: Lanham, Maryland : Rowman & Littlefield, 2025. | Includes
   bibliographical references and index. | Summary: "Arum and King provides a
   unique, behind-the-scenes look at the most iconic boxing promoters in the last 100
   years-two very different men with very different backgrounds who have promoted
   such notable superstars as Ali, De la Hoya, Pacquiao, Mayweather, Tyson, and
   Fury"—Provided by publisher.
Identifiers: LCCN 2024023963 (print) | LCCN 2024023964 (ebook) | ISBN
   9781538184127 (cloth) | ISBN 9781538184134 (epub)
Subjects: LCSH: Arum, Bob, 1931– | King, Don, 1931– | Boxing—United States—
   History—20th century. | Television broadcasting of sports—History—20th century.
   | Matchmakers (Boxing)—United States—Biography.
Classification: LCC GV1132.A775 C67 2025 (print) | LCC GV1132.A775 (ebook) |
   DDC 796.830973—dc23/eng/20240730
LC record available at https://lccn.loc.gov/2024023963
LC ebook record available at https://lccn.loc.gov/2024023964

CONTENTS

FOREWORD

"**M**arty, you are in for the ride of your life!"
I never said those words aloud to him, but that's what I was thinking as we sat down, just the two of us, for dinner in Mexico City. The year was 1994, and Marty had just been named Don King's executive producer for television services. This dinner would be the first of many I would share with Marty: a young, gregarious, hardworking television producer who would prove, over the years, to be a master storyteller. This talent held him in good stead—and me, highly entertained—as Marty would be privy to the inner sanctums of Don King. A decade later, Marty would take the same position for Don's rival, Bob Arum, thus becoming a department head for the two most enigmatic, most powerful, most intriguing men in boxing. He is, as far as I know, the only person to bridge the divide between these two archenemies.

Marty's tenure with these promoters came during what I consider to be a golden age of boxing. It was a time that featured many of the most legendary names of the sport, names such as Tyson, Holyfield, Chávez, De La Hoya, Pacquaio, Mayweather, and so many others. It was also a time when great fighters fought great fighters, especially if the money was right. But no matter how breathtaking, or how savage, or how memorable the bouts in the ring may have been, they pale in comparison to the behind-the-scenes maneuvering of arguably the two greatest promoters in all of sports.

To be a successful boxing promoter, much less a great one, you must have the promotional instincts of a P. T. Barnum and the political maneuverings of Machiavelli. And nobody did it better than these two hardworking, brilliant polar opposites: Don King, a self-taught, former numbers runner from the streets

Lennox Lewis after his November 1999 win over Holyfield. He lost the WBA title right after this picture was taken. Lennox said it was the only picture he ever saw holding them all. Marty Corwin

of Cleveland; and Bob Arum, an accomplished Harvard-trained lawyer from New York City. But after battling for boxing supremacy for the past half century, their careers are coming to a close. So, what happened behind the scenes? What did the cameras not catch? How epic were the battles between King and Arum? What secret deals were made? Marty may be the only one who knows the whole story from both sides.

—Jimmy Lennon Jr.

Jimmy Lennon Jr. is boxing's most prominent ring announcer. He has worked extensively with a host of promoters including Don King and Bob Arum and, for the past five decades, has been the voice of Showtime Championship Boxing. He was inducted into the International Boxing Hall of Fame in 2013.

INTRODUCTION
Arum And King

I'm a television producer and director who has, for the past 30+ years, specialized in producing boxing telecasts, words I NEVER expected to say. From five years old to my junior year in college, I was headed to med school. But, as I always told my kids, you never know what life may throw your way.

The reason I am writing about Bob Arum and Don King, with a little Mike Tyson thrown in, is that I am uniquely qualified to do so. I am the only human who has been a department head for both Don King and Bob Arum. I was also Mike Tyson's producer/director while he fought for Don King, for Showtime after leaving King, and for the shows he promoted as Iron Mike Productions.

I am a producer, director, and production manager with more than forty years in the TV business. After a brief career as a recording studio manager and engineer, I moved into television, specializing in audio. I started as a TV engineer with a first-class FCC license. My audio experience led to a job as a lead audio mixer for *Night Watch* with Charlie Rose and *Face the Nation* with Lesley Stahl at the CBS Washington Bureau before winding up, a fluke is the best way to explain it, in sports production. I produced and directed 110 games a year, for almost ten years, for the Washington Bullets of the NBA, Washington Capitals of the NHL, and Baltimore Orioles of Major League Baseball before winding up in boxing.

I have covered boxing as a television producer and director since 1993 and have learned a great deal from some of the greatest experts in the sport while doing so. My knowledge about boxing, techniques, and the ins and outs of becoming a master fighter, comes mostly from sifting through other people's expertise and deciding what I would accept as true expertise and dismissing

Don King and Marty Corwin at the WBA banquet, 1996. Marty Corwin

what I believed was purely opinion. I have been fortunate enough to spend time with some of the legends of the sport: Manny Pacquiao, Julio César Chávez Sr., Tyson Fury, Mike Tyson, Felix Trinidad, Larry Holmes, George Foreman, Lennox Lewis, Sugar Ray Leonard, Miguel Cotto, Vasiliy Lomachenko, Floyd Mayweather, Roberto Duran, and hundreds of others.

My expertise is live sports television production—specifically, currently, covering boxing for broadcast. I've worked with many great sports producers and directors. I've seen pure boxing coverage for the dedicated and knowledgeable fan, and I've seen circus productions designed to attract viewers with production frills where boxing was almost secondary.

HBO's, Showtime's, and ESPN's Top Rank boxing are examples of the former. They were dedicated to the best coverage of the sweet science possible. Cedric Kushner's Heavyweight Explosion, although fun to watch, was an example of the latter. We dressed the entire set in purple and had strippers dancing on boxes next to the ring. Currently, circus events such as internet "influencers" fighting non-boxers are modern examples of events making great buckets of money but not the favorites of boxing purists. When a social influencer makes money pretending to be a professional boxer, or when a professional boxer fights an MMA (mixed martial arts) fighter, in my opinion, it diminishes the sport. It gives credence to the conspiracy notion that boxing is dead. You can't poison the patient and then act surprised that he appears to be declining. Several smart people in boxing tell me that because these events attract younger viewers, they are good for the sport, despite the nontraditional nature.

I'm best described as a quiet team player. I try to do my job with as little fuss and friction as possible. I'm never the loud, flashy, aggressive employee or the squeaky wheel to the corporate managers. I try to honestly and transparently give clients the best shows their budget can afford.

My greatest expertise is in getting the biggest bang for the client without padding the bill. I've been doing this for almost forty years, and I'm confident in saying that the most expensive technicians and talent, or the most aggressive salesmen, or the squeakiest wheels, might do very well for a time, but they never have longevity. The promoters I have worked for have never been accused of wasting money on extra staff. Therefore, my job was to wear multiple hats, make people work together on a budget, always keep my word, and deliver what I promise or take responsibility if I don't.

Bob Arum and Don King share a common dislike for bullshit when it comes from others. I share that trait, which makes us three of a kind in at least one regard. I have lasted this long in boxing by keeping my head down and my opinions mostly to myself. Working for promoters rather than the networks has allowed me to stay away from the politics as well. I don't do well in that environment. My years with Viacom, Paramount, and CBS, in my first fifteen years in TV, taught me that I can't swim with sharks without displaying my feelings for all to see. I often got into trouble wearing my emotions on my sleeve.

I've truly enjoyed the experience of meeting many amazing people that my move into boxing has afforded me. Celebrities and political notables have always flocked to the sport. The fighters themselves are always fascinating to me. Unlike the thousands of other athletes I've known, boxers are very different because of the world they perform in. Topping the list for me was the opportunity I had to meet and work with Mike Tyson. Mike Tyson is a truly unique individual, a generally misused label. I covered Mike's fights from Razor Ruddick through the end of his career for Don King and with Showtime after that. When Mike became a promoter, starting Iron Mike Promotions, I was asked to be his producer/director and was privileged to join the team. Mike is, in my opinion, greatly misunderstood, due in no small part to his off-putting nature. He is extremely intelligent and curious about many subjects that would surprise you. He is also one of the greatest boxing historians and expert on past fighters I have ever known.

For nearly eight years, I was a VP, director of TV, for Don King Productions, and for more than twenty-five years I have been the live event line producer, director, production manager, and director of TV production for Bob Arum's Top Rank Boxing. Many people have worked with both men as associates but no one else I'm aware of was a department head for both. I was responsible for live shows and world feeds of live shows when there was another broadcaster for the U.S. domestic show, such as Showtime, HBO, or ESPN. We created every type of show imaginable for worldwide distribution including full boxing shows with no other broadcast partner, weigh-in shows, red carpet shows, shows for foreign markets, pay-per-view events with and without partners, social media feeds, and shows created from other international promoters from Japan, Mexico, England, Australia, and more.

I was unbelievably fortunate to start my boxing career in the top category of boxing. My first events in boxing were pay-per-view events with Julio César Chávez Sr. and Mike Tyson. The Colonel, Bob Sheridan, my first boxing play-by-play announcer, remarked to me that I had no idea how lucky I was to start this way. It was like becoming a new baseball director whose first game was in the World Series. I would, I hasten to add, have my share of "A league" events in lesser venues later in the story.

This book attempts to give facts, tell stories, and offer a glimpse behind the scenes of boxing promotion. Very few people know what it takes, or what it looks like behind the scenes, to make a live sports television production. It's a smaller community than you'd think at the top level. The first time someone steps into a control room or mobile production truck, he is mesmerized by the wall of monitors revealing the number of cameras, switcher configurations, and video choices the director has at his disposal. Couple that with the audio choices, graphics elements, special effects, announcer direction, stage managing, event timing, and translation requirements, and the scope of the production becomes massive. Watching the single monitor at home and listening to the completed audio track while enjoying the graphics and animations, you never imagine so much is going on behind the scenes. After a while it becomes much less daunting as you become adept at knowing where to focus your attention rather than looking everywhere at once. I will pull back the curtain from this process and tell some amusing stories about what can, and often does, go wrong.

This is not intended to be a tell-all book unmasking scandals and taking down the careers of its subjects. I know about most of the controversies these three remarkable men, Mike Tyson, Don King, and Bob Arum, have been associated with. I talk about them as factually as I can throughout the book. I don't ignore or whitewash the details. My purpose, however, is not to focus on them but instead to highlight the accomplishments of the men. If what they did was easy, everybody would be trying to be a promoter and succeeding. Few try, and fewer succeed. It is my opinion that what they accomplished was unbelievably difficult and these men should be recognized for it. My favorite example of this comes in a series of comments made by comedian Bill Burr. He said, and I paraphrase here, while talking about people criticizing Arnold Schwarzenegger after his soiree with the housekeeper, "Really, he's not a great man anymore? How many of you could move to another country, learn the language, become a rich athlete, then become a huge movie star, then marry into that country's political royal family, and then become governor of the state with the biggest budget?"

I decided to include stories throughout the book of my travels around the world for Bob Arum, Don King, and Mike Tyson in the company of my longtime announcer and best friend, Colonel Bob Sheridan. The Colonel, as everyone calls him, was a former scholarship baseball player for the University of Miami, a class A player for the Orioles farm system, a pro bull rider, a cattle rancher in Ireland, and yes, a colonel in the Ancient and Honorable Artillery Company of Massachusetts, the oldest military organization in the United States and the third oldest in the world. The Colonel and I, along with a remarkable genius, Pancho Limon, our 7-foot tall, 480-pound, Mexican friend, had a few adult beverages together along the way and have some interesting, funny, and flat-out ridiculous stories you might enjoy hearing. The Colonel and Pancho are no longer with us. It's a miracle that the Colonel lived as long as he did, after the life he led, with little regard for his personal health and safety.

Everything in this book is as true as my memory and notes allow. I apologize in advance for any unintentional memory lapses or regrettable omissions.

BOXING—HERE, THERE, AND EVERYWHERE

First, a little boxing history . . .

The first boxing we know about occurred in the third millennium BC depicted in Sumerian relief drawings and carving.[1] We don't know the promoters' names, but I am sure there was one there. Ancient Romans boxed with leather thongs around their fists. They boxed in circles drawn into the sand on the amphitheater floor. This might be where the concept of the ring was started. My wife's favorite boxing joke is about boxing being all about accessories: rings, belts, trunks, and purses.

In the sixteenth century in England, bare-knuckle fighting was referred to as prize fighting for the first time. In 1719, James Figg was known as the bare-knuckle boxing champion, in the first known recording of the term boxing. Recently there has been a resurgence of bare-knuckle boxing. The UFC has ginned up an audience that wanted more violence and the illusion of greater danger. I've covered bare-knuckle Muay Thai fighting in Thailand, which is an homage to the origin of the sport.

The first boxing rules, the Broughton rules, were introduced by Jack Broughton in 1743. There was no hitting a man who was down; and if a man was down for thirty seconds, the fight was over. In 1867, the Marquess of Queensberry rules were adopted. Rings were twenty-four feet or smaller. Gloves of "fair size" were required. Fights were divided into three-minute rounds with one minute rest intervals. The "ten count" was adopted for a downed fighter, which resulted in the match being ended if the fighter couldn't recover. All forms of wrestling were barred, as were kicking, elbowing, or biting. A few years ago, while Don King and I were on a press tour, when asked about MMA being a

Don King with Muhammad Ali and Joe Frazier at the Thrilla in Manila, July 1, 1975.
Marty Corwin

threat to boxing, he said, "I thought we got together a few hundred years ago to make up some rules to stop this shit."

The first known heavyweight championship fight under the Marquess of Queensberry rules was in 1892. The fight matched John L. Sullivan versus "Gentleman" Jim Corbett, and it occurred at the Pelican Club in New Orleans. The first-ever known incident of film censorship occurred in 1897. The censored film showed boxing from Nevada, where it was legal.[23]

There are many levels of boxing events. From amateur fights to pay-per-view quality championships, there are events of every description in between. I describe the different levels of boxing to a boxing newcomer, who knows baseball, as being like baseball's Triple A ball, the Major Leagues, and the All-Star Game. The first level of pro boxing events involves fighters with some midrange level of talent or fighters on their way up hoping for a title shot. This is my AAA league.

The "show," or Major Leagues, is the class of fights where athletes are positioning themselves or competing in title fights. The greatest number of fights on network and high-end premier cable channels include these events. Often there are undercard fights of boxers who are close to fighting for a title and a headline fight that will provide the winner with a belt or lets him keep his championship belt.

The third and highest level of events, which I compared to the All-Star Game, involves pay-per-view quality events, which include elite champions fighting for closely contested championships or unification of multiple belts. Pay-per-view events often include "mandatory" fights, or unification fights, where the two top fighters in a division are required or choose to fight each other because the payday will be huge. Often in these fights the outcome is impossible to predict, even to insiders. And that is very unusual. Most fights have a predictable outcome. Fights aren't fixed anymore because they don't need to be. There is enough money in properly assembling and marketing events to create huge paydays for the parties involved. Even the appearance of a "fixed" fight is, as Robert Duvall as Tom Hagen said in *The Godfather II*, "bad for business."

AAA events happen almost every day, Major League events happen weekly, and All-Star events happen twice or three times a year for a promoter.

The best promoters attract the best fighters and therefore, produce the greatest events. Having an All-Star or pay-per-view quality fighter is mandatory if you want to reach the elite promoter status. The revenue from an AAA event is just enough to pay the bills. The Major League events can be lucrative if all the legs of the shaky card table are there, as I will describe later: a venue deal that is good, a broadcast network that pays its share, fighter purses that are reasonable, and a public that buys the product. But it is the All-Star Events, the pay-per-view events, that tip the needle into the black. At Don King Productions in the Tyson era, the foreign broadcasters who wanted the big events had to also take several lesser events to stay at the table. This made the events between the pay-per-views more economically sound.

On April 10, 1980, Bob Arum began the longest boxing series of its time with ESPN as Frank "The Animal" Fletcher took on and beat Ben Serrano.[4] This series combined the AAA concept, fighters waiting for a title shot, with the Major League concept, championship fights. Future stars got the marketing exposure they needed to move up the ladder. Part of the great success of the series was the ability to market to boxing fans that the show would be seen every week on the same night at the same time. This created an audience of boxing fans that could rely on the show being there so they wouldn't miss it. The series also gave the fighters more exposure on a regular basis, so they get fans behind them as they climb the ranks. This concept was also used very successfully by USA Networks with its Tuesday Night Fights, formerly Friday Night Fights, then Wednesday Night Fights, and then Thursday Night Fights, before settling on Tuesday Nights. The show aired from October 1988 to August 1998. Al Albert, the play-by-play announcer, was teamed up with Angelo Dundee, Randy Gordon, and finally "The Champ" Sean O'Grady as color commentators.

Most boxing fans only get interested in a fight when they know at least one of the combatants. Once they learn something about the fighter, like his personal struggle or family story, they have a connection with the person behind the boxer's name and image, and hopefully, care about the fighter, giving them a vested interest in the event. Tuesday Night Fights, usually sponsored by Budweiser, didn't carry championship bouts, and often came from smaller venues like The Blue Horizon in Philadelphia, the Felt Forum—now the Theater at Madison Square Garden—or Casino Magic in Mississippi. A notable exception was when Vinny Pazienza, a month before breaking his neck in a car accident, captured the WBA (World Boxing Association) junior middleweight title from Gilbert Delé on Tuesday Night Fights on October 1, 1991.

When a boxer develops a win streak, especially with impressive KOs, the fans get behind him like a groupie. This is the same as the followers of a NASCAR driver, winning NBA star, successful pitcher, or football standout. These AAA fights, with a main event that is hopefully a championship, also set the stage for the pay-per-view events that happen a few times a year, with the elite fighters in a much talked-about, must-see-it-live event. The biggest of these pay-per-view events contain two such fighters, and the outcome is a toss-up prior to the first bell. This does not consider "carnival" events such as a top boxer taking on an MMA fighter or big-name fighter in their fifties. These events make a lot of money but are curiosities rather than great fights. When asked if I watch these sideshow fights, I answer that I agree with the former host of the *Sports Machine*, George Michael, a Washington, D.C., sports journalist who wasn't a big hockey fan. About the Stanley Cup Finals, he said, "If it was in my back yard, I'd pull the shades."[5]

I call boxing a true gladiatorial sport because, like gladiators, the fighter knows his life could end, or at least change forever, win or lose. It is hard to fathom the level of fear that must be ignored so that fighters can focus and perform. In other sports, such as football, the player knows he *could* get injured, but he certainly doesn't expect to get injured. A boxer takes continual blows to the head, which might lead to irreparable damage or a life-shortening injury, even if he wins.

On February 25, 1995, Gerald McClellan was winning his fight after nearly taking Nigel Benn out in the first and second rounds when he suffered his life-changing brain injury and never walked or talked the same again. This twenty-seven-year-old knew the risks, put them out of his mind to enter the ring, and suffered a tragic life-changing injury from participating in his chosen sport. That is what being a gladiator is all about.

Boxing is a truly global sport. Although the NFL leads the ratings in the United States, and the Super Bowl has garnered audiences of nearly 115 million viewers (as in 2015 when the Patriots met the Seahawks),[6] boxing has netted as many as one billion viewers because of the international interest. The biggest boxing PPV netted 50 million viewers in the United States alone.[7]

In 1997, Tyson versus Holyfield II was transmitted to 100+ countries. I know that because I produced the world feed and saw the transmission schedule. Millions watched the spectacle. France, England, Japan, Mexico, and Scandinavia had their own TV trucks to enhance the feed with exclusive content. I seated 40+ announcers ringside speaking six languages. And that is just the audience that was legal. Many millions more saw the fight on a "pirated" feed. In the nineties, it was much harder to catch refed, illegal feeds downlinked in one country and fed to another. On a couple of occasions, we caught an announcer from South America sitting in a good audience seat on a cell phone calling the fight. We knew they were adding that audio to an unlicensed feed back home. (Otherwise, if legitimate, the announcer would have been seated in the press section.)

The success boxing has enjoyed, reaching a global audience almost as big as the World Cup for soccer, is entirely due to the work of the promoters. Without a league to advertise and promote the sport, the work of the promoters has elevated the audience to record proportions on big events. When Tyson Fury fought Deontay Wilder for the third time in 2021, the worldwide audience was estimated to be more than five million. This is thanks to the efforts of UK promoter Frank Warren and Bob Arum, who obtained the rights for ESPN in the United States. When Floyd Mayweather fought Manny Pacquiao on May 2, 2015, the fight reported 4.4 million buys in the United States alone.[8] The number of people watching internationally was estimated at nearly a billion viewers in a hundred countries.[9]

The appeal of boxing for the ardent fan is the mastery of style and strategy coupled with athletic talent. Some fans, of course, just enjoy watching the damage one person can do to another in a fighting sport. People can't look away from a traffic accident. But most boxing lovers I speak with talk about styles, matchups, and ring intelligence when describing their favorite fighters.

Promoters, using their telecasts, social media efforts, broadcast partners, promotion and marketing teams, and personal interviews, make an effort to educate the public on the sport of boxing, promote the sport as ambassadors, and increase the public's familiarity with their fighters. When fans get to know a fighter and care about him, empathizing with his story, they are much more likely to seek out his next fight and watch. Overcoming the tremendous number of choices available to potential viewers is one of the hardest tasks of a promoter. Selling the event as one you shouldn't miss live is their best tool.

There are four main styles and two main types of boxers: punchers and boxers.[10] Tyson was a puncher and a "swarmer" known for relentless aggression.

"Sluggers," such as George Foreman and Deontay Wilder, have a devastating punch. An "out-boxer"—Floyd Mayweather and Muhammad Ali—is also known as a pure boxer, outlasting and outscoring his opponent. A "boxer-puncher," such as Manny Pacquiao or Terence Crawford, is great at all the above, thinking constantly in the ring and mounting an excellent defense.

Mike Tyson might have been mostly one dimensional, with power being his primary weapon, but the power in his right arm was too much for anyone for decades, like that of Deontay Wilder. This power made him so feared that many opponents, as I like to joke, lost during the instructions when they saw Mike across the ring from them. In my opinion Evander Holyfield beat Mike twice by standing up to the power and not giving in to the bully. That is much easier to say than to do. In their second fight, Mike bit his ear, like a child throwing a game board, when he realized that he couldn't intimidate Evander this time either and was going to lose again. Top Rank's Manny Pacquiao was an all-around great boxer. He outthought his opponents in the ring and did whatever he had to do to win. If the jab was ineffective, he came at his opponent with shots from angles he couldn't defend against. Terence Crawford adapted inside the ring, during the fight, to the style that would win against this specific fighter on this night.

That ring intelligence is the most valuable asset a boxer can have, according to experts who have shared their experience with me. Watching a match is most exciting if you have well-matched fighters with the ability to adjust their game plan during the fight. The last Ali–Frazier fight was remembered as one of the greatest fights of the century because they were so well matched, not because either fighter was in his prime. One-dimensional fighters can outperform their opponents if their primary weapon is enough, but they often shy away from fighters who aren't a good match for their style.

Boxing is a sport that honors its past. The 150-year history of boxing, since the Marquess of Queensberry rules, has made many fans appreciate the time-honored tradition with few changes since the rules were standardized. I believe the championship limit of twelve rounds, down from fifteen, was a good amendment. Fights such as Norton versus Holmes were fifteen-round marathons that probably caused the fighters too much damage. Holmes won the never-ending slugfest with Norton despite a torn biceps muscle he had injured sparring with Louis Rodriguez the week before the fight.

Promoters have grown the sport remarkably over the years. Boxing has several factors that make it a fan favorite.

Boxing is an "everyman" sport. Anyone, at any size and shape, can compete. You don't have to have a single body type, weight, or height to participate. There is also a strong appeal in rooting for the fighter that comes from your community or reminds you of yourself or your circumstances. Bob Arum and Don King both saw early that true boxing lovers, such as the Latino and Filipino fans, would be the best target audiences. Bob had Oscar De La Hoya, Erik Morales, and Puerto Rican stars such as Miguel Cotto. Don had Salvador Sánchez, Julio César Chávez, and Ricardo López. Eventually Bob added Filipino superstar Manny Pacquiao for the same reason: devoted, loyal, adoring fans.

Boxing is exciting and unpredictable. Boxing matches can be very hard to watch without getting involved in the action. Many events, especially big pay-per-view events, have enough hype and promotion leading up to the event that viewers are fully engaged at the first bell. Boxing is also glorified in film and in games. Numerous films going back to the turn of the twentieth century have immortalized the struggle of fighters with their opponents or life's difficulties as a metaphor for boxing. Video games have always loved the competition of fighting as a digital sport.

It is a global sport with universal appeal. Fighters from every country give their countrymen pride and a rooting interest. Promoters also try to assist the event with their choice of venues. A local fighter draws a larger paid attendance, which makes the event more exciting to viewers on TV due to the energy in the building, exuded by the announcers on site.

The matchmakers, who work for the promoters, generate the most interest in the promoters' fighters with matches that build up their records, protect them as assets, and generate the most excitement with a well-matched pair of combatants. It doesn't help the promoter to have every match for his star be a one-sided walkover. Fans see through that quickly. Boxing also promotes fairness and sportsmanship. With few exceptions, boxers glorify the sense of fair play and sportsmanship by following rules intended to give an opponent a fair chance. You can only fight when both fighters are on their feet. You cannot wrestle, grapple, or hit with an unpadded body part such as a knee or elbow. You cannot hit below the belt, behind the head, or at an opponent's back. Even some of the trash talking that goes on to hype a fight is ultimately turned into a winner's respect for his opponent and a sportsmanlike hug or handshake after the match. There are a few exceptions, such as Deontay Wilder's refusal to shake hands after losing to Tyson Fury.

The number of stars, due to the seventeen weight classes and the international pool of talent, also makes boxing as popular as it is. There are amazing stories and exciting talented boxing stars fighting constantly and new stars coming up all the time—plenty of choices for viewers to latch onto.

Promoters have long known that their broadcast deal was key to their success. Ticket sales and sponsorships alone can't pay the bills. Over the years Don King and Bob Arum have entered into deals with CBS, ABC, NBC, Showtime, HBO, ESPN, FOX, and many others. Selling tickets in a venue has had up-and-down success. Prior to the 1960s when television was not a revenue option, everybody saw live boxing in person. The rise of television caused some to predict the demise of live gates in favor of TV studio fights with only a TV audience.

In 1955, boxing historian Nat Fleischer said, "Within five years title fights will be held in TV studios. The only people on the spot will be the reporters."[11]

That ominous forecast was close to true at the time. The World Boxing Council (WBC) heavyweight title fight on September 28, 1979, between Larry Holmes and Earnie Shavers was witnessed by a live crowd of just forty-eight hundred at Caesars Palace in Las Vegas, a mere trace element compared with the forty-six million who saw it on the ABC network in the United States. The live gate amounted to $700,000, approximately the price that Caesar's Palace had paid for the right to sell tickets (and, of course, link its name to the event for publicity purposes). The real payoff was in the television rights, for which ABC had paid an estimated $4 million.[12]

When Don King finished a long-term deal with HBO, he expected to get a big pay raise with his new contract. It was reported that in October 1990 he walked away from a very large amount of money, eight figures, for a new ten-year deal that included Tyson, which he felt was too low an offer. HBO thought they had King in a "take it or leave it" corner that he wouldn't be able to walk away from. Much more on this later.

Don King also worked with several partners over the years and sought partners who accepted his vision for broadcasting the sport. Don King always saw future possibilities. While in Atlanta for a WBA banquet in 1994, he received an award for promoting forty-seven world championships in one year,[13] a first for a boxing promoter. He and I went to the parent company of a revolutionary broadcaster, where Ted Turner's pictures adorn the lobby, to negotiate a deal for five fights on their network. We entered a conference room, just Don and I, in relatively casual business attire, and faced six suits across the table. The meeting started very cordially. Don was his usual effervescent self, acting like a caricature of himself, something he often did in public. About ten minutes into the meeting, the leader of the other team told Don they had a proposal for the venture that he would be very pleased with. The launch would contain a great deal of free marketing for him, free mentions on their network, and free promotional spots for a month leading up to the first event.

"How much?" Don asked, cutting to his only question.

After some preliminary explanation, the other side of the table finally stated a price.

"What?" Don bellowed. "That isn't going to cut it. I need more for a show." And he threw out a much higher number.

"No, Don, we are proposing that amount for the five shows. Not per show."

"What???" Don said, standing up. "What are you trying to do? Bankrupt me?"

With that, Don walked out of the room with his phone in his ear gesturing for me to stay seated. I had no idea what to do. I was stunned and completely at a loss as I was now left with the six of them, and Don was gone. I was only there to address production questions. I was neither an international salesperson nor a business negotiator of any kind.

That didn't stop them from expressing what they thought of the "Only in America" man: "He's impossible." "He has no idea what he's talking about." "Why are we wasting our time with this nonsense?" "He can't come in here and strong-arm us."

Over the next hour or so, Don came in and out of the room several times. He became even more caricature like, gesturing wildly like an unstable man, making statements about television revenues I was unaware of and wanted to get home to research. The six suits changed their tune completely when Don was in the room, trying to reason with him, explaining how valuable the venture would be for both parties. They assured him that they would sweeten the deal with this or that and kept upping the base offer each time DK returned to the room.

They also continued to speak freely in front of me like I wasn't there when Don bolted from the room, sounding more concerned that the deal was going away, since I'm sure they had been told by superiors to make it happen. At the end of what seemed like hours, Don shook their hands on a verbal deal for a high figure. I was exhausted after the encounter. In the limo leaving the building, I said to Don, "I'm sorry you didn't get what you wanted."

"What the hell are you talking about? I would have taken half of that," he said and belly laughed.

This was a valuable lesson for me on several fronts. First and foremost, it confirmed the brilliant quote from the early twentieth-century Italian diplomat Daniele Varè that diplomacy is the art of letting them have your way. Don couldn't have cared less what they thought of him. His words, actions, and antics were all designed to allow him to pursue his objective: a good deal. He was in control by appearing to be out of control. Brilliant.

The story of boxing being recorded or covered live goes back to 1894 when Thomas Edison filmed a boxing exhibition. The first known radio broadcast of boxing featured Jack Dempsey knocking out Georges Carpentier in Jersey City in July 1921. In August 1933, the first television broadcast of a fight was engineered by the BBC, showcasing Archie Sexton and Lauri Raiteri. In 1939, pay-per-view boxing was born, again in England, when the fight between Eric Boon and Arthur Danahar was shown in movie theaters in London.[14] In June of that same year, the first notable fight was shown on U.S. television between Max Baer and Lou Nova. Max was the father of Max Baer Jr., who played Jethro Bodine on *The Beverly Hillbillies*.

The first reported live pay-per-view boxing event included Joe Louis and Jersey Joe Walcott.[15] The early PPV broadcasts were closed-circuit feeds that fans could view in a venue such as a movie theater. These closed-circuit type pay-per-view events peaked with the Rumble in the Jungle, by Don King in 1974, drawing fifty million buys,[16] and the Muhammad Ali fights of the sixties and seventies. The Thrilla in Manila in 1975 boasted 100 million buys worldwide.

HBO would put its first boxing on pay television on January 22, 1973, with George Foreman fighting Joe Frazier in Kingston, Jamaica. Showtime aired its first boxing match, Marvin Hagler versus John Mugabi, in March 1986. HBO pay-per-view launched in April 1991 with Evander Holyfield versus George Foreman.

Don King and Bob Arum arranged events in the best-suited venues. They promoted shows in many venues both unique and difficult from a broadcast standpoint. We broadcast from some very difficult locations with less-than-ideal local equipment. Although Showtime and HBO demanded that foreign broadcasting sites feel just like home and shipped or traveled in equipment at amazingly high prices, King and Arum never told me money was no object. They also occasionally booked us into venues with events the night before, making setup almost impossible. Tyson versus Mathis occurred at the Spectrum in Philadelphia the day after a Flyers/Rangers game. We couldn't even start the normal three-day setup for a pay-per-event until 4 a.m. on show day.

Every year Bob Arum books us into Madison Square Garden in December, the day after the annual "Jingle Balls" event, which causes the same frantic setup nightmare. Somehow, we always get it done. Perhaps that is our mistake.

Both Don King Productions and Top Rank expected me to furnish a world feed with whatever facilities I could obtain locally at a reasonable cost. I became an expert at this. On a Miguel Cotto fight in Puerto Rico, while Showtime was in a truck they floated to the island from Miami, I was in a minivan from a local public television station. It's a misnomer to say that I was "in" the minivan. This tiny production vehicle was so small I had to stand outside the van with my head only inside directing the show. Todd duBoef, Bob's stepson and now president of Top Rank, saw my entire backside out of the truck and asked, "What the hell are you doing?"

"I'm directing the show; there's no room for me inside the van," I answered.

He erupted in the heartiest laugh I've heard from Todd to this day. He was holding his abdomen laughing as he walked away, presumably to tell someone.

In Tijuana, I worked from an even smaller truck called "La Maquina Deportiva," the Sports Machine. The tailgate opened, and a couple monitors were propped up. I sat behind the truck on a lawn chair and directed the show like I was tailgating. A tarp was put on poles overhead in case it rained, which it always seemed to do. Once while working this way, during the main event, the video seemed to get darker, like a brownout in a big city. The engineer shook his head and said, "The generator, she is bad again." I ran into the venue and asked a familiar face where the generator was. He said, looking worried, "It's in the room in the corner, but please do not go there, sir; it is very bad."

Ignoring the advice, I ran to the corner room. The door was open slightly, and smoke was pouring out. The entire generator was engulfed in flames. "Oh, my God," I yelled.

The engineer saw me and said, "Don't worry, señor, the fight is almost over, and this should burn for another ten or twenty minutes." The man knew his disasters. I ran back to the truck, the fight ended, I told the Colonel to get off the air in thirty seconds, we went to black, and everything in the truck and venue went dark one second later. All hell broke loose; the scene was a disaster, bedlam ensued, but on the air looked good. I decided I would put that on a T-shirt.

At big events, other promotional events were intended to market the main event. Press conferences and weigh-ins were often televised with elaborate shows around them. For pay-per-view events, there were often satellite media tours, where the radio and TV networks around the world could get a slot to ask questions of the fighters and promoters to personalize their coverage.

On one such day, December 7, 1994, the Wednesday of fight week before the Julio César Chávez versus Tony Lopez event in Monterrey, Mexico, there was a problem. Mexico had just changed presidents. The satellite truck we were waiting for was stuck at the border on the U.S. side because the new customs officer was not in place, and all traffic was held up. The drive from the Nuevo Laredo border was two and a half hours, and the satellite media tour was in three. I told the World Boxing Council (WBC) president, José Sulaimán, who was a friend of the president. He made a call, and almost immediately the U.S. military searched for the satellite truck, ordered them to follow the military vehicles to the border, then passed them through to the Mexican Federales on the other side, who escorted them to Monterrey.

The truck pulled up to the hotel fifteen minutes before the event was to start. I had them park in front of the hotel right below the window of the room we were in. We hustled power, video, and audio cables up to the room, tossed them out the window, set up cameras and microphones in record time, and came up on the satellite with a minute to spare. I ran up to Don King, seated next to Julio César Chávez and said breathlessly that we were going to be all right; we'll make it on time, barely. Julio leaned to Don and said, "I don't know why this man is taking credit. It is my magic, Don."

I never liked him as much after that.

With either Don King or Bob Arum's Top Rank, one of the most enjoyable parts of my job was working with the foreign broadcasters. My friends from Teiken, Japan; TV 1000, Scandinavia; BBC, ITV, and Sky, UK; Premiere, SAT1, and RTL, Germany; Telepiu, Italy; Canal+, France; CCTV, China; ABS-CBN, Philippines, and hundreds of others around the world made the job always interesting and enjoyable.

On a Tyson show where we had broadcasters from eight countries show up in Vegas with their own trucks and office trailers to facilitate their unilateral coverage, it was like a mini- Olympic village. One day I walked to the Japanese trailer to make sure they were receiving our signals and were happy with the video and audio. The director from Japan was the only one in their trailer. I asked if he had any problems. He said, "Hai," which I knew meant yes in Japanese. I ran to find the technicians to try to figure out what the problem was. I ran back with the engineer and the Japanese facilitator who spoke English, who asked me what was wrong. I said, "The director told me something was wrong. I asked if he had any problems, and he said, 'Yes.'"

After a long conversation in Japanese between the two, he said, smiling, "No, there is no problem. You spoke in English, which he doesn't understand. He said, 'Hi,' not 'hai.' He tried to speak in English, and you tried to listen in Japanese."

Macau was a great new horizon for Bob Arum and Top Rank boxing. Since the middle of the nineteenth century, Macau had gambling. The Portuguese government, which controlled the region at that time, officially legalized gambling in 1850. When China took over control of Macau and made it an SAR (special administrative region) like Hong Kong, it was the only place in China where gambling was legal. In 2001, when the Chinese ended Stanley Ho's monopoly ownership of Macau gambling, other countries began investing in Macau properties in the hopes that their casinos would be hugely successful.

In 2007, the Venetian Macau opened to great fanfare. A sister to its Las Vegas Sands property, it boasted the largest casino floor in the world. On April 6, 2013, Bob Arum held his first of nine events at the Cotai Arena in the Venetian Macau. The main event included Zou Shiming, three-time Chinese Olympic boxing medalist. With his two gold medals, he was a national hero in China. Hawaiian Brian Viloria was also on this first Top Rank card in China. Other Chinese and Asian stars on the shows included Rex Tso, Ik Yang (or Lian Hui Yang), and Kuok Kun Ng. Manny Pacquiao fought Chris Algieri in Macau at the Venetian on November 12, 2014.

It was a pleasure to work with the Chinese production people from Hong Kong we used for the event. After our first show there in 2013, I saw the HBO people we worked with regularly back in Vegas for another fight. Several were annoyed with me that I hadn't brought them to the event. I said that I couldn't bring anyone due to the budget restrictions and only used camera, audio, utilities, and technicians, as well as using a "fly-pack" production setup brought in from Hong Kong by boat. They were incredulous, saying that they watched the show and were sure I brought in other boxing people from the United States because it looked too good. I said thanks and showed them a picture of me in the middle of three dozen production people from Hong Kong.

Those production people were honored to work on this show for a national hero, Zou Shiming. They dedicated themselves to helping me produce a quality show despite the language barriers. I learned seven words in Cantonese: up, down, right, left, in, out, and stop. Despite being TV professionals, they knew nothing about boxing. Not only weren't they boxing TV people, but mostly they had never seen boxing. It just wasn't something shown there. I spent two days prior to show day of the first event with my wife, Wendy, and stage manager, Tami Cotel, in the ring pretending to box, teaching the camera people and audio people how to cover the sport.

We had a big, elaborate, lighting truss and screen display above the ring. I wanted to give Top Rank their money's worth showing off the beautiful display on the telecast. I met with my Jib operator, a camera on an extended arm used for beauty shots and alternate angles of coverage, who spoke absolutely no English. Through a translator, I tried to explain the wide shots and how I wanted to show off the light truss occasionally. He wasn't really getting it. The translator kept telling me that he thinks I don't want to show the lights, because they learned not to shoot a light because it's not good TV. I said no, I *want* to show the lights because they are very expensive, and I want people to see the big display. After a while he said, "Show me the money," a line from the movie *Jerry McGuire* with Tom Cruise. Yes, I said excited, "Show me the money!"

For the next nine events, whenever I wanted a wide shot that included the truss, I said, "Show me the money" and got perfect pans of the entire truss. Todd duBoef, president of Top Rank, was in the control room once when this happened and asked, "Why the hell did you say that?"

"Because it works."

The people of Macau, the people who worked at the Venetian, and the great technicians from Hong Kong made it a wonderful experience I was very grateful to have had.

To help you understand the multitude of broadcast platforms for boxing, let's look at the types of broadcasts. OTA, or over the air, refers to a broadcaster who sends signals, either VHF, very high frequency, or UHF, ultra-high frequency, from their broadcast transmitter(s) directly to your house to be received by an antenna. This was the only way we received TV signals in our homes from the 1940s to the late '60s with the narrow exception of CATV to rural locations. The VHF television band, occupies frequencies between 54 and 216 MHz and the UHF band, between 470 and 608 MHz. In general, VHF channels are numbered 2 to 13 and UHF channels 14 to 36. Prior to the 1960s, this was all there was in TV transmission. And we had to drag our butts off the couch to change the channel. My kids find that hard to believe, like the fact that cars could run with only an AM radio.

The advent of cable television allowed an unlimited number of channels to be sent to your house on a copper cable from the cable head end to your house. Cable TV dates back to the 1940s when CATV enabled rural consumers to get television, when no other methods existed for them. A large network of repeaters and amplifiers was required to make this happen. Since then, state and local governments have allowed cable companies to build a cable network nationwide. The cable companies promised low costs to consumers, public service access, and no commercials. I remember movie theaters all running petition drives to "stop pay TV." They were afraid that if you received movies in your house every day, people would stop going to theaters. Cable companies promised to be pro-consumer, pro-competitive, and strongly in the public interest. But we pay far more for broadband internet access, cable television, and home phone lines than people in many other advanced countries, even though the services we get aren't any better. All too often, they are worse.[17]

As Rob Miraldi wrote in *USA Today* in October 2021, "even cable television companies control the market, controlling your internet and television; they have a near monopoly." Congress and the courts have declared it perfectly acceptable to have few regulations over pricing one of the most important utilities we get into our houses and places of business. There is a good reason why few feel sorry for cable companies as competitors, such as TV streaming services and competitor fiber companies, edge out some of the business from these monopolies. I mention this because this became the most important highway for boxing shows to get to the public for decades.

Now, OTT (over-the-top) broadcasts are a modern streaming approach for delivering videos directly to viewers over the internet. OTT bypasses traditional media networks such as cable, broadcast, and satellite TV providers. So, individuals or broadcasters can deliver original video content without the traditional media companies being involved, although they require an internet connection that, for many, brings you right back to a cable company. In boxing, for example, pay-per-view events can be sent directly to consumers by a promoter without them having to pay In Demand, cable companies, or other networks for using the highway they traditionally provided. Those fees were normally 50–60 percent of the purchase price. So, you can instantly see the attraction of OTT options to promoters.

Social networks are basically OTT operations for sharing social content. But they also provide a platform for distributing video content. Instagram, Facebook, X (Twitter), LinkedIn, and several others allow streaming.

Part of the problem with this freedom to self-distribute content, in my opinion, is that there is almost no regulation or oversight over the process. Twitter used to censor known false allegations voluntarily, but that doesn't stop conspiracy theories or outright falsehoods from getting through. In boxing I've watched an alarming number of social broadcasters, masquerading as journalists, feeding their opinions directly to the internet with inaccuracies, lies, and intentionally targeted attacks to serve their disturbing agenda. These uncontrolled falsehoods can't always be identified by average consumers. Average fans don't know who's promoting these attacks. The speed with which falsehoods and rumors can populate the dialogue is alarming because once a falsehood takes hold, it is nearly impossible to go back and correct the record. When newspapers, magazines, and broadcast news covering boxing came from identifiable journalists, you had some accountability. Some untruths were still reported; but at least, because you could identify the reporter, he had some incentive to try and get it right or face the backlash.

Great boxing writers, such as Alan Goldstein of the *Baltimore Sun* and Joe Maxse of the *Cleveland Plain Dealer*, were examples of writers who did a great service for boxing fans. Nat Fleischer, founder and writer for *Ring* magazine until 1972, was one of the most influential of the last century. Bob Arum and Don King have had to adapt to the new playing field and broadcast strategies and pitfalls. Top Rank, at least, has embraced the social platforms and uses them to a distinct advantage. Top Rank has a large, talented young staff blanketing all social media platforms with news, highlights, and historic content. It is much easier now, if you want to see Muhammad Ali's fifteen-round TKO win over Oscar Bonavena after three knockdowns with only fifty-seven seconds left from 1971 in Madison Square Garden, for example, than ever before.

Back in the seventies and eighties, Bob Arum was with ESPN and HBO. He aired a weekly show on ESPN that ended after sixteen years, making it the longest running weekly series in boxing. When Don left HBO for Showtime, HBO leaned toward Top Rank events. Now, starting in 2018, Top Rank is back with ESPN. I directed almost all the early fights on the new ESPN+ app. The future of boxing, on direct-to-consumer broadcasts, will be with us from now on.

The outlets for boxing videos have also had to embrace the social platforms as well. The fights themselves are now streamed to new viewers, clips are offered to the ADD generation on YouTube, Instagram, TikTok, Facebook, Pinterest, and others. There are countless boxing "reporters": anyone with an iPhone and an opinion, pretending to be an expert. A great deal of the opinion they spew has little thought behind it and no production quality at all.

Every time a reality show is watched, a book dies.

That is also true, in my opinion, of the new streaming platforms. Every time a viewer becomes used to receiving raw streamed video and opinion replaces thoughtful, researched, educated analysis, it diminishes the work produced by the extremely talented producers, researchers, editors, graphics artists, and directors who bring them well-constructed broadcasts from the ESPNs and Showtimes that care about the sport and the quality of their presentations. We should celebrate quality work, not lower the bar.

2

PROMOTERS—A TOUGH JOB

Many people over the years have asked me what a boxing promoter does. Very few people understand how difficult and risky trying to put on a promotion is. They see a promoter at a press conference or in the ring after a fight and assume it's mostly being a celebrity. Nothing could be further from the truth. In the week I am writing this, two big scheduled events lost their main events or went away entirely. Kenshiro Teraji lost his Tokyo championship unification fight, only two weeks away, when his opponent Jonathan González got sick. On the same day, they officially killed the upcoming Tyson Fury versus Oleksandr Usyk heavyweight match, scheduled for Wembley in a month, due to a disagreement over the rematch clause in the contract. Few businesses could weather these types of regular multimillion-dollar setbacks.

Creating and promoting a boxing event can be best described as endeavoring to construct a shaky card table to feed important guests. The four unstable legs of the table are the fighters, the broadcasters, the venue, and the public.

The promoter must convince the fighter, his manager, and their entourage that the proposed fight is the best choice for his career at this moment and answer every boxer's favorite question, as the late great boxing man Duke Durden used to ask, "Is the *sugar* right?" Boxers rarely feel they are being paid enough. A fighter sees other fighters receiving millions and wonders why he is only getting six figures. Like some company's stock prices inflated well above their valuations, much of their future worth is based on perception.

The broadcaster or broadcast network must be convinced that this fight card headlined by the main event is worthy of their programming schedule. A money deal between the promoter and broadcaster, containing a thousand elements

Bob Arum at Caesars Atlantic City. AP Images

defining the relationship, must be proposed, negotiated, and accepted. Broadcast networks are almost always run by executives who have sales backgrounds, not a love for sport, which means that the bottom line trumps what might be any passion for the athletes.

The venue must believe that the public will want this event and that the proposed deal for branding, tickets, concessions, staffing, profit sharing, etc., is a good deal for them. There is a myriad of deal types that venues can sign with an events promoter. One type is a four-wall deal, where the promoter pays a set price for the space and gets all the revenue from tickets, etc. Another type of deal is a barter deal—the most common type—with varying degrees of profit sharing, with certain items going to one side or the other. The revenues from ticket sales, concessions, advertising, sponsorships, and broadcast deals are divided up according to the deal. Both sides try to get the best deal for themselves in the process.

And finally, the public must want to see the event. They must believe that it will be a great show, care about the sport and fighters, and want to watch it despite a thousand other potential choices available to them on that day, at that hour.

Being a boxing promoter means selling all these entities on the benefits of becoming one of these "legs" to the event all at the same time. If any of these incredibly shaky legs falters, the entire card table collapses. That's a lot of pressure before an event can be successful. That is why boxing promoters aren't like other people. A successful event includes a staggering number of cards on that table. Often one or more of the legs collapses, and the cards scatter. A fighter gets injured, a broadcaster has a better event on that night, a venue has a conflict, or the public becomes disinterested in the event because of a newly announced alternative vying for their attention. It happens all the time. Sometimes it is even an "act of God," such as a pandemic.

Sometimes it is just a difficult partner. In April 1991, Top Rank and Main Events entered into a deal in Atlantic City to have an event at Trump's failing casino. Evander Holyfield, promoted by Dan Duva's Main Events, and George Foreman, promoted by Bob Arum's Top Rank, met at Boardwalk Hall. As usual, they wanted a casino sponsor. Trump's bid of $11.5 million topped Caesars $11 million for the event. Arum still wanted Caesars, but Duva convinced him to go with the slightly higher bid. Trump's Taj Mahal was in desperate financial straits, built on $675 million of junk bonds, in or near bankruptcy, so Trump told both promoters he couldn't pay them ten days before the event. He claimed that the Iraq War constituted an act of war, so his contract didn't have to be honored. Too late to cancel they had to commandeer the gate plus a million from Trump and eat the $2.5 million they were short.[1]

"Yesterday I was lying. Today I'm telling the truth." This was a quote allegedly uttered by Arum[2] to a group of writers while enjoying a drink one evening during the promotion of Sugar Ray Leonard's welterweight title defense fight against Larry Bonds in Syracuse in 1981. The writer who noted it said it was a throwaway line Bob might have offered as a joke. but then again it might sum up a skill promoters need to do their job. Promotion, like any sales endeavor, uses truth "flexibility" to attract buyers.

Boxing promoters aren't like other people. They must combine the skills of a master salesman with a lawyer, a street hustler, and a child psychologist. Boxing promoters are team owners without a league. In the NBA, NHL, MLB, or most other sports, there is a league with a commissioner and other officers. The league has binding rules to control the actions of the team owners and to make sure they conform to the league formats, branding regulations, conduct guidelines, rules, and agreements. In boxing, the promoters make the deals, handle their fighters however they like, make deals, and negotiate with other promoters, or just have their own fighters fight each other.

In other sports leagues, commissions usually run the show, and teams only promote their own merchandise and ticket sales. The job of promoting the sport is left mostly to the league or commission in partnership with their major broadcasters and media vehicles.

There are associations such as the WBA, WBC, WBO, and IBF but they often lack the ultimate ability to make the promoters conform to their wishes. When preferable, the promoters go around the associations and avoid sanctioning fees in the process. HBO boxing went as far as to never mention the WBA, WBC, IBF, or WBO and refer to championships only by their weight. The associations, it appears to me, usually consider the promoters' wishes to avoid losing those fees. The fighters can negotiate the best deal possible with the promoter, but ultimately everyone works toward the best paydays. UFC has cut through the red tape by deciding who fights who, where, when, and for how much. If a fighter objects to a match or a low purse, he is shut out with few or no better options.

Television broadcasters tried in the past twenty years to take away some of the promoters' power and become promoters themselves, but these efforts have generally failed. A notable example of this is HBO, which considered promoters such as Don King and Top Rank to be adversaries and sought to control the events themselves. I was told by an HBO exec that it needed to remain distanced from the promoter to maintain journalistic integrity. Thirty years earlier, HBO told Don King that their $85 million renewal deal, a fraction of what Don wanted, was a "take-it-or-leave-it" offer. It was also rumored that Don and Mike Tyson wanted Larry Merchant, a Tyson antagonist, removed from the broadcast.[3] Seth Abraham, president of HBO, inducted into the International Boxing Hall of Fame in 2023, reportedly said no to that demand. Whenever you back Don into a corner with no apparent choices he'll come up with one that you hate. He turned down HBO's offer, called Tony Cox, the head man at Showtime, then a very distant competitor to HBO as a premium movie channel, and promised to make Showtime number one in boxing if Showtime cared to trust him in a partnership. Tony did, and Don kept his promise. Within five years Showtime had the top three pay-per-view events of all time. The negotiations for Tyson's services were another example of Don's street hustle that landed the heavyweight legend at Showtime and other promoters and HBO crying foul.[4] Now, ironically, five years after HBO got out of the boxing business, Showtime is also getting out of boxing. The landscape of boxing broadcasting is shifting dramatically at the very same time that sports broadcasting, and broadcasting in general, is also evolving from networks to direct-to-consumer streaming services and digital app delivery. Much more on this later.

Boxing promoters aren't like other people, and Bob Arum and Don King are nothing alike. In my role as a member of the board of directors of the Nevada Boxing Hall of Fame, I had the pleasure of delivering the introduction speech for the induction of both men into the Hall of Fame. As a member of the board of directors and the only person who had the pleasure of being a department head for both promoters, I was a reasonable choice. I truly admire both men for their accomplishments. In the world of business, there are few industries I consider harder to achieve greatness in than boxing promotion. Any success that might be achieved is tempered by unavoidable perils along the way, including the considerable sniping and downright sabotaging of your efforts, not only from your competitors but from your own fighters and partners as well. With the number of potential land mines and traps that must be avoided, any success deserves applause. Any achievement of prolonged success in the industry, as Don King enjoyed for decades and Bob Arum has enjoyed for an unbelievable fifty-plus years, is more remarkable than can be adequately recounted in a standard introductory tribute. I had to try.

My tribute to Bob Arum was mostly a recounting of his unprecedented endurance as a promoter. His brilliant Harvard Law School mind allowed him to maneuver through the perilous waters of event promotion. From Muhammad Ali, Joe Frazier, and George Foreman through Sugar Ray Leonard, Roberto Duran, Marvin Hagler, Tommy Hearns, Oscar De La Hoya, Floyd Mayweather, Erik Morales, Julio César Chávez, Manny Pacquiao, Vasiliy Lomachenko, Tyson Fury, Teofimo Lopez, Terence Crawford, Shakur Stevenson, Xander Zayas, Jared Anderson, and Keyshawn Davis, Arum has been at the top of the sport since his start in 1966 with no close rival.

My introduction of Don King for induction was a far trickier matter. I was no longer in Don's employ, or good graces, since I now produced and directed all the events for Arum and Top Rank, his hated rival. Let me say here that it wasn't my choice to leave Don. By 1998 I had started my own company and was an independent contractor for Don and others. I was asked by a friend at Top Rank to direct a show because they were in a bind. Because I was no longer staff and not exclusive to DKP anymore, I agreed to help this one time. Apparently, someone at Don King Productions found out that I did a job for Top Rank and that was that for my career at DKP. That first fight I directed for Top Rank was Oscar De La Hoya versus Ike Quartey on February 14, 1999. I've been with Top Rank ever since—twenty-five years and counting.

So, my speech for Don King attempted to give him credit for his accomplish- ments, which were certainly impressive, while being a little less deferential. The speech was being given while Barack Obama was campaigning for president and a lot was being made of his history as a "community organizer" in Chicago, as if that weren't praiseworthy. King in his youth was a well-known street hustling gambling boss, numbers runner, and an associate of unsavory characters in Cleveland, Ohio. He had in fact killed two people, one in self-defense, and for the other he was incarcerated for three years on homicide. These facts led to my best line in the speech:

> Like Bob Arum, Don King also achieved greatness as a boxing promoter. Both men reached the pinnacle of their sport promoting some of the greatest fights of all time. But both men didn't start at the same place. Bob Arum, a Jewish law scholar from Brooklyn, a Cum Laude honored Harvard lawyer who went from Robert Kennedy's Justice Department to a Wall Street law firm and then to box- ing, and Don King, who as a young man in Cleveland started as some kind of "Community Organizer."

That line got me the best sustained laugh, nearly two minutes, I have ever received while speaking publicly.

I have often heard people who watch boxing or are on the perimeter of the sport claim that they could be Don or Bob. They have no idea what it takes. They have no idea how many hours and how much high-level negotiating, usually on the spur of the moment, that is required. One slip up, one bad deal, and you're out of business. You're either broke, indicted, or consid- ered an unworthy partner as your sales pitch goes out the window. You also need thick skin and an unbelievably resilient character to bounce back from failures. They always come, and they are never advertised in advance. Only a great promoter such as Bob or Don can rebound from the type of adversity these men faced and prevail. Don did it for decades, and Bob is still doing it after nearly sixty years.

Whenever I meet someone who thinks he could be a boxing promoter, he is always completely unaware of the unbelievable number of hours promoters work and how much intense negotiating and maneuvering they must do at all hours of the day and night. These men work almost around the clock with a rare, almost inhuman dedication to their profession. People believe that what they see of promoters on TV from press conferences, weigh-ins, and being in the ring after a fight is what the job is mostly about. Those instances are a min- iscule fraction of the job. Don, while I worked for him, had no hobbies, took almost no days off, and took no vacations. He worked at least twelve to fifteen hours every day and expected his people to be on call around the clock. He was once quoted as saying that he was a success because he hadn't taken a day off since leaving prison. That's not far from true.

Another misconception people have is that promoters always make money hand over fist. They hear about the multimillion-dollar paydays of mega pay-per-view events and disregard what it took to set them up. A lot of break-even events or ones that lose money for a variety of reasons are necessary to set up the big paydays. The fighters get the huge purses you read about in the papers, not necessarily the promoters. And then there is the overhead. A successful promoter with a successful promotion company has a lot of expenses to keep things working: office expenses, insurance, taxes, commission fees, medical fees, legal fees, business fees, entertainment expenses, utilities, and office supplies. Next are costs related to broadcast deals, fighter-related costs such as training camps and gym operations. Then there is a staff of matchmakers, PR people, social networking people, finance/accounting people, lawyers, travel managers, event managers, TV producers, directors, lighting people, audio people, video technicians, executive assistants, marketing managers and their assistants, foreign broadcaster rights managers, brand managers, and more. That is quite a nut to cover. New, young promoters are rarely prepared for this. Russell Peltz, a great promoter from Philadelphia, who has six decades of boxing promotion under his belt like Bob, said about starting up in his twenties, in his book *Thirty Dollars and a Cut Eye*, "People think the promoter always makes money. Few have a clue as to what goes into promoting. I made $2,192.37 from my first 5 cards. An average of $189.64 from the next 4."[5]

When Bob Arum celebrated his ninetieth birthday, Top Rank staff assembled a video montage of birthday wishes. My favorite of the videos came from Russell Peltz. He said, "Bob and I have a lot in common. Bob has been a promoter for six decades. I've been a promoter for six decades. Bob is from the Northeast. I'm from the Northeast. Bob is a lawyer. I'm also a lawyer. Bob has become a multi-millionaire as a promoter. I'm also a lawyer."

Bob Arum at ninety-two is still in the office almost every day and only takes time off at the insistence of his wife and family. Don King, also ninety-two, is having his second event in thirty days in Miami. I'm not sure there will ever be any other promoters who will do the job with the skill and complete dedication that these two men have displayed.

No other promoter rose in my eyes to the status of a Bob Arum. Don King was also at the highest echelon for decades. The number of high-end champions they have had and their longevity at the top are why they are both legendary figures. Even their detractors, who compete with them or are owed money or were out-negotiated, give them credit for their achievements.

In 1987, Bob was a partner in a racehorse. Merchant of Baghdad was owned by CBS commentator and boxing trainer Gil Clancy, Bob, and others. On the week the horse ran in the Belmont Stakes, Bob received his stable pass that listed him as owner-gentleman. "All the years in boxing, nobody ever called me a gentleman."[6]

The main reason that Bob has enjoyed unbelievable longevity is his character and attitude about the people around him. Whereas Don insisted on handling absolutely everything himself, Bob has trusted some very good boxing brains to run Top Rank and keep it on top. Bob has said that he built his company with the mind-set of a technician. "If you're a technician," Arum explains, "then you build up an organization." So, he might be Top Rank's founder, but there's an infrastructure, a president, chief operating officer, vice president of boxing operations, matchmakers, and anyone else needed to keep the fights going to survive past him.[7] His stepson, Todd, is a good example. Bob entrusted Todd as a successor, and he has become a great boxing businessman in his own right, crafting new deals that will carry Top Rank for decades to come. Todd also moved the company forward with social networking developments and by embracing new technology to keep the company moving forward. As Albert Einstein said, "Success in life is like riding a bicycle, to stay balanced you have to keep moving forward."

Todd's sister, Dena, has been the marketing executive with Top Rank who made possible the hundreds of events she has handled for decades with the ticketing and complicated marketing requirements they have. Bob had close associates to head boxing operations and work as matchmakers, event operations directors, marketing directors, and creative managers. Bob's HOF senior matchmaker, Bruce Trampler, has been with him for several decades, expertly working with Hall of Fame matchmaker Brad Goodman, another of boxing's best matchmakers. Bob's head of boxing operations, Carl Moretti, who came over from Main Events, told me that it was the best move he ever made. Brad Jacobs, another Hall of Famer, the chief operating officer at Top Rank, who makes the event operations run smoothly, had a long career with Tuesday Night Fights at USA Network before joining Top Rank. Arum trusted these people and dozens of others in accounting, production, legal, etc., to do their jobs for the benefit of Top Rank and its prominence in the boxing business.

Arum always believed in delegating the right job to the right people. He wasn't against working with someone he disagreed with as long as he was the right person to disagree with. In 1980, seven years after Top Rank incorporated, Bob hired Teddy Brenner as his matchmaker. Teddy, a rival of Arum's who worked as matchmaker for Madison Square Garden boxing for twenty years and more recently as an independent promoter, was considered the right man for the job by Arum despite their differences. Brenner was a realist about the union, stating, "Marriages sometimes end in divorce."[8]

An agreement between Brenner and Arum was considered an upset. But now Arum was talking about the "great matches" Brenner would make, which would free Arum to concentrate on the increasingly complex business of making the deals to put on the fights.

"You were always better at that anyway," Brenner told his boss. Brenner likes cross-divisional bouts between stars, just as the Leonard-Duran fight matches a superb young welterweight against one of the great lightweight champions in history. Brenner suggested such fights as Aaron Pryor, the undefeated lightweight slugger, against Antonio "Kid Pambele" Cervantes, the legendary forty-year-old Colombian boxer who held the World Boxing Association junior welterweight title, a match Arum had already been working on; and Eddie Gregory, the WBA light-heavyweight champion, challenging Mike Weaver for the WBA heavyweight title. Arum said, however, that he was working on Gregory defending against either Rudy Koopmans of the Netherlands or Mustafa Wasajja of Denmark. The point here is that Bob respected Brenner's knowledge, instincts, and experience. He wanted those assets for Top Rank.[9]

Don King, by contrast, had problems allowing managers to use their own judgment or trusting others to exercise authority. When Don was indicted for wire fraud in 1997 over an agreement with a British promoter, Frank Warren, the court case brought out details of their contract. Don exclaimed in court that "his people" handled things like that and that he didn't know what was in every contract. We, the department heads of Don King Productions, thought that was very funny. Not only did Don, with his photographic memory, know what was in every contract he ever signed, he was almost always the only one who did. He was acquitted of that charge, by the way, and invited the entire jury to the Atlantis Resort and Casino on Paradise Island in Nassau. I'll tell you more about that later, including the CNN cameraman I found hiding in the bushes.

Some unflattering stories about these promoters are probably true, as the type of negotiations and hustling required in this job is less transparent than in other industries. Don has been accused of cheating fighters and hustling deals. In his defense, occasionally it might be a case of a disgruntled fighter going to the media. Occasionally a fighter might agree to a fight for Don, and later his friends tell him he was cheated. More likely he was out-negotiated by a very savvy street lawyer.

Let's take the case of a hypothetical pay-per-view fighter. Let's call him Joe Boxer. The hypothetical Mr. Boxer, while training for a fight, shows up at Don's office on a regular basis and requests advances for "walking around" money. After the fight, Joe Boxer gets his check from which he must pay his people and taxes. Left with less than the newspaper said he made on the fight, he wonders where the money went. The contract, Mr. King points out, requires the deduction for training expenses, management fees, the promoter's percentage, and any advances. Remember those? If the fictional Mr. Boxer goes to the media and says he was cheated, was he right? The greatest likelihood is that he was unaware of the clauses in the contract and absentminded about how much he received in advances. If you sign a promotional contract without a lawyer, or at least an experienced, trusted, adviser, as it was reported many young fighters did when a promoter dangled cash in front of them, you are naive at best or foolish at least.

Arum, as a lawyer, negotiated contracts with great detail. He occasionally was accused of a contract flaw but almost always was vindicated.

In my thirty years in boxing, I've worked with dozens of notable promoters. Other promoters' fighters were either on a Don King or a Top Rank card or on a show I produced. Cedric Kushner, the Duva family, Dan Goosen, Lou Dibella, Roy Jones Jr. Productions, and Mike Tyson are a few of the other promoters I've worked for or alongside.

When Mike Tyson began Iron Mike Promotions, I was asked to be their TV producer/director. With Arum's permission, which I always asked for when another boxing entity requested my services since he was my main client, I did all but one of his events. The most notable international promoters I've worked with include Frank Warren, Eddie Hearn, Klaus-Peter Kohl, Wilfried Sauerland, Fernando Beltrán, Akihiko Honda, the Acaries brothers, Thai promoter Thohsaphol Sitiwatjana (also known as Master Toddy), and Yvon Michel.

Throughout history there have been thousands of great self-made individuals. Some might argue that all great steps forward came from these individualists. We wouldn't have developed space travel if the brave and brilliant bicycle shop owners, the Wright brothers, hadn't had the vision to fly their motorized glider at Kitty Hawk. We wouldn't have had a successful industrial revolution without the brave, brilliant, and ruthless individualists such as Carnegie (steel), Rockefeller (oil), Vanderbilt (railroads), and Astor (real estate). We wouldn't have cured diseases without the brilliant and visionary works of Salk (polio vaccine), Pasteur (bacterial disease), Lister (antiseptics), Curie (radioactivity), and Jenner (smallpox vaccine). We wouldn't even understand the human existence without the work of Watson and Crick in explaining the DNA helix and how the human body works.

Although not all self-made leaders and ambitious individualists do noble things or achieve greatness, proof that greed is not a virtue, they do share a common ability to think for themselves and look ahead toward the big picture. Boxing promoters, in my opinion, are like these individualists. Working without a commission or governing board, as in most other sports, they need to act as individuals in the interests of their fighters, broadcasters, and ultimately their fans. The two promoters this book focuses on, Bob Arum and Don King, are both self-made men and individualists.

Arum went from Harvard Law to the Justice Department, which easily could have set his career path for the rest of his life. He chose instead to pursue a risky, uncertain, path that had no guarantee of success. He not only made it work, but he has also done so for six decades and counting; he is arguably the greatest promoter ever. That career path might never have happened if Willie Mays had known boxing. It was James Brown, who Bob Arum approached to be a color commentator for Lester Malitz on a George Chuvalo fight after Mays said he didn't know boxing, who suggested that Bob become a promoter.

King went from a rough and dangerous youth, which landed him in prison, to a new path in a new world he had no guarantee of success in. Using only his intelligence, which I know from firsthand experience is formidable, he used the intuition he honed as a street hustler and his amazing endurance to outwork and outmaneuver many rivals. While I worked for him, King worked incredibly long hours. He didn't have other hobbies, never took vacations, rarely took days off, and could remain sharp at the end of a grueling work period. We, the staff, struggled to keep up with him.

The reason I left my staff job as VP of television at Don King Productions and started my own company in 1998 was because I couldn't keep up with him every day. I wanted to provide the same services, as I told Mr. King, which is what I always called him out of respect, as an independent contractor to preserve my sanity. The turning point for me was when I went home to Maryland on Wednesday of Thanksgiving week in 1997 to keep a promise I made to my nine-year-old daughter and twelve-year-old son that I'd be there for Thanksgiving. An hour after I arrived there, Don King called me and told me to get to an airport to go to Atlanta and cover a football game between Southern U and Grambling, where he'd be announced at half time. While still on the phone I saw my daughter standing in the doorway crying. That was the Rubicon for me, which I decided not to cross. I left Don's staff and started my own company so I could better manage my time priorities. He became my first client.

Both men had the intelligence, fearlessness, and vision to make it to the top of their new careers. And both did it quickly. Bob Arum had Muhammed Ali as his first client and an ESPN series shortly after.

Don King was the principal promoter of the Rumble in the Jungle and the Thrilla in Manila within five years of entering the sport. The Thrilla in Manila was also a milestone as the first continuous satellite broadcast of a fight.

Comparing these two individuals to other boxing promoters, it becomes evident that this group of businesspeople, promoters, are mostly individualists. And some are self-made entrepreneurs.

Let's look at some of the past and present competitors, some of the other great promoters of all time:

Tex Rickard

George "Tex" Rickard was perhaps the first great boxing promoter. For thirty years he promoted boxing in addition to being an Alaska gold miner, saloon keeper, gambler, founder of the New York Rangers NHL team and builder of the third Madison Square Garden in 1925. His most famous match was Gene Tunney versus Jack Dempsey in Chicago in 1927. Tex also staged the historic fight between Jack Johnson and James J. Jeffries in Reno in 1910.

Max Hoff

Hoff was a gambler in Philadelphia during the 1920s who built the largest stable of prizefighters and was the first to incorporate a group of boxers as Max Hoff Inc. Hoff was involved in a famous lawsuit with Gene Tunney and his manager regarding his first fight as a heavyweight champion against Jack Dempsey. The suit for $350,000 was mysteriously dropped.

Chris Dundee

Chris Dundee, owner of the 5th St. Gym in Miami, brother of Angelo Dundee, who was Muhammad Ali's trainer, was a promoter in Miami for more than twenty years. The 5th St. Gym was one of boxings most prestigious gyms from the 1950s until it was torn down in 1993. Ali trained there throughout the sixties. Chris Dundee promoted the first fight between Cassius Clay, later Muhammad Ali, and Sonny Liston. Born Chris Mirena, he changed his name to Dundee after his older brother, Joe, a fighter, took the name of another boxer, Johnny Dundee. He put on the first interracial fight in Florida when welterweight champion Kid Gavilan, a Cuban, fought Bobby Dykes in 1952. Joe Louis and Rocky Marciano also trained at Dundee's gym.

Aileen Eaton (Eaton Promotions)
Aileen Eaton was the queen of Southern California boxing for nearly forty years. She promoted more than ten thousand fights, including one hundred world championships at the Olympic Auditorium and Dodger Stadium between 1942 and 1980. She recommended Cal Eaton to Frank Garbutt, president of the Los Angeles Athletic Club and owner of the Olympic, to straighten out financial irregularities in the commission. She later married him. She was, according to most involved, the real force behind the promotions.

Jack Solomons
Israel Jacob "Jack" Solomons was Britain's greatest boxing promoter for nearly fifty years. His landmark fights included Jack London versus Bruce Woodcock, Randy Turpin versus Sugar Ray Robinson, and Henry Cooper versus Muhammad Ali in 1963. Jack promoted the fight where Sugar Ray Robinson lost his middleweight belt to Turpin. His home venue of Harringay Arena in north London held many of the biggest British bouts in those years, including some of his twenty-six world championships.

Cedric Kushner
South African boxing promoter Cedric Kushner was the promoter of record for heavyweights Chris Byrd, David Tua, Hasim Rahman, Shannon Briggs, and Oleg Maskaev. He made noise in the boxing world with his TV series, *Heavyweight Explosion.* I was involved occasionally in the series as a director or production manager. Cedric started in the United States as a music promoter handling acts such as Fleetwood Mac, Queen, the Grateful Dead, the Rolling Stones, Steppenwolf, and others.

Dan Goossen (Ten Goose/America Presents/Goossen Tutor Promotions)
Dan Goossen promoted boxing through several entities. Beginning with Ten Goose Boxing, he later guided America Presents and finally Goossen Tutor Promotions. Throughout his decades as a promoter, he was involved with many notable fighters including Andre Ward, Chris Arreola, Michael Nunn, Terry Norris, Gabe and Rafael Ruelas, David Tua, James Toney, Bernard Hopkins, Joel Casamayor, and David Reid. After Floyd Mayweather left Top Rank, for whom Dan formally worked, he promoted two of Mayweather's fights. Known as a great PR man, Dan Goossen also represented Pete Rose and Mr. T.

Duva Boxing (Main Events)

The Duva family has long been one of the dominant forces in boxing. Lou Duva is one of the greatest trainers of all time. His sons, Dan and Dino, and daughter-in-law Kathy Duva have promoted some of the greatest boxers of all time, including Evander Holyfield, Lennox Lewis, Pernell Whitaker, Meldrick Taylor, Arturo Gatti, Vincent Pazienza, and Mark Breland. When Dan passed away, his wife, Kathy, took over the company with his brother Dino as president until he left to start Duva Boxing. One of the most notable fights for Main Events was the 1981 battle between Sugar Ray Leonard and Tommy Hearns. Main Events was the copromoter with Arum on the fiasco event where Donald Trump shorted them both in Atlantic City.

Wilfried/Kalle Sauerland (Sauerland Promotions)

Wilfried Sauerland was one of Germany's premier promoters. He promoted champions such as Axel Schulz, Alexander Povetkin, Henry Akinwande, David Haye, Henry Maske, Mikkel Kessler, and Sven Ottke. His son, Kalle, recently merged the company with Wasserman Boxing.

Klaus-Peter Kohl (Universum Boxing)

Klaus-Peter Kohl became Germany's top promoter with the Klitschko brothers' domination of the sport's heavyweight division for decades. Before the Klitschko era, Universum also helped stage the fight between Felix Sturm and Oscar De La Hoya in LA in 2004. Klaus-Peter Kohl also entered into a contract with HBO in 2003 while he was still broadcasting on ZDF in Germany. My friend Bernd Bönte, after leaving Premier, the German version of HBO, was an executive with Universum for the reign of the Klitschkos. I loved conversing with Bernd in my lousy German when he attended Tyson fights, my first chance since high school.

Frank Warren (Sports Network, Queensberry Promotions)

Frank Warren deserves his own book, and he told me it is in the works. His forty years and counting as a promoter include some of the greatest champions of all time: Lennox Lewis, Nigel Benn, Tyson Fury, Frank Bruno, Prince Naseem Hamed, Joe Calzaghe, Amir Khan, Chris Eubank, and Ricky Hatton. He was a part owner of the London Arena and lost a fortune in East End London development interests. He was also shot in 1989 by an unknown assailant. The bullet missed his heart by an inch, taking part of a lung. A former Warren boxer, Terry Marsh, was charged but never convicted. In 2011 Warren started BoxNation TV, a subscription boxing channel. Frank's first fight with Don was

Azumah Nelson versus Pat Cowdell in Birmingham in 1985. He remembered DK as a great deal of fun on the promotion. His first with Bob Arum was Don Currey versus Colin Jones in 1985 in Birmingham as well. The night before the fight, Frank had problems with the Inland Revenue Authority. The British Boxing Board of Control was also not a friend to Frank, favoring Mickey Duff over him at the time. They should have helped with Inland Revenue but didn't. Bob went full defense lawyer on them telling them to f-off. He asked who the hell they thought they were, in full aggressive mode. Frank had to remind Bob that he would still be living there after Bob got on his plane, and things calmed down. When I began in boxing, Frank and Don were partners, and we had one or two fights a month all over the United Kingdom. These Nigel Benn, Prince Naseem, and Lennox Lewis fights were some of the best I've been part of.

Barry/Eddie Hearn (Matchroom)
Since 1983, starting as a snooker promoter, Matchroom's Barry Hearn eventually became a boxing promoter. In 1987, Hearn was involved in the match between Frank Bruno and Joe Bugner at Tottenham Hotspur Football Ground. Hearn kept his interests in pool and later darts and ping pong while also being involved in boxing. Son Eddie has taken over the company recently and heads the PGA/Euro tour. Their most famous boxer was Canelo Álvarez, who they promoted through DAZN pay service. Other notable fighters include Anthony Joshua, Julio César Martínez, Lawrence Okolie, Joseph Parker, Luke Campbell, Conor Benn, Demetrius Andrade, Dmitry Bivol, Juan Francisco Estrada, and Devin Haney.

Oscar De La Hoya (Golden Boy)
Since 2002, Oscar De La Hoya, a former champion and close protégé of Bob Arum and Top Rank, has promoted boxing under his company Golden Boy Promotions. As a boxer he won eleven world titles in six weight classes. As a promoter he has risen to the top of the promotion world with fighters such as Canelo Álvarez, Devon Alexander, Marco Antonio Barrera, Adrien Broner, Nate Campbell, Danny Garcia, Ricky Hatton, Bernard Hopkins, Jorge Linares, Paulie Malignaggi, Lucas Matthysse, Carlos Molina, Erik Morales, Humberto Soto, Winky Wright, Deontay Wilder, and Shane Mosley.

Al Haymon (PBC)
A former music promoter for Mary J. Blige, Whitney Houston, and MC Hammer, Al became a boxing promoter, first managing Vernon Forrest. He founded the Premier Boxing Champions entity in 2015. Rarely photographed or interviewed, the controversial promoter, due to his alleged managerial as well as

promotional role with his boxers, has promoted Luis Ortiz, Floyd Mayweather, Manny Pacquiao, Guillermo Rigondeaux, Andy Ruiz Jr., Errol Spence Jr., Deontay Wilder, Devon Alexander, Andre Berto, Adrian Broner, Artur Beterbiev, Anthony Peterson, Carl Frampton, Abner Mares, and Antonio Tarver.

There have been other, notable, short-term promoters such as Triller, who burned out quickly, proving my assertion that it's a difficult, risky, and often financially perilous undertaking.

As we examine what a promoter is, we should look at promoters in other industries. Perhaps the greatest promoter of all time was P. T. Barnum. Barnum defined what a promoter is for the modern world. He created an attraction and then created a need to see it. Starting with a variety troupe and a museum collection, he later started the first massive circus, Barnum & Bailey. Barnum's museum of curiosities, some real, drew massive crowds of nearly a half million visitors annually until it burned down. He promoted Tom Thumb and paid the highest fee ever to a performer, Jenny Lind, to draw patrons. He is credited with the phrase "never give a sucker an even break," although that hasn't been confirmed conclusively. When faced with crowds lingering too long in his sideshow tent at the circus for only a dime, he put a large, ornately painted sign at the end of the tent with an arrow that read, "This way to the egress." Once outside the tent, since egress is another word for exit, they had to pay another admission charge to reenter. In the early 1850s, Barnum invested heavily in a company developing Bridgeport, Connecticut. The company went bankrupt, taking Barnum's fortune with it. Like every good promoter he picked himself up, grabbed what assets he had left, such as Tom Thumb, and rebuilt. He also was an innovator, creating the country's first aquarium. At sixty years old, he entered the circus business and became the world's greatest circus showman.

Perhaps the greatest promotion job outside of boxing is the UFC. This sport combines several fighting disciplines into one sport known as mixed martial arts, was created out of a promotional plan. The origins of the UFC's mixed martial arts, or MMA, was tough man contests. Combatants, using whatever fighting skills they had, met, often in unmatched weight classes, to amuse the blood lust of fans, who were often treated to brutal, often bloody matches. Unlike boxing, where rules, artful skills, and discipline made the matches more civilized, these were brutal and often savage fights. Banned in most cities, these events were typically held out of the control of state athletic commissions. Venues such as tribal reservations and locations that were less strict about fight commissions were the only locations they could use.

In 1993, the UFC was created by Bob Meyrowitz, along with Art Davie. A few years later, I was brought on as production manager. The UFC, despite a loyal and growing fan base, lost money throughout this early evolution. Lorenzo Fertitta and his brother, Frank Fertitta III, owners of the Station Group Casinos Las Vegas, bought the franchise in 2001 for $2 million, creating Zuffa LLC. After losing money for a few more years, they built a franchise worth more than $4 billion. That's the figure they received for selling a majority interest in Zuffa in 2016. From a money loser to a multibillion-dollar company has to be regarded as the greatest promotional feat of all time. You have to take your hat off to them.

The way UFC accomplished this feat is multifaceted. First, they became an eight-hundred-pound gorilla. They fought off competition and bought those they couldn't fight off to be the biggest, baddest MMA franchise on the block.

Second, they locked their fighters into iron-clad exclusive contracts with few personal rights, so the fighters became, in my opinion, restrictively contracted to UFC. UFC owned their fights, merchandising rights, and their ability to even make personal appearances. If you complained about this, you were released and would probably lose your meal ticket. That eight-hundred-pound gorilla status also allowed them to set the fighters purses, so the UFC was primarily, with few exceptions, the only one getting rich. Some joked that UFC stood for the Underpaid Fighter Conspiracy.

Third, they knew their audience. They knew the people who would become loyal fans. They also made the clear distinction between their multi-discipline "sport" for branding purposes.

Fourth, they changed the sport to make it acceptable to athletic commissions such as the Nevada commission so they could reach a better audience with larger, classier venues. Biting, crotch punching, and eye gouging were no longer allowed. I know: they ruined the sport, right?

Fifth, they were brilliant at branding. Like wrestling, the model they most closely followed, they elevated TV production values and created myriad media outlets for their product. They were geniuses at getting on TV, radio, social media platforms, and news broadcasts. Writers who spoke ill of them, even if the criticism was fair, were banished. In the undemocratic world of UFC, no detractors were allowed. Fans learned this, too.

Somebody got the idea of trying to turn boxing into a UFC-type operation. Al Haymon, in my opinion, talked his investors into bankrolling his attempt to turn boxing into another UFC model. I believe he wanted to have UFC-type control of boxing. Harold Smith had tried this in 1980. Unfortunately, because boxing had been around for hundreds of years and had too many working parts to take over, after hundreds of millions of losses for his investors, Haymon failed to put Arum, De La Hoya, Hearn, and others out of business to become boxing's new eight-hundred-pound gorilla.

Wrestling promotion is another fantastic success story. The entertainment value alone has created a large, fiercely loyal fan base. Few would argue with the statement that Vince McMahon is one of the greatest promoters of all time. The character development of the wrestlers and soap-opera narratives make for fun, compelling shows enhanced by second-to-none production value: amazing lighting, pyrotechnics, audio, cameras, screens, animation, and in-arena entertainment elements. Jason Robinson is the brilliant lighting/staging/event attractions master behind this effort.

As a kid, I turned on the Spanish-language channel in New York to watch lucha libre—wrestling. The champion aways seemed to be Bruno Sammartino. I loved watching Ivan Koloff, Andre the Giant, George "The Animal" Steel, midget wrestling, and the fabulous Moolah. But I'll bet they didn't rake in the dough back then.

I was in my teens when wrestling started to come into its own financially, with Hulk Hogan, Randy "Macho Man" Savage, Rick Flair, Captain Lou Albano, "Rowdy" Roddy Piper, and Jake "The Snake" Roberts. Since then, professional wrestling has continued to raise the promotion value for their steadily increasing popularity through the development of stars such as Bret Hart, The Rock, Triple H, and Steve Austin. The newest stars include Roman Reigns, Seth "Freakin" Rollins, Asuka, Rhea Ripley, and Ronda Rousey. Here, too, a financial basement dweller became a fabulously profitable operation through great promotion.

On April 3, 2023, an announcement was made that WWE and UFC would merge into a $21 billion company. Endeavor, the current parent company of UFC, announced that it would acquire the WWE. Endeavor would own 51 percent of the new company; WWE, 49 percent. It is unknown at this time what the merger would mean to viewers, but the expectation is that it will be a major event in sports broadcast television. Likely little will change in the UFC or WWE product, but their status as a monster powerhouse of broadcasting revenue will make them the heaviest hitter at the bargaining table for a broadcast deal. Likely they will demand and get the biggest platform, with the most marketing concessions from the network, of any sports company. Even the NFL can't deliver the dollars of the combined enterprise. In 2025, when some of their deals expire with ESPN and others, they will likely move all their properties to one broadcasting platform that offers them the best deal with the most perks. For example, they might wind up on NBC and Peacock for everything. The network might have to pony up the most crossover promotion, free marketing, and other show platforms on the network and streamed on their social web ever offered before.

As I stated earlier, being a promoter is very difficult. People might get the false impression that they can do a job just because they have seen a small portion of it or that they have the temperament, tenacity, or intellect for the job. I've also dealt with a few dramatic failures in unprepared rookie promoters.

On August 27, 2005, a first time "promoter," Canadian Darryl Wolski—"Beef" to his friends—was a beer-league hockey organizer from Manitoba, Canada. Wolski tried to start a pay-per-view event series called Hockey Enforcers. Hockey players known for fighting would meet in a boxing tournament on ice. I was suckered in to do the television coverage and got ripped off by this rookie. Beef was so unprepared to be a promoter he had to fight until the last minute to have his event happen and revealed himself as a deadbeat whose word was worthless when he couldn't pay his bills.

Another favorite rookie promoter story I was unfortunately involved in concerned the famous flop of an event between Christy Martin and Mia St. John at the Detroit Silverdome on December 6, 2002. The rookie promoter was named Peter Klamka. He made his money with a cell phone accessory company. His first mistake was thinking that being a promoter was easy. His second was picking the Pontiac Silverdome. The Silverdome, former home of the Detroit Lions, had a seating capacity of eighty thousand. I believe fight night ticket sales were about three hundred. We set up on one end of the stadium prepared for approximately ten thousand. One big reason for the massive failure was that at the weigh-in on Friday, the night before the fight, Christy Martin told the press that the fight was off. She was expecting to be paid the day before the fight, something I've never heard of in a fight, and Peter hadn't been prepared for that. I don't have any idea what was in her contract; I was, after all, only the TV guy. I do know, however, that the company that provided the speaker system for the event threatened to remove everything a couple hours before the event because they hadn't been paid. Peter was nowhere to be seen the afternoon of the event. He did, however, as I indicated earlier is required of new clients, pay our contract in advance. I never heard of another Peter Klamka boxing promotion.

In 1980, Bob Arum and Don King were confronted with a rival promoter who took their playbook and seemed to run with it for a while. Harold Smith, the thirty-seven-year-old head of MAPS—the Muhammad Ali Professional Sports Inc., a name he paid the champ to use—put on big, splashy, expensive events that drew attention. He paid huge purses, such as the $8.1 million he guaranteed for a February 23, 1980, Madison Square Garden event featuring Gerry Cooney and Ken Norton, which ultimately was canceled as the FBI searched for a missing Smith, along with his wife and young son. He was being sought for an investigation into a $21 million embezzlement from Wells Fargo

Bank. The money presumably had been used to finance his boxing promotional scheme and lifestyle. Smith had in mind an early version of the same plan it appeared Al Haymon attempted thirty years later: use a great deal of other people's money to take control of boxing. Smith was also a music promoter, like Haymon, before switching to boxing.

"Harold's plan, he told me, was to take over boxing by buying all the champions with big money," said Dr. Ferdie Pacheco, the boxing consultant for NBC. "Once he got all the fighters away from the other promoters, he was going to tell them the fun's over; now it's back to reasonable prices."[10]

Don King, unsympathetic to rivals, said, "He [Smith] has no morals, no ethics and he's devoid of any respect for contractual agreements. The man is Satan in disguise."[11] "Any fool who goes out on a street corner and hands out money will attract attention," King added.

I bring up these notable failures because I believe it demonstrates what I said about how difficult promoting is, even for a single event.

The most impressive new promoter I ever worked for was Calvin Ayre. Calvin was the son of a farmer from Ontario, Canada. He became a billionaire with his genius for promoting sports betting online, online casino gaming, and music promotion. Calvin was also a big fan of MMA. He started BodogFight because of his love of the sport and for the branding value to his Bodog gaming corporation. I was hired as producer/director to produce and direct live events. BodogFight produced live events and four years of reality shows in Vancouver, Canada; St. Petersburg, Russia; and Costa Rica. When I was hired, I was asked to produce events that are as high end as Showtime, HBO, or UFC. I told them, thinking that I should be showing my expertise, that the cost might be higher than they realize. Calvin said, and I quote, "Who asked you about the cost?" I'd never heard that before from a promoter, and I've never heard it since.

In discussing King and Arum, Marc Rattner, one of the best Nevada Athletic Commission executive directors of all time, now with the UFC, said his first experiences with Don King were surprising because the bigger-than-life King acted bigger even in person. He remembered Bob as a businessman but marveled that if it was beneficial to them, they could work together just fine.

One of my wife's favorite stories is about how she met Don King. She has accounting and law degrees from Pepperdine. She worked in the tax division of Price Waterhouse and ran a business in LA as controller for Iranian businessmen with factories around the world. She worked with some of the highest-powered LA CEOs and giants of the entertainment world. I mention this because her opinion was based on experience.

She and I were dating when she joined me at a press conference for a pay-per-view event. She sat at a rear table taking it all in. Don King, his lawyers, the billionaire owner of the MGM Kirk Kerkorian, Matt Blanc and Jay Larkin of Showtime were all seated at the next table. Unable to avoid listening to Don's voice, which carried well, she heard him conducting business, in her words, "like any Fortune 100 CEO." He talked about asset depreciation, long-term investments, ROI, and business plans that would cross any mortal businessman's eyes. She was fascinated because of her preconceptions about Don. His public persona didn't jibe with his real brain for business. At one point Mike Marley, Don's PR director at the time, told Don it was time for the presser to start. "DK, it's showtime."

She saw him finish his business as he stood to leave, make final remarks, pick up his flags, put on his "Only in America" jacket and start, slowly, toward the stage. She characterized his move from the table to the stage as a "de-evolution" of man. She described it as that evolution depiction drawing from ape to man in ten steps to the reverse process. She said he went from an aggressive Gordon Gekko to a cartoon character in only a few minutes. As the jacket went on, and the cigar went in his mouth, and he started waving the flags, he started changing his speech from "next quarter these events will gross you 2.4 million against the pittance of the initial 800,000 investment," into "Ah, ah, ah, only in America don't you ever forget it. We ain't looking for pie in the sky when we die, we want somethin' sound, on the ground, while we around, ah, ah ah."

Bob Arum was the opposite of Don King. While Don was a P. T. Barnum-like figure, promoting and playing that cartoon character my wife saw, Bob Arum was never a cartoon *or* a wild, outlandish character. Bob was genuine on or off camera. He reminded me of my favorite uncles. He has a brilliant legal mind, which tends to make him pitch an event with facts, not bluster. Bob talks about the quality of a show and the skills of his fighter because he believes they are unmatched. He hypes with testimonials that he believes to be true. I respect the man for his passion and tenacity. Bob has, on occasion, gotten himself into trouble with his honesty. He has said negative things to defend himself, his fighter, or his beliefs. Bob seems like my favorite uncle. Don seems like the distant cousin who always scares you a little bit.

3

ARUM AND KING

Before They Were Promoters

Robert Morris Arum was born near the beginning of the Great Depression on December 8, 1931. His parents' home, Crown Heights, a Jewish neighborhood in Brooklyn, would be the scene of a "stop the violence" march I would record with a TV crew sixty years later as Don King marched with Hasidic Rabbi Shea Hecht and Al Sharpton to try to stop the continuing violence between the Blacks and Lubavitch Hasidic Jews a few years after a Black child was killed by a Hasidic man in a car and a 29-year-old Hasidic student was killed in retaliation.[1]

Bob was an excellent student, graduating from Erasmus Hall High School and eventually graduating cum laude from Harvard Law School. That prestigious honor allowed him to land a job with Robert Kennedy's Justice Department during John Kennedy's presidency. While at the DOJ, in 1962, Arum was assigned to confiscate proceeds from the Sonny Liston versus Floyd Patterson fight. This was his first known association to boxing.[2]

After the Kennedy assassination, Bob moved to a prestigious Wall Street law firm, Phillips, Nizer, Benjamin, Krim & Ballon. It was here that Bob did research work for senior partner Louis Nizer, who wrote the foreword for the famous Warren Commission Report about the assassination of President John Kennedy.

Bob had three children with his first wife, John, Richard, and Elizabeth. Bob's son John, a brilliant lawyer and environmentalist, tragically passed away in a mountain climbing accident in the North Cascades National Park in August 2010. John, age forty-nine, was writing a book about climbing in Washington State. Bob said, "When you lose a child, I don't care what anybody tells you, you lose part of yourself, it does not get easier over time."[3]

Muhammad Ali and Jim Brown on set of The Dirty Dozen, *August 5, 1966.* AP Images

Bob told a reporter, "John argued successfully before the Supreme Court on behalf of an Indian tribe. He was an environmental lawyer and one of the country's leading experts on water rights. He found those topics interesting; I found them incomprehensible."[4]

Bob's other son, Richard, also attended Harvard and became a professor of sociology.

* * *

Don King was born in Cleveland, Ohio, on August 20, 1931, five months before Bob Arum. He was the fifth of Clarence and Hattie King's six children. His father, Clarence, died in a steel plant explosion when Don was only ten. Hattie used the insurance money to move the family to a better neighborhood. She made money making pies and selling peanuts. As a young man, Don and his brothers put numbers into the bags of peanuts. This was a form of "playing the numbers," a street lottery on the black market. This boosted sales and began Don on his way to an early career in numbers gambling.

Even his enemies, including Arum, admitted King was a genius. He was known as Donald the Kid back in Cleveland when he was one of the leading numbers racketeers there. It started as a summer job, as a runner for a numbers game. King hoped to earn enough money to go to Bowling Green University and study law. But one day, he forgot about a policy slip, "I can still remember the numbers," King said, "zero one four." He didn't turn it in to his boss. King had to pay the winner out of his savings, so he had to stay on the job. He soon took over the business.

* * *

Don took a different path than Bob to becoming a hall of fame promoter. Despite being quite intelligent, in 1949 Don dropped out of Western Reserve University, now Case Western Reserve University, after only a year.[5] His departure was likely due more to his demeanor than his capabilities. Don was always known as a hustler capable of making a good living on the streets. From his early childhood, he had a talent for numbers running. His photographic memory would be a huge asset. In this pursuit, Don became a bookmaker in the basement of a record store on Kinsman Road in Cleveland. In 1954, Don shot and killed Hillary Brown.[6] The homicide was deemed self-defense and justifiable because Brown was threatening him while robbing King's gambling establishment.

In the mid-'60s, King ran a numbers operation in Cleveland. He was known to carry a .38 in his belt and smoke big cigars. This put him squarely in association, and sometimes at odds with, Alex "Shonder" Birns, a Jewish mobster in Cleveland who, along with Angelo Lenardo, ran his own large syndicate. Shonder Birns demanded that King pay him a tribute as a protection fee to operate in their territory. King initially went along but eventually stopped paying. On May 23, 1957, at 3:45 a.m., the front of King's home was blown up. Don wasn't injured.[7] Shonder Birns and rival Cleveland mobster Danny Greene were well-known bombers. Birns also bombed Greene's house, and Greene eventually killed Birns with a car bomb.[8] Greene also died by car bomb.

King decided to testify against Birns for the bombing of his home. King was ambushed and assaulted at his home prior to testifying by several men and sent to the hospital with severe bruises to the head and back. There were also shots reported being fired. King ultimately decided not to testify.[9]

In 1961, Don King directly led to one of the most important U.S. Supreme Court rulings in history. Known as the Exclusionary Rule, it states that a person cannot be prosecuted with evidence that was obtained by violating an individual's Fourth Amendment rights. Dolly Mapp worked with Shonder Birns in his gambling operation. Her boyfriend was Virgil Ogletree. In May 1957, the police, acting on a tip that Ogletree was at Mapp's home, tried to gain entry to search for Ogletree and evidence of her involvement in gambling. She denied them entry without a search warrant. Thirteen hours later, they busted in her door, searched her home, and handcuffed her. They found Ogletree, who they were trying to get as a witness in the bombing of Don King's house, and some betting slips and pornographic magazines that she said had been left by a former tenant. They charged her with possession of pornographic materials. The case eventually wound up at the Supreme Court where the Exclusionary Rule was launched, all because of a police desire to question a man about the bombing of Don King's house. I was told that amazing story by Alan Dershowitz at Harvard in 1996. Don was there to speak to law students.

At thirty-six, Don was heavily tied to gambling and street hustling in Cleveland. He wouldn't escape the law after his second brush with homicide. In 1967, he went to prison, convicted of second-degree murder for stomping to death Sam Garrett, an employee who owed him $600. The victim's rumored last words were, "I'll give you the money, Don."[10]

When this went to trial, the charges were reduced from second-degree murder to involuntary manslaughter. Manslaughter is appropriate in a fit of passion when the accused is incapable of controlling his emotions.

He served his time at Marion Correctional Facility. While there, he decided to change his life for the better. Don said he read everything he could get his hands on, from Machiavelli to Shakespeare, to enhance his education. After dropping out of college, where he entered wanting to become a lawyer, his criminal activity seemed like it would dictate the rest of his story. Now, in prison, he decided to change his path. He began to think about his future and how he could use his talents to get ahead legally.

A short while after his release in 1972, Don became associated with Muhammad Ali, who agreed to box in an exhibition to benefit a Cleveland hospital. The event grossed more than $80,000. Don was then associated with two events at the Cleveland Arena in August and November 1972, with fighters such as Johnny Griffin, Sam McGill, Jimmy Dupree, and most notably, Larry Holmes involved. Don King Productions began in 1974. Don's first major promotional event was the Rumble in the Jungle when he convinced Muhammad Ali and George Foreman to fight in Zaire. The poster he created for the event was a drawing of slaves in chains and included the phrase, "From the Slave Ship to the Championship."

* * *

Bob Arum got into boxing through a side door. He didn't grow up in poverty, where many boxing stories begin, or hang out at a boxing gym, he wasn't part of a boxing family or an athlete who was attracted to the individual achievement lure of the sport. Bob was an attorney, the son of an accountant, with a distinguished background as a Harvard law graduate with honors, which landed him in Robert Kennedy's Department of Justice.

In 1962, Bob worked for Justice in the Southern District of New York and headed the taxation group that held up the purse of the first Floyd Patterson versus Sonny Liston fight, because of reported illegalities by one of the promoters and infamous criminal lawyer, Roy Cohn. They wanted to make sure proceeds didn't wind up in Switzerland, according to one reporter.[11] Cohn, the promoter, was planning to take the money overseas and pay Patterson on a payment plan, which was illegal. Arum seized close to $5 million from the event, then for ten days took Cohn's testimony. Through that he learned all about the boxing business even though he'd never watched a fight.

"Liston came to my office," Arum recalled. "He was owed about $160,000 for the fight. He was a real scary, tough-looking character. And here I am a little pipsqueak behind a desk in horned-rimmed glasses. Liston says to me, 'Hey, you so-and-so, where's my money?'

"I said, 'I'm an assistant United States attorney, behave yourself.' He was a bit of a coward.

"He said, 'Oh no, I didn't mean it.' He finally got his money."[12]

It was during that investigation that Bob met Lester Malitz, boxing promoter, CCTV pioneer, and former vice president at Leo Burnette and Co., a Chicago advertising agency. At this meeting the germ of his new career path was born. Arum, assigned to the tax division of Justice in the Southern District of New York, was tasked with taking action against the fight as the department investigated whether criminal activity was involved. The Liston versus Patterson fight, the first of their two meetings, was held on September 25, 1962, at Comiskey Park in Chicago. It was the third defense of Floyd Patterson's second title. More than 600,000 people watched the two-minute apparent massacre of Floyd Patterson. More than nineteen thousand were in attendance, many more at 264 closed-circuit locations. Frank Sikora was the referee. Despite being the champion, Patterson was the underdog. Many felt like he looked like a light heavyweight against a much bigger man. Liston was only two inches taller but had a massive thirteen-inch reach advantage and twenty pounds on Cus D'Amato's fighter, Patterson. *Sports Illustrated* reporter Gilbert Rogin wrote that the myth of the fight being fixed was proven false by Patterson's comments after the fight. He didn't remember the hook that nailed him, getting up to a knee, or the end of the fight. He reportedly told his trainer D'Amato that he must have blacked out. He worried that he could have started taking off his trunks in the ring, thinking he was back in his dressing room.[13]

After John Kennedy's assassination in 1963, Bob moved to the prestigious Wall Street law firm of Phillips, Nizer, Benjamin, Krim & Ballon and did research for Louis Nizer. Three years later, Bob reconnected with Lester Malitz to act in a legal capacity for the promoter. Malitz was trying to promote the George Chuvalo versus Ernie Terrell fight. Interest in this event was relatively low, which is why Bob suggested a star Black athlete as an announcer to add interest to the broadcast. Bob knew how to contact Willie Mays and suggested him first. It was already evident that Bob had the brain of a promoter. After trying Willie Mays, who turned Bob down because he said he knew nothing about boxing, he contacted Jim Brown, star running back for the Cleveland Browns, to add star value to the announcing team.

It was Jim Brown who first suggested to Arum that he try promotion as a career. Brown agreed to do the fight, and Arum said he did great.

"Afterward, he said to me, 'You shouldn't be behind the scenes, you should be in front as the promoter,'" Arum said.

"I said, 'What do I know about promoting boxing?'"

"Next thing I know, I'm getting a call from Ali. He's going through all his legal issues with the government for refusing induction into the army, and he's going to fight Chuvalo in Canada, and he asks me to help him promote the fight. I told him the same thing I told Jim, and Ali said, 'Don't worry about it. I'll do all the talking.' We became friends, I was accepted by Elijah Muhammad and the Nation of Islam, and the rest is history."[14]

Ali talked with Elijah Muhammad for more than an hour. "We started talking very, very interesting business for about twenty, thirty minutes. And then his eyes would glaze over," Arum says of the Nation of Islam's late leader. "He would start with the blue-eye devils coming down his spaceship. But I let that pass and then we continue talking business."[15]

That talk ended with Arum as Ali's lawyer and promoter. As promoter, Arum would pay Ali 50 percent of his fight's gross profits instead of the 40 percent that was the standard then. That's how the decades-long relationship between Ali and Arum began. And there was no better way to have a firm grasp on boxing than to promote the transcendental Ali, so Arum never left after that.

"When I first started in the business, it was a terrible problem with all the mobsters involved in the sport," Arum says. "Everywhere you looked there was a mob guy."[16]

On November 22, 1965, Muhammad Ali fought Floyd Patterson in one of the first bouts of his newly formed Main Bouts promotional company. This match came after Patterson had lost twice, both in the first round, to Sonny

Liston. It was one of these bouts where Arum was assigned to confiscate the purses while he was working for the Justice Department under Robert Kennedy.

Muhammad Ali's won his fight with Canadian heavyweight champion George Chuvalo on March 29, 1966, by unanimous decision. The fight, at Maple Leaf Gardens in Toronto, Canada, was widely considered an epic brawl for fifteen rounds. Chuvalo had been ringside a year earlier for Ali's fight with Sonny Liston, still arguably one of the last suspiciously ended fights in boxing, which made some question whether it was fixed. Chuvalo booed loudly, according to his companions, after the conclusion because he would have gotten a title fight if Liston had won. He surged into the ring with other fans. Chuvalo himself was involved in a fight with questioned mob ties. In 1965 his fight with Ernie Terrell was rumored to have a referee, Sammy Luftspring, threatened by Chicago mobsters to help Terrell win. Chuvalo went the distance in that bloody fight. Prior to the fight with Ali, Chuvalo, a 216-pound fighter, had never been knocked out.

4

BOB ARUM—THE EARLY BOXING YEARS

B ob's first event, the Ali versus Chuvalo, was a landmark fight. On March
29, 1966, Muhammad Ali met George Chuvalo in Maple Leaf Gardens
in Toronto, Canada. The fight was controversial, meaningful, and brutal. Bob
Arum called the event the toughest he ever had. He said, "Everything I've
had since then was easier. And I'm grateful for that because this was like basic
training."[1]

Ali was supposed to fight Ernie Terrell, but Terrell backed out right before
the fight, and Chuvalo was called seventeen days before the event. The fifteen-
round epic was as notable for the pugilism in the ring as the human story of the
two men outside the ropes. Ali was dealing with the fallout of his conversion to
Islam and his draft stance, and Chuvalo was trying to quiet accusations of mob
ties. One year earlier, Ali had defeated Sonny Liston with the "phantom punch"
that was widely considered an obvious fixed fight. Ali had been stripped of his
title by the WBA after he joined the Nation of Islam. The WBC still listed him
as champion. Chuvalo was the Canadian heavyweight champion for eight years
leading up to the fight. He usually ended fights in the first or second round.
In 1965, he lost to Floyd Patterson in Madison Square Garden in what *Ring*
magazine called the fight of the year.[2] In 1963, Chuvalo fought Mike DeJohn in
Ali's hometown, Louisville, Kentucky. His total destruction of DeJohn, despite
the ref helping DeJohn recover after knockdowns, made Ali rethink a fight with
Chuvalo. He preferred Ernie Terrell.

The Toronto event was also tied to local promoter Harold Ballard, a colorful
hustler who, for example, sold tickets to two Beatles concerts when only one
date was planned.

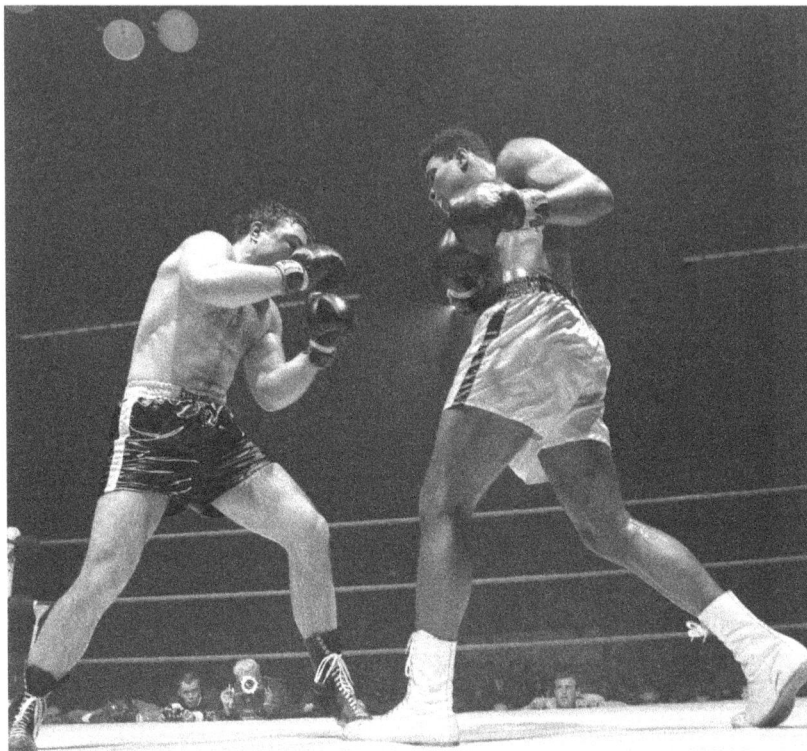

Muhammad Ali versus George Chuvalo, March 29, 1966, Maple Leaf Gardens.
AP Images

The Ali–Terrell fight was supposed to be in Chicago but was turned away by anti-Ali sentiment. Rookie promoter Arum shopped the event before finally thinking that Montreal would work. Arum was partnered with football star Jim Brown; Mike Malitz, son of Lester Malitz who had helped Arum get into boxing promotion; Herbert Muhammad, son of Elijah Muhammad, founder of the Nation of Islam; and John Ali, the secretary of the NOI. Two hundred mayors across America, though never asked, also stated that Ali couldn't fight in their cities. Montreal, with the mayor on board, gladly welcomed the event. When announced, the American Veterans Association announced that it would boycott Expo 1967 in Canada if the event took place. The mayor had a change of heart. Step in Harold Ballard, co-owner of the Maple Leafs, who managed Maple Leaf Gardens. When Maple Leaf Gardens was announced as the venue, Conn Smythe, who built the Gardens and had owned the team since 1927, objected. Smythe, a veteran of two wars, objected to Ali's anti-induction stance. According to Milt Dunnell, a *Toronto Star* reporter who died in 2008 at 102, Conn Smythe quit the Maple Leaf Gardens board and sold his shares in the team because of the event and never entered the building again. If you thought setting up Arum's first promotional event couldn't get stranger, hold on to your spit cup. After the fight was set, Ernie Terrell backed out.

Welcome to the world of boxing promotion, Bob Arum!

George Chuvalo was suggested as a replacement a little more than two weeks from the event. Ontario politicians decided to vote on whether to allow the event. Nobody was optimistic. Irving Ungerman, Canada's "chicken king," came to the rescue. He managed George Chuvalo. Arum said that Ungerman sent all the Parliament turkeys, and that did the trick. The event was saved by a single vote.

Many underestimated George Chuvalo as an opponent for Ali. He claimed that he never understood why he was such an underdog. The fight turned into an unusually difficult one for Ali. Nobody expected Chuvalo to beat Ali on points, but no one appreciated how tough George was and how much difficulty Ali would have with him in the later rounds. The fourteenth and fifteenth rounds saw George landing multiple lefts on Ali's chin. Legendary announcer Don Dunphy shouted excitedly on the air, "He may have hurt Clay. This is as wild as a night in the Yukon."[3] Ali called Chuvalo the toughest man he ever fought.

* * *

This was the start of Arum's promotional career with Main Bouts. Bob started as VP and secretary of Main Bouts, Ali's promotion company, with Jim Brown in charge of publicity. Malitz, a pioneer in closed-circuit and pay-per-view events, was also a partner in the venture, which would eventually become Top Rank. Incorporated in 1973, this also included Lester Malitz's son, Mike, who remained with the organization for more than three decades. Herbert Muhammad and John Ali of the Nation of Islam rounded out the team.

Arum hadn't been thinking about breaking into boxing promotion. His move came when he was introduced to Muhammad Ali. The idea was that Arum would help promote a fight and then continue as his lawyer, but they wound up spending more than twenty years together. Ali became a legend and Arum a legend maker. Bob promoted twenty-seven Muhammad Ali events.

"I could tell who a good person was, who was not, who was a selfish person, and who was an OK person, and who was a great person," Arum says. "And Ali was a great person. I'm talking about what was in his heart of hearts, what was he deep down, what was he made of."[4]

Another of boxing's colorful characters who spotted what Muhammad Ali would become while he was still Cassius Clay was journalist Harold Conrad. Harold, who saw Muhammad Ali in the 5th St. Gym in Miami before anyone knew his potential saw the greatness in him and exclaimed to friends that he had just met the next champ. Bob Arum met, befriended, and worked with Conrad on the Toronto event as well. In the suite that Main Bouts held for the promotion, Arum beat some writers out of a little over a hundred dollars. Harold told him, "You're supposed to lose to those guys." Lesson learned. It was also Harold Conrad who Bob said introduced him to pot. Bob and marijuana had a lifelong relationship. Harold, it was said, was as comfortable with gangsters as with executives. He mingled with Meyer Lansky, Ben Segal, Tony Accardo, and the most important fight promoters, hotel owners, and movie moguls in the same week. Conrad, in January 1974 while in the Top Rank offices on the thirty-first floor of a Park Avenue location, said about Arum, "The fun is all gone, he's here to stay."[5] Harold Conrad was considered something like a well-thought-of monsignor at the Vatican, close enough to hear the whispers behind cupped hands but never too close for his own good.[6] Harold, who knew shadier boxing promoters, was implying that the "funny business" would stop with Arum; an honorable sheriff was in town. Teddy Brenner, Arum's matchmaker, said that Bob was "not down with the fighter's blood and sweat." Bob was more a businessman and negotiator.

Muhammad Ali had Bob Arum hooked on boxing. Coincidentally, Ali also helped Don King get his start as a boxing promoter.

In 1971, Wilt Chamberlain almost fought Muhammad Ali. Cus D'Amato, Mike Tyson's mentor and first major trainer, was going to train Chamberlain. A press conference to announce the fight was slated for the Houston Astrodome. "Don't start needling him," Arum told Ali while waiting for Chamberlain to arrive at the news conference. "I need him to sign the contract."[7] As Chamberlain arrived, the seven foot one NBA star bent over to get through the door. Ali yelled, "Timmmmberrr." Chamberlain whispered something to his lawyer, said he needed to use a phone in a private room, called Lakers owner Jack Kent Cooke, made a deal, and left. Good-bye promotion.

Ali versus Patterson II was presented on September 20, 1972. Floyd Patterson was the number one contender for Muhammad Ali despite losing to Sonny Liston twice in first round KOs. His wins against Eddie Machen and George Chuvalo put him right back in position. In their first fight in 1965, Patterson lost by TKO in the twelfth round. This time the thirty-seven-year-old Patterson, in what turned out to be his farewell performance, only made it to the seventh round. With cornerman Bundini Brown shouting, "Let's go to war" from Ali's corner, Ali performed flawlessly in this fight, setting him up for his most memorable fights to come with Frazier, Foreman, and Norton. The fight ended when referee Arthur Mercante called it a TKO; Patterson's left eye was completely shut. In the lead-up to the first bell, Joe Frazier, undefeated heavyweight champion, who beat Ali in their first match, was introduced to the crowd. Ali made a theatrical display of trying to get at Frazier, setting up their rematch fourteen months later. Patterson never fought again, although a retirement was never announced.

* * *

Bob Arum has been in not one but two movies. In 1999, Bob was ringside during Woody Harrelson and Antonio Bandares's film *Play It to the Bone*. He had a much larger role in the 1975 cult blockbuster *The Marijuana Affair*, made by his friend Lucien Shen who, in 1973, promoted the "Sunshine Showdown" between George Foreman and Joe Frazier in Jamaica. In this film Bob, recently off a stint in the real U.S. Department of Justice, played a crooked DEA agent who trafficked cocaine and wanted to interfere with the rival marijuana trade because it cut into his business.

* * *

On January 28, 1974, Ali–Frazier II was held at Madison Square Garden. Top Rank promoted the event. In commenting on how the negotiations went with Mike Burke, president of MSG, then owned by Gulf and Western, Bob Arum said, "We did no negotiating with Teddy Brenner on Ali–Frazier. We made the deal with Mike Burke over dinner at '21." Why Burke instead of the old tradesman Brenner? "Because," Arum says, "Mike Burke is a very intelligent, sophisticated man. And Teddy Brenner is a good matchmaker." He pauses: "I categorize Brenner as an honest person. Extremely unimaginative. He is a boxing purist and a traditionalist. He still doesn't understand the impact and importance of the TV aspect of boxing."[8] Bob didn't get along smoothly with Yank Durham, Frazier's manager, either. Bob said he never understood why Durham didn't like him.

The fight, called Super Fight II, was held on Monday, January 28. Ali was a slight favorite. The fight, billed as the NABF heavyweight championship, was Ali's chance to avenge his loss to Frazier in their first meeting and to secure a fight with George Foreman, who had dethroned Frazier. The fight was the least admired of their three events. It went the distance, giving a unanimous decision to Ali.

In September 1974, Bob promoted another American icon, Evel Knievel. Knievel attempted to jump the Snake River Canyon on a jet-propelled motorcycle. Bob was brought on board to help this pay-per-view event succeed, even though Evel Knievel told Arum to his face that he hated "lawyers, Jews, and New Yorkers,"[9] a trifecta when talking about Bob. Arum proved he could work with anyone.

The event went to Arum after ABC refused to pay Knievel's price to air the jump on the *Wide World of Sports* program. Knievel's investors included Vince McMahon, who took a loss on the event. Some thirty thousand fans watched as his parachute deployed prematurely, and he crashed into the canyon wall on the side he launched from. He had to be rescued from the bottom of the canyon.

In October 1975, Bob Arum, along with Don King, copromoted the Thrilla in Manila, the third and final fight between Muhammad Ali and Joe Frazier. The fight took place at the Araneta Coliseum in Cubao, Quezon City, Philippines, located in Metro Manila. The fight got its name after the always entertaining Muhammad Ali said, leading up to the fight, that it would be "a killa and a thrilla and a chilla, when I get that gorilla in Manila."

The announcement of the third fight took place in June 1975, after Muhammad Ali defeated Joe Bugner in fifteen rounds in steamy Kuala Lumpur, Malaysia. Ali appeared with Joe Frazier only hours later to announce the fight. The Thrilla in Manila came about, according to Arum, when he was approached by a Malaysian major, Thomas Oh, who put him in touch with Luis Tabuena, the Philippines' commissioner of the Games and Amusements Board (GAB) and manager of the Manila airport. "The deal was, the government would put up the money for the fight, a $4 million guarantee. But they taxed the two fighters a total of $1.2 million. So, the net dollars the government put up was only $2.8 million. But the government also provided 300 first-class tickets from San Francisco to Manila on Philippine Airlines."[10] Don King mostly agreed with this story. He said, "We were negotiating with Tabuena, who would take the deal back to Marcos for approval." The government put up $4 Million for the purses and gave the fighters a tax credit of $3 Million which was credited to their US taxes, dollar for dollar."[11]

Both promoters also thought they had side deals with Marcos. King claimed Ferdinand Marcos wanted him to be a representative of Philippine sugar, "selling sugar to other countries." Arum who, along with a New York friend, was invited to Manila by Imelda Marcos, the president's wife, discussed a casino deal. "We worked out a deal where the profits from six hotel casinos would be split 60 percent for us, with Imelda getting the other 40 percent," Bob Arum recalls. "But then Marcos himself found out about our deal and we got the word that we had to make a deal with him too. So, we agreed to give him 40 percent and keep 20 percent, which was still a bonanza. But when Imelda found out about that, she called off the whole thing."[12] Rumors about the fight swirled for years around the contract, including a secret payment to Marcos through a California company that King stiffed him on—a claim he denies.

Frazier's chief second, Eddie Futch, wanted to prevent Ali's tactic of holding Frazier's neck down as he did in the first two fights. Futch claimed that Ali got away with holding more than a hundred times. To prevent this, he wanted to replace referee Zach Clayton with somebody else. He enlisted the help of the Manila mayor and other local officials of Ferdinand Marcos's government, telling them that appointing a Filipino referee would be a matter of pride for the nation. It worked. Carlos Padilla Jr. replaced Zach Clayton as referee. Ali wanted, and received, concessions for a larger ring, allowing him to move more easily, and eight-ounce gloves.[13]

The heat inside the arena was staggering. The metal roof and humidity of the Manila morning—the fight took place at 10 a.m.—made it well over one hundred degrees Fahrenheit in the ring. Ali said he lost five pounds during the fight. The first six rounds were a brutal exchange of blows evenly distributed by both fighters. Ali engaged his "rope-a-dope" strategy, but it enabled Frazier to fight inside, which he preferred. Trainer Angelo Dundee kept yelling at Ali to "get off the damn ropes." After the sixth round, Ed Schuyler, reporter for the *Associated Press* said, "They told me Joe Frazier was washed up," to which Frazier retorted, "They lied."[14][15]

The fight turned for the last time in the thirteenth round when Ali landed dozens of shots to Frazier, who was having great difficulty seeing. Futch stopped it in the fourteenth.

Widely regarded as the best of the trilogy between the two fighters, it was a brutal fight. It was estimated that a billion or more people watched the fight, one hundred million on closed-circuit in movie theaters.[16][17] This was the first fight sent live continuously by satellite to viewers in the United States. In the early seventies, closed-circuit television was the key to broadcast success. Movie theaters, bingo halls, convention centers, and any room large enough and accessible enough to handle the signal and crowd would suffice.

Arum, building on the success of pioneers such as Lester Malitz and Lou Facigno, was becoming a force in the United States. Some other notable global event managers at the time were George Parnassus in the Far East (and any other place he chose to alight), Tito Lectoure in South America, Rodolfo Sabbatini in Italy and France, and Jarvis Astaire in Great Britain. Bob could contact any of them to work out deals. His network was impressive and growing.[18] And Bob Arum was very, very, good for Mexican boxers. Arum and his team made many Mexican fighters wealthy.

The big spectacles make up most of the year's profits for a great promoter. Smaller events throughout the year keep the lights on, but the big event makes the enterprise profitable. Bob's first Vegas fight was in 1978, when Muhammad Ali fought Leon Spinks at the Las Vegas Hilton. After that, Bob forged a long and notable relationship with Caesars Palace; its outdoor stadium thrived as a boxing mecca until the mid-1990s. The Ali versus Leon Spinks fight, on February 15, 1978, was for the WBA and WBC heavyweight belts. The fight came about after Ali got a unanimous decision over Ernie Shavers. Spinks, the 1976 Olympic gold medalist with only seven pro bouts, was chosen by Ali despite knowing that he needed to fight Ken Norton for the fourth time or risk losing the WBC belt. WBC President Jose Sulaimán allowed the match to proceed but required that the winner of this bout face Norton. Both fighters had to agree in writing to this provision.

Spinks, a 10–1 underdog, shocked the boxing world by handing Ali his only championship loss in a ring through a split decision. *Ring* magazine called it the upset of the year. Spinks was later stripped of the WBC belt on March 18 for refusing to fight Norton, instead opting for a rematch with Ali. Arum promoted the fight because it was what Ali wanted. "It was one of the most unbelievable things when Ali agreed to fight him because you look at the fights he had up to then and he was not only not a top contender but shouldn't have been a contender at all," Arum told the Associated Press. "He was just an opponent but somehow he found a way to win that fight."[19]

Ali told Arum to arrange a quick rematch. Bob said that he believed Spinks lost focus between the matches and celebrated way too much. He was even photographed in a bathtub with champagne and a cigar. In the elevator of the hotel in New Orleans a few days before the rematch, Arum encountered Spinks, who had collapsed on the floor. Arum, thinking that Leon was drunk early in the morning, asked him if he was crazy for drinking so much. Spinks replied that he was just coming in from roadwork.

On September 15, 1978, at the New Orleans Superdome, Bob Arum put on an event with a record-tying four championship fights: Ali-Spinks II, Victor Galindez versus Mike Rossman, Danny Lopez versus Juan Malvares, and George Lujan versus Albert Davila. By defeating Leon Spinks, Ali won his third title. Ringside tickets were $200, and ABC paid $5.3 million to broadcast the fight.

In June 1979, Ali sent an official letter of retirement to the WBA. Bob Arum said he paid Ali $300,000 to announce his retirement because Ali's reluctance had delayed the scheduling of a fight between John Tate and Gerrie Coetzee for the vacant WBA title. "We knew Muhammad Ali was going to retire," Arum said, "but as long as he delayed, I couldn't make definite plans."[20] However, in October 1980, Ali returned to face WBC Champion Larry Holmes but was stopped by TKO in the tenth round. He then retired for good after a lackluster loss to Trevor Berbick in December 1981, thus making the second Spinks fight the final win in Ali's career.

After Ali's retirement, for the first of several times in his career, rivals predicted that Bob Arum was through. Bob knew that his superstar attraction needed to be replaced to keep the operation in the black. His genius as a promoter was his ability to keep the system in place with many top fighters leading the next wave such as Sugar Ray Leonard, Marvin Hagler, Tommy Hearns, Oscar De La Hoya, Erik Morales, Manny Pacquiao, and Floyd Mayweather. Today, Top Rank's streak continues as Arum and his stepson, Todd duBoef, president of Top Rank, have showcased Tyson Fury, Terence Crawford, Shakur Stevenson, Teofimo Lopez, Naoya Inoue, Oscar Valdez, Mikaela Mayer, Edgar Berlanga, Miguel Berchelt, José Ramírez, Artur Beterbiev, Josh Taylor, Xander Zayas, Richard Torrez Jr., Janibek Alimkhanuly, Devin Haney, Jared Anderson, Keyshawn Davis, Tiger Johnson, Muhammad Ali's grandson Nico Ali Walsh, and many other up-and-coming superstars.

Arum was always an innovator. Bob wanted to attract attention to his events any way possible to make the biggest splash possible. That was good for business and therefore, good for the gate. He also never shied away from possible political land mines either. His fight in Zaire with King, the fights in China, and doing business with Ferdinand and Imelda Marcos proved that. In 1979, Bob went to South Africa—a location often banned from sports attention due to apartheid—and brought a Black American, Big John Tate, to fight a white Afrikaner in his backyard. On October 27, 1979, Tate (19–0) met Gerrie "the Boksburg Bomber" Coetzee (21–0) at the Loftus Versfeld Stadium in Pretoria, Gauteng, South Africa. Both fighters were twenty-four years old and evenly matched in size and reach.

South Africans latched onto this WBA heavyweight fight as a chance to showcase South Africa and use some international exposure to blunt the perception that fans of worldwide sports should look down on their athletes. At Arum's insistence, apartheid was suspended in the rugby arena for this event. No small thing. He dangled the possibility that ten more events could follow. If Coetzee won, and most white South Africans believed he would, they could show the world that they deserved notice on the world sports stage. Eighty thousand people were in attendance. Businesses spent huge amounts busing clients to the event, including dinner and drinks, many of whom had never seen a boxing event. In the end, Tate was too much for Coetzee, winning a wide unanimous decision. There were celebrations in the Black communities of Johannesburg and Pretoria where, although they said they would have liked to celebrate a South African doing well, this was about apartheid.

After this fight, Tate was proposed as an opponent for Larry Holmes. The match would bring Arum and King together again. They talked separately about an uneasy truce for a Holmes–Tate match. Ultimately, the fight never happened. Arum, who once remarked that Holmes "has the courage of a mouse," said that he would gladly stage a winner-take-all bout. "That just doubles the profits," he said.

"Arum isn't the kind of person I want around me," says King. "But for a one-shot deal, under the right conditions, I'll work with him. I'll do it for Larry. I want to unify the title." And sell a lot of tickets, too.[21]

5

ENTER DON KING

Don's introduction into boxing came shortly after he was released from prison when he worked with Muhammad Ali on a charity boxing exhibition promotion in Cleveland, Ohio. The event helped save the Forest City Hospital in Cleveland. Ali, as he had done for Bob Arum, gave Don his start. It was reported, however, that although the event made a reported $85,000 in ticket sales, the hospital allegedly only ever received $1,500 of it.[1]

> *I made Don King. I made Bob Arum. I am the greatest name in boxing, and I will be the biggest promoter. Everyone will come to me. I will use my name and I will run things. —Muhammad Ali*[2]

Don's real start as a promoter was made possible when he met Don Elbaum, a promoter with a company called Video Techniques, who promoted fights in Pennsylvania and Ohio. Elbaum was mesmerized by King. King worked with Elbaum on fights that included heavyweight Joe Frazier. In 1974, Don was the mastermind behind the Rumble in the Jungle between Muhammad Ali and George Foreman, officially promoted by Don Elbaum of Video Techniques and Hemdale Film Corp., a British company founded by producer John Daly and actor David Hemmings. King managed to get Ali and Foreman to sign for $5 million each, a record at the time. Fred Wyman, an adviser to Zaire dictator Mobutu Seso Seko, convinced him to stage the fight for the benefit of Zaire, which is now known as the Democratic Republic of the Congo. Libya's Muammar Gadhafi put up the money in support of Mobutu.

Don King, March 17, 1975. AP Images

Fifty years ago, January 22, 1973, after attending a heavyweight title fight in Kingston, Jamaica, between George Foreman and Joe Frazier, Don King uttered a line that might well serve as his epitaph: "I came into the ring with the champion," he said, "and I left with the champion." King was invited by and rode to the ring with Frazier in a limo with police escort. As the fight started to go Foreman's way, he moved closer to his corner. He jumped into the ring after Foreman won by stoppage and said to him, "I told you!," leaving with Foreman. George Foreman had just scored one of boxing's most shocking upsets.[3] Don had been courting Foreman leading up to the fight, just in case, volunteering to pick up his family at the airport as they arrived.

In the seventies, King worked with the biggest names in boxing, including Larry Holmes, Wilfred Benítez, Roberto Durán, Salvador Sánchez, Wilfredo

Gómez, and Alexis Argüello. For the next twenty-plus years, talented fighters flocked to King, hoping to headline a card and earn big paydays.[4]

The best description I can muster about Don King is paraphrased from William Manchester. In writing about Douglas MacArthur, Manchester summed him up by writing that he was as wise as a man can be without ethics and as great as a man can be without morals. I think that applies beautifully to DK.

King was larger than boxing. Over the years, he met with Nelson Mandela, Mikhail Gorbachev, Vladimir Putin, Leonid Brezhnev, two popes (John Paul II and Benedict XVI), Tony Blair, Fidel Castro, Ferdinand Marcos, and eight U.S. presidents. Also, as he once recited, "most of the people who have been president of a country in Africa, some Chinese heads of state, every president of Mexico for thirty years, and more senators, governors, and mayors than you can count."

Seth Abraham, the architect of HBO's boxing program, once observed that "Don was incredibly creative in making his fights bigger than just a boxing match and infusing them with sociological importance. Look at how he turned Ali-Foreman into one of the major cultural events of the 1970s by taking the fight to Zaire."[5]

King went on in very short order to promote major fights including the Thrilla in Manila with Ali and Frazier, solidifying his meteoric rise to the top of boxing promotion. This was his first promotion in partnership with Bob Arum, an uneasy partnership that cropped up sporadically for several decades.

Don King was notable for many firsts as a promoter. He was the first notable Black promoter, elevated to that idea by Muhammad Ali, who thought it was about time we have one. But, as Mike Tyson noted, he was not always appreciated. Mike said on ESPN, "I found out that someone I believed was my surrogate father, my brother, my blood figure turns out to be the true Uncle Tom, the true n****r, the true sellout. He did more bad to Black fighters than any white promoter ever in the history of boxing."[6]

It must also be noted that King made at least ninety fighters millionaires. "When I came into boxing, when it was more out of control, no fighters got an opportunity to fight," King said. "I came in; everybody got an opportunity to make a living in America."[7]

King was the first promoter to put up $10 million as a purse, which was the guarantee in Zaire. He was also the first to pay a fighter $10 million. That was what Sugar Ray Leonard was promised for his first fight against Roberto Duran.

In 1976, Don King approached television network ABC about hosting a national boxing tournament on TV. After ABC was on board, King reportedly paid *The Ring* magazine to write fake rankings and records on the competitors to make the event sound more exciting. During the tournament, one of the fighters went to the media saying that the tournament had been rigged so that competitors who had contracts with King would win. The man would further explain that before he even got to the ring, he'd been told he lost the next fight. Once this man came forward, others stepped up and said they had similar experiences, and others claimed there were payoffs. ABC canceled the tournament to put the issue to rest.[8]

Sometime in the late 1970s, a U.S. attorney in the Southern District of New York, where Arum once worked, called to tell him they had information that his life was in danger.

"Who is it?" Arum asked.

The attorney told him he couldn't say.

"So why the f--- are you calling me?!" Arum responded.

Through an FBI agent, Arum found out it was King. He took the threat so seriously that for days after, every day, he changed his walking route to work. When it all got settled with the help of a criminal lawyer who had represented mob guys, King called Arum. King laughed and told him he hadn't been serious.[9]

Boxing is an assembly of interesting people like no other collection of humanity I have ever been exposed to. Through twelve years of school on the outskirts of New York City, four years of chemistry-zoology premed studies at George Washington University in Washington, D.C., bartending and wine captaining, managing a recording studio as chief engineer in D.C., audio engineer at CBS Washington Bureau, and twelve years as a producer/director for the Washington Bullets, Washington Capitals, and Baltimore Orioles, I met special people—but no group like the ones I'd meet in boxing.

Several years after joining Don King Productions, I ran into an old NBA broadcasting friend. He was quite curious about my new life in boxing. I said, "Well, Don King, Mike Tyson, and Al Sharpton all consider me a friend now and boy is my mom proud."

In the fall of 1994, a month after I worked on an NBA preseason game, I was standing on the circular dirt floor of the Plaza del Toros, the most famous bullfighting ring in Mexico City, meeting with people, including Showtime TV people, about the upcoming Carbajal-González fight I was tasked to produce and direct for Don King. I had a momentary pause at one point, wondering how the hell I got there. Seriously, I had only directed sports in clean, well-equipped, "safe" arenas in the United States. Within a month I would work in two Mexican cities; Las Vegas; Quito, Ecuador; and two European cities. This was going to be very different.

To give you some sense of my time with Don King, it's important to know Colonel Bob Sheridan, who had been Don King's announcer for more than twenty years, and our adventures together with Don King Productions. The week of that Carbajal–González fight, my first for Don King Productions, I needed to meet the Colonel. Having worked with several play-by-play announcers in basketball, hockey, and baseball, many of whom I considered life-support systems for overinflated egos, I was more than a little apprehensive about meeting the Colonel. For one thing he called himself "the Colonel." And, because he had been with Don for twenty years, if things didn't work out between us, who, I theorized, would get the boot? Him, or me? On the day before the fight, weigh-in day, I asked one of the Showtime people if they could point out "the Colonel" to me. They pointed to a large gentleman leaning over the rail at the bullring. I walked up to him and asked, "Are you the Colonel?" "Yes," he replied, "are you Mahti?" (That was Boston speak for Marty). "If you're going to be my new pra-doocer, we have to get something straight right off the bat!" Oh God, here it comes, I thought, probably rolling my eyes, "What is *that*, Colonel?"

With a menacing look he said sternly, "I'm in charge of the whores. I've always been in charge of the whores, and I'm always going to BE in charge of the whores. Do you got that?" he asked.

"Did you say 'whores'?" I asked, confused. "Yeah, I got that."

With that he smiled like a kid on Christmas and gave me the biggest bear hug I had ever gotten. Years later, he told me that he was equally concerned about our meeting, having only worked with one producer in his twenty years with Don King, David Fox. He decided to check me out with that joke. If it worked, he guessed, I must have a sense of humor, and we'd get along fine.

I guess it worked. The Colonel was my best friend for the past 35+ years until his passing in 2023.

The Colonel was a cross between John Candy and Spanky McFarland from the Our Gang comedies. He is included here, in a book about Bob Arum and Don King, because the Colonel called great fights for both promoters. He started with King in the seventies, and after I became director of TV for Top Rank, he called fights for Arum for years. That meant that in addition to all the great Tyson, Chavez, Christy Martin, and Felix Trinidad fights, he also called the great Pacquiao, Mayweather, and Crawford fights. The foreign countries that took the shows in English always appreciated his exciting calls and ability to make good fights great and great fights unforgettable. Broadcasters often recited Colonel lines from the telecasts to me like I wasn't there.

The Colonel was not, I should mention, without his issues. Bob was a gregarious Irishman from Boston with all the trimmings. A hard drinker, a quick-to-respond fighter and the best friend you could possibly have due to his loyalty and great sense of humor. Traveling with him had its downsides, however. Especially if you threw the Colonel's former sidekick, Pancho Limon, in the mix. On a flight to New Zealand from LA, we sat in a three-across row with me sandwiched between the two big men. Bob was three hundred pounds then, and Pancho tipped the scales at a slim trim 480. I was their "little friend" at six foot five and 250 pounds. Pancho used seat-belt extenders to make one seat belt across the three of us. He asked the male flight attendant, who was a little timid, for three glasses. When the attendant gave him the glasses Pancho pulled out a bottle of private stock tequila. The attendant, horrified, said, "You can't have that on the plane; get rid of it," and left. Pancho proceeded to pour full glasses of tequila and made us drink it quickly. In about eight minutes, when the attendant returned, Pancho handed him the empty bottle. "I said you can't drink that on the plane," said the flustered employee. "No, you said get rid of it," Pancho corrected. I don't remember much of that seventeen-hour flight.

Bob Sheridan worked more championship fights than any other announcer by a huge margin. The Colonel called more than a thousand championship fights and more than ten thousand fights overall. To put that in perspective, Jim Lampley, HBO's longest and most prolific hall of fame play-by-play announcer for thirty years, has probably called 15–20 championship fights a year for those thirty years or about 400–500 total. The Colonel's number is unmatched because he called all the fights Don King did, including championships that weren't on the broadcast, as well as working longer than almost any announcer except maybe CBS radio's Bob Wolff, Vin Scully of the Dodgers, or Johnny Most of the Celtics. Bob's was likely the longest career of a boxing play-by-play announcer. In 2016, the Colonel was inducted into the International Boxing Hall of Fame in Canastota, New York. This was his fifth Hall of Fame induction.

When Don King hit the boxing scene, it was Angelo Dundee, Muhammad Ali's trainer, who suggested Bob as an announcer to Don Elbaum at Video Techniques and Don King. Bob was twenty-nine years old.

By our third fight together, the colonel and I were already becoming fast friends. I had already met Pancho Limon in Ecuador, a seven-foot tall, 480-pound Mexican, who would be another great boxing acquaintance who stayed a close friend until he passed. Pancho was a certifiable genius. His IQ was off the charts. I told Pancho that the next day he'd meet the Colonel, who was a very interesting guy. Pancho said that he'd be the judge of that. After he met the Colonel, Pancho told me at the airport that I was the first person who ever said that to him and wasn't wrong.

The Colonel's call of the "Rumble in the Jungle" from 1978 is still the one you hear to this day. The U.S. announcers for ABC's *Wide World of Sports*, who weren't in Zaire by the way, despite the fictional account in the movie *Ali*, couldn't be re-aired due to contract issues. It is the Colonel's call, which can also be heard in the 1974 documentary about the fight, *When They Were Kings*, despite that they never got his permission, credited him, or paid him.

One time, while we were staying at the Britannia Hotel on the Isle of Dogs to cover Nigel Benn at the London Arena, the lead boxing writer for the *London Times* asked Bob why he didn't stay at a better hotel in central London. "Why would you stay on the Isle of Dogs?"

"Well," Bob answered, "apparently there is no Isle of Pigs, and the Isle of Bastards wouldn't have us."

There was a terrible brawl at the Britannia one night. And I'm afraid, we were in the middle of it. We were there covering Don King's event starring Tom "Boom Boom" Johnson fighting Prince Naseem at the London Arena. Tom's entourage included six foot five trainer Vonzell Johnson, no relation, a 22–3 light heavyweight who fought Michael Spinks, along with six foot ten cutman Jeff Grmoja and five foot six sparring partner Virgil "Peanut" McClendon. We stayed at the Britannia hotel all week. We frequented the tiny lobby pub, where the Colonel tipped big despite the barman's insistence that it wasn't necessary or expected. "We're American," he said, "we love tipping."

After the sanctioned fight, which Tom lost, the lobby was slammed with fight patrons. The tiny pub had a line stretching across the lobby. When the barman saw the Colonel, he waved him up to the front. A young, intoxicated hooligan, waiting on the line, took offense to the Colonel walking back past him with a tray of pints. "Hey, you, Yank, why don't you consider waiting on the queue?"

"Why don't you consider tipping?" said the colonel.

"Oh, I know you," said the brave, five foot five lad, "you're wiff that n****r fighter."

Stunned by what he heard, despite spending much of his life in Boston, the Colonel began to laugh. "What did you say?"

"You heard me," the young man continued, and he repeated himself.

"Just a moment," the Colonel said, "I want my friend to meet you." And he proceeded to set the drinks down at our large table on the other side of the lobby and tell Vonzell Johnson he had to come and meet his new British friend. Now, standing in front of the kid with this very intimidating looking Black athlete, Bob said, "I'd like you to meet the fighter's trainer." He fully expected the kid to shut the hell up.

"Right," the brainless youth continued, "you're brave now, you have your n****r trainer wiff you." Vonzell was visibly stunned by what he heard.

The Colonel couldn't stop laughing. With tears in his eyes, he egged the kid on. "Say that just one more time."

The fool obliged. He barely got the "N" out this time. He tried to push Vonzell away and took a right cross from somebody, which caused him to taste the floor. A dozen of his friends stepped up and started to brawl. I was being handed pints from our guys, who knew I was useless in a bar fight, including Don King's boxing matchmaking legend Bobby Goodman, and the melee started in earnest. The Colonel, who had ham hocks for fists and knew how to use them, also wore several giant championship boxing rings he had received from the Hall of Fame, as well as fighters Tom Johnson, Christy Martin, Oliver McCall, Francois Botha, and others. Those rings, along with his nearly three-hundred-pound frame behind his swing, made quick work of the attackers two at a time. Vonzell defended himself brilliantly. One hooligan, probably thinking that he'd get "the little guy," decided to go after "Peanut" McClendon, a diminutive southpaw who, unbeknownst to said hooligan, had recently been released from prison, charged with two murders and convicted of a parole violation for a prior assault that landed him in prison for two years. Big mistake.

After taking a cheap shot to the back, Virgil turned around and delivered a twenty-punch combination that resembled a Popeye cartoon fight sequence after the spinach can was opened. He hit him from so many angles that the kid couldn't fall down.

Don King's daughter, Debby, ran upstairs and pounded on cut man "Big" Jeff Grmoja's door. "Jeff, there's a fight. They need you." Jeff jumped out of bed, naked, grabbed a robe, which, of course, was made for an Englishman, not a 350-pound, six foot ten American, and ran down the stairs to help. He dropped combatants with a single punch, bare backside with his manly equipment swinging in the breeze from a bathrobe that barely covered half his butt. The colonel had the original mouthpiece that started this fight in the lobby, and as he readied to land another straight right, yelled, "and my boss is a n****r, too."

The hotel staff, who liked us for tipping all week, alerted us to the police being called and their imminent anticipated arrival by urging us to retreat to our rooms as fast as possible. On the stairs to the second floor, the Colonel apologized to Jeff Grmoja for getting him involved. Jeff said, "Are you kidding, Colonel, that's the most fun I've had since high school."

At 5 a.m. I went to the Colonel's room to get him up for our flight from Heathrow back to the United States only to find him naked on top of his bed snoring with a right hand the size of a prime rib with broken knuckles. I told him I was disappointed to have a "hooligan" for an announcer . . . a line he repeated regularly, always laughing heartily when he did.

Don King had an amazing head for business. His education, which came from the street, not the Wharton School, taught him how to communicate, compete, negotiate, muscle, and outsmart his competition. By the early 1980s Don was not only a strong competitor of Bob Arum and Top Rank, but he surpassed them in many respects. He was a clever competitor and quick study on the fight game. In 1982, King staged what he called his "end run" for the Mike Weaver–Michael Dukes match. Weaver, then the WBA champion, had signed for a voluntary defense against Randall "Tex" Cobb. King claimed that Weaver had also signed with him to meet Dokes. To make sure Dokes, his fighter, got a chance at the WBA title, King signed Cobb to fight Holmes for the WBC championship.

"Give me credit for my genius," King laughed.[10]

Don revolutionized the fighters' pay scale. Nobody ever accused him of underpaying fighters. He achieved many firsts in purses to a main event, individual fighter payments, and total purses on a card.

Many of his detractors accused him of underhanded tactics such as monopolizing a division through intimidation, but the results were there to prove his success. Nobody ever denied that Rockefeller, Getty, Morgan, Vanderbilt, Ford, Astor, or Carnegie were ruthless when they referred to them as aggressive, successful barons of industry. Don faced numerous investigations, insinuations, and rumors. But he was never convicted of a single crime in his boxing career. His competitors and some fighters who weren't pleased with his dominance in the sport complained that he controlled boxing's premier division. In 1983, King had six of the top ten heavyweights. He promoted thirteen of the twenty-seven world champions. Don's matchmaker, Bobby Goodman, who I always thought resembled Barney Rubble a little, said they had 110 fighters in their stable, including a near monopoly of the lightweight and heavyweight divisions. When asked about accusations of wrongdoing, King said, "All I'm doing is working in the tradition of America. I am a pioneer, a trailblazer. I'm tired of chasing rumors."[11]

King had a strong relationship with Caesars Palace, like Bob Arum, until Caesars' top man Cliff Perlman went to the Dunes. Don King followed. On May 20, 1983, Larry Holmes, formally managed by Don King, met Tim Witherspoon, managed by Carl King, at the Dunes in "The Crown Affair," what many believe was the greatest heavyweight contest of the '80s. These two undefeated fighters ebbed and flowed to a twelve-round split decision that ultimately went to Larry Holmes. The ninth round was named round of the year by *Ring* magazine as Witherspoon nearly ended the fight with an assault on Holmes. After he hurt him and threw several unanswered blows, he made a mistake that probably came from his lack of experience in long fights, and looked to referee Mills Lane as if to ask, "Are you going to stop this?" Holmes capitalized on the mistake, went to the well, and launched a counterattack that probably kept him alive to the next round.

This card highlighted King's ability and preference to stock an event with only his fighters. Michael Dokes, managed by Carl King, defended the World Boxing Association version of the title against Mike Weaver. Greg Page and Renaldo Snipes, the top two WBC contenders and both under promotional contract to Don King, met to determine the next WBC challenger. In addition, Osvaldo Ocasio, who has promotional ties to Don King, defended the WBA junior heavyweight title against Randy Stephens and, if Stephens had won, he would have owed Don King options on three title defenses. That King tried to lock up titles so his fighters could fight for them is an accusation I can personally attest to. When Mike Tyson was released from prison in Indiana, Don had lined up two of the heavyweight belts by securing promotional agreements with Bruce Seldon and Frank Bruno. Mike would grab them both after tune-up fights with Peter McNeeley and Buster Mathis Jr.

Working for Don King was a bit like juggling knives for thirteen hours a day, wearing a blindfold and muzzle, on one leg, balanced on a tightrope, suspended over a pit of starving wolverines. I'm only exaggerating slightly. After twelve years in broadcasting, starting as a first-class FCC engineer in a UHF station, managing a recording studio, working as an engineer on the first two years of the BET network, a decade of producing and directing 110 MLB, NBA, and NHL games a year on the road, I was surprised to be completely unprepared for the new position as VP of TV production for Mr. Don King. He was unlike any person I had ever met, any boss I had ever had, and ran a company that was unlike any I had ever imagined. And I bet you'd be surprised to learn that the six department heads of the company when I worked there included three women, three Jews, and all were white.

I started with Don King Productions at the end of 1993. The job I had as executive sports producer covering the Bullets, Capitals, and Orioles was coming to an end. The general manager of the Paramount station in Washington, D.C., that the games aired on gave me a confidential heads-up that this would be our last season. Paramount was launching a third *Star Trek* show, *Babylon 5*, to go with its *Star Trek the Next Generation* and *Voyager* series, which meant that it was looking to ditch the poorly rated Bullets basketball and Capitals hockey games so as not to preempt the Star Trek shows. So, when I got an unsolicited call from a production company in Florida, calling themselves TVP Productions, offering me an executive sports producer position for live sports broadcasts with good salary and benefits, plus international travel and full control over the department, I was interested in hearing what they had to say. The story of my hiring at Don King Productions, although I apologize for its length, tells you a lot about Don and his company.

I flew from my home in Silver Spring, Maryland, to the interview in Oakland Park, Florida. Upon arriving at the three-story building, where I was supposed to report for the interview, I noticed a Don King logo behind the receptionist's desk. I asked if this was, in fact, the office for TVP. The confused receptionist said she had never heard of TVP. I apologized and said I must have the address wrong because I was supposed to meet a certain person at TVP. She said, "Yes, she is here, but she works for Don King Productions."

Thoroughly confused, I confessed to my interview contact that I was unaware that TVP was owned by Don King, and I immediately confessed that I wasn't a boxing person. I had produced and directed many sports but never boxing. She said that she was afraid that if she mentioned Don and boxing, I might not come to the interview. I confessed I wouldn't have. I had the same prejudices as others about Don's background and reputation. For the next four hours, I was introduced to the department heads of Don King Productions and told that they got my name from a satellite vendor they partnered with who knew about me in D.C. Their producer, who was with them since Don King started as a promoter, was injured, unable to work, and they needed a replacement. They had heard that I had similar qualifications to their producer, which meant I could combine the skills of a producer, director, production manager, tech manager, and department head, and they needed someone very quickly due to pressing upcoming events. It wasn't until well after I started that I learned that David Fox, Don's sixty-one-year-old producer of twenty years, was horribly beaten at the MGM in Las Vegas, listed as a John Doe for three days at the hospital, and nearly died with bones broken in his face and brain damage. The reason he was attacked in the men's room at 3 a.m. is still listed as unknown. A small Brit with a gray/white ponytail, David had won playing craps. He might just have been a robbery victim.

Don was supposed to be at the interview but was away on business unexpectedly. I left that interview thinking that it had been an interesting way to spend a day, but there was no possible way that I would consider working with those people. For one thing, I wasn't a boxing guy. I had never directed boxing. I was also a bit of a pacifist who didn't like fighting, didn't know anything about boxing, and couldn't remember ever watching more than a few seconds of a match. Couple that with my negative impression of Don King based on a few bits of information about him I'd come across, like him killing two people, and I went back to Maryland to look for other possibilities.

The very next day I got a call from the person I met with, asking me to come right back to Florida to meet Don, who was very apologetic that he had been called away. He really wanted to meet me urgently. As I've told my kids for the past 30+ years, always try to keep an open mind. You can always say no later, so I said I would come back. After all, how many chances do you get to meet a guy like Don King? I went back two days later and was met warmly with another apology that Don had been called away again. I met a few new people and was even more firmly convinced that these people were borderline crazy and out of control and I'd never fit in.

Back to Maryland.

A couple days later, I was called and told that a first-class ticket was being overnighted to me to fly to London to meet Don King. See previous post-interview thoughts above for my thoughts on this call, as well.

The day after the ticket arrived, I was told that Don was leaving London and wanted me to meet him in Las Vegas. I had to meet this guy.

I went to Vegas and was supposed to meet Don after a press conference he was holding at the MGM. I was in the audience taking in this strange new world of boxing and its unique group of people and atmosphere. The new hitch, and I'm sure you knew there would be one, was that on this day Don was indicted by the federal court in the Southern District of New York for wire fraud. Bob Arum, who you remember came from the DOJ, had many close friends at the Southern District Court, so Don immediately accused him of arranging the indictment.

The press conference quickly slid into a rant by Don about how he was being persecuted, not prosecuted, by Arum and his friends at the SDNY court to keep the Black man down. He claimed, in increasingly hostile tones, that they were lynching him because they can't compete with him fairly. He went on for quite a while. "The problem with this country," Don King said, "is the Jewish prudence system!" That got my attention. Besides thinking that that was a genius play on words, I immediately realized that I was afraid of Don. I asked my contact at DKP sitting next to me who, like me, was Jewish, if Don was always like this. She realized that her prospective new hire shouldn't be hearing this volatile rant and whisked me away to speak with cooler-headed, safer people. I left for home without meeting the man a third time.

Yup, you guessed it: the day after returning home, an even more apologetic call beckoned me back to Florida to meet Don, who was now in a real hurry to meet me. He had big, complicated international shows in a couple of weeks. I decided that despite not being interested in joining that world, I would benefit in life from having met this powerhouse of a man. I couldn't resist the unique opportunity. I always felt that any job interview was a learning opportunity that should be experienced.

This fourth interview would be completely different. Not only was Don there, but he treated me like a celebrity and lavished his attention on me for hours, in what I realized too late was a sales pitch. He can be very charming when he needs to be. He asked me questions about myself and my TV background, praised my skills and accomplishments, which I'm sure he knew absolutely nothing about, and listened to everything I said in a completely convincing act of interest. He asked what I knew about St. Patrick's Day, because he wanted to have a St. Pats fight in Boston. I said that I didn't know much other than that Saint Patrick chased the snakes out of Ireland. He seized on that elementary school wisdom, calling it brilliant. Within an hour he was on a scheduled conference call in his office with me standing next to him telling a large gathering of boxing beat writers and reporters that he was coming to Boston on St. Patrick's Day and, "as my favorite TV guy Marty Corwin says, we're going to chase the snakes out of town just like old Saint Patrick did in Ireland." I couldn't believe Don was quoting me to reporters. I was completely fooled into being flattered.

I watched Don for hours in his office smoking a big, fat cigar, lavishing attention on me, while he was handed things to sign, speaking with people popping into the office, handling calls, quoting philosophers and writers, educating me on the greatness of boxing as a sport, and barking instructions to people outside his office about urgent meetings and tasks to come.

I had never seen a dynamo like Don King. He clearly had a photographic memory, and I believed him to be one of the smartest men I had ever met and that he possessed the business skills of a Fortune 500 CEO. I knew absolutely nothing of the character of the man.

At about 3 p.m. Don walked me around the office to again meet some of the department heads I had already met. In front of several of them, he asked me what it would take to bring a great television guy like me into his organization. I asked, "Do you mean salary?"

"Yeah, man, I don't know what you make."

I threw out what I thought was a very big number as I had no intention of working there and wanted to get back home on my flight in a couple hours to tell my friends and family what I saw. "I like you," he said and shook my hand.

"Make sure he's on the plane in the morning," he barked at Jim Merila, his head of pay-per-view events, and left the room.

"Our flight is at 6 a.m. tomorrow," the PPV manager said.

"No, I have a flight in a couple hours to Maryland," I said, standing there confused in my three-piece suit holding a small briefcase with no luggage as I was only there for the day. They all started to laugh at me.

Another of the department heads said, "The man asked you for a number, you gave him one, and he shook your hand. You work here now. We leave for Mexico City at 6 a.m." It took several minutes to sink in. What would I tell my wife and two small children back in Maryland expecting me for dinner? It turned out that I didn't see them again for a month. I was taken to a store with a company credit card where I purchased clothes, toiletries, and a suitcase. The next day I was on the dirt floor of that famous bullring, Plaza del Toros, in Mexico City, trying not to look like a four-year-old being asked to drive a car.

In the next four weeks, I learned how much I would enjoy Mexico and its people. I found out how little I knew about tequila. I flew on the presidential plane with the acting president in Ecuador. I visited palaces in Quito and Guayaquil with Don. I met one of the richest men in Mexico, the owner of Maseca Flour in Monterrey.

This was my first of hundreds of boxing trips all over the world and began my new affection and deep respect for other cultures and people outside the United States.

A month later when attending my first department head meeting, seated next to my new friend Carl King, Don's stepson, I wasn't concerned about anything. Carl and I became friends because we were close in age, and both of us worked in the conference room at Don King Productions because our offices weren't sorted out yet at the Oakland Park building. Carl loved the NBA and, since I had just left it, talked about it to me for long periods of time. I didn't know he was Don's stepson initially. I never asked his last name. I learned who he was when another manager at DKP joked that I was sucking up to the boss's son. At the department head meeting, I had information on upcoming shows, I had my work caught up, and was used to giving reports on my department after my years at Viacom and Paramount. Don was in a foul mood for some unknown reason. He started screaming at everyone in turn about one thing after another. I still wasn't concerned because I was the new guy and hadn't done anything I could get yelled at for, as far as I knew. When he got around to me, he had thought of something to yell at me about. "I thought I told you to call," somebody or other. "He called me and said he hadn't heard from you. When I tell you to do something . . .", all at the top of his lungs. I guess I looked like a deer caught in the headlights because I was stunned. Nobody had ever yelled at me like that at work before. After Don went on to the next person, Carl King leaned over to me and whispered to me, "I guess now you know?"

"Know what?" I asked.

"We're all n*****s on this bus," he said.

After this introduction by fire, I settled into a steady diet of interesting adventures with the Colonel and Pancho in fabulous and not-so-fabulous locales. It made no difference to DK as long as the deal was right.

With my head swimming in the strange new world of boxing, I was working everyday with the Colonel. Mexico City, Merida, London, Quito, Las Vegas, all in my first month.

The first event of which I was fully in charge was the world championship match between Bernard Hopkins and Segundo Mercado in Quito, Ecuador, on December 17, 1994. If I had thought about it longer, I might have run and hid at that point. I was feeding Showtime back in the United States because they chose not to be there. Bernard Hopkins's manager was Rock Newman. I knew Rock from Washington, D.C. He was Marion Barry's campaign manager for his return as mayor after his crack cocaine incident. When Bernard and Rock arrived in Quito, right before the fight, they toured the venue. Their dressing room had a water leak and was freezing. Rock asked me if it could get fixed. I talked with the building people and took care of it, including adding a space heater. Don read me the riot act and told me to mind my own business. Another boxing wake-up call.

Three days before the fight, Don handed me a check for $17,000 and told me to go with the local promoter, a car dealer, to convert the check into Ecuadorian money so he could pay the locals in cash. The Ecuadoran currency was Sucres at that time; now, U.S. dollars are the national currency. In 1994, the currency exchange was 2,800 Sucres to the U.S. dollar. So, Don's check was worth 47,600,000 Sucres. I spent three hours being ferried in the back of a Jeep by the local promoter from one business to another, then one bank to another, to collect that many Sucres. I hung on for dear life, being buffeted back and forth on bad roads around hairpin turns, counting 10,000 Sucre notes, one million, two million, three million, like a cartel banker being pursued by the police. When I arrived back at the Oro Verde hotel Don yelled, "Where is my money?" I held up five shopping bags. He roared in laughter at the sight. My crew and I, by the way, stayed at the Quito Inn, which had no hot water and almost no staff. I called Don to ask why we weren't at the Oro Verde because the conditions at the hotel I nicknamed "Mo's Quito Inn" were so bad. Don screamed at me never to ask a question about a hotel again. I never did.

A month before the fight, we went to Quito on a site survey. I brought my friend and cameraman Steve Greenbaum from Florida on the survey. We traveled on the president's jet, dined at the Palace, and were toured like dignitaries in Guayaquil and Quito. On a street in Guayaquil, an extremely old woman exited a seven-hundred-year-old church. As we passed, she raised her hands and said, "Don King," in a deferential voice. I wondered how she could possibly know Don here in Ecuador. Then I realized that everything about Don added to his notoriety. Boxing was universal, and Don King had a great Q rating, also known as quotient factor. I always told that story when somebody asked why he wore his hair like that and acted like a living cartoon character.

Quito was where I met Pancho Limon. Pancho, whose real name was Jose Francisco Hernandez Limon, was the most intimidating person I had ever met. Pancho's father was one of the three men who founded San Felipe, Baja, Mexico. Pancho didn't need to work but liked us and boxing, so he was a great friend who occasionally, as in Ecuador, saved the show. Pancho was also a brilliant man. He purported to be a wizard, of the Carlos Casteñeda, *Teachings of Don Juan*, variety. He regularly called me out of the blue when I was thinking of him, made people do things that seemed impossible, and was the most influential person I had ever met. So, I believed he was.

I could write an entire book about only Pancho, and he deserves one. This first meeting will show you what I mean.

Quito was my second or third fight for Don King. So international television broadcasting arrangements were new to me. Especially a huge "fly-pack" production in a difficult place such as Ecuador. A "fly-pack" production is where all the equipment comes in cases and needs to be assembled. This contrasts with a production truck rolling up with the equipment already installed. My production manager, Chuck Haifley, arranged for forty cases of rental gear to be shipped from Los Angeles, which collectively weighed nearly ten tons. They arrived on Wednesday at Quito customs and needed to be completely set up by Friday. So, they had to be at the arena by Thursday morning at the latest. Chuck thought it would be a good idea to bring his friend Pancho, who was Mexican and fluent in Spanish, to be a coordinator. Pancho, he said, was very influential and would undoubtedly be helpful. That was the biggest understatement of all time. That event would have never been televised without Pancho.

I was immediately surprised at his size when we met. He was approximately 7 feet tall and weighed more than 450 pounds. He was bigger than any NBA player I had ever worked with. I stood next to him looking up, despite being six foot five myself. I asked, "How tall are you?"

"Well," he answered in a powerful, calm bass voice, "you don't have a bald spot."

"That's pretty tall," I said.

On Wednesday of fight week, I met Pancho for the first time at customs in Quito. After discussing the logistics of the equipment and event, Pancho walked over to the customs officer with the paperwork that I handed him and talked to a man, who was nearly two feet shorter, in Spanish before returning to me. "It can't happen," he said.

"What?" I asked, "Thursday delivery? How about Friday?" That would make it very difficult to be ready on time.

"No," Pancho said, "getting the equipment through customs this month. The fastest this much equipment has ever cleared customs is two weeks, but they're a little backed up now so it will be longer."

"Oh, my God," I said out loud. The fight was in three days, and I was going to get fired in four.

"How important is this stuff?" Pancho asked. I told him it was irreplaceable. The show wouldn't happen without it.

"I'll be back," Pancho said in a very calm voice. I was thinking of nothing other than whether I could get another job in the NBA or NHL to replace this one I was definitely losing. After all, I had met the president of the country on his private plane and promised a great event. Showtime was also counting on me as they weren't in the country.

I watched Pancho, who was twenty yards away, speak with one and then a second, more senior, man, gesturing toward me and taking out his huge cell phone. The men kept holding Pancho's arm so he wouldn't use the phone and speaking with him, becoming more animated as time went on. Pancho remained calm throughout. After about fifteen minutes, Pancho came back to me. "Where do you want the stuff delivered?"

I told him where the arena was but said I hired a trucking company that was waiting for my call to alert them when to come to the airport.

"Cancel them," Pancho said. "Your boxes will be there tonight," and walked away.

Almost afraid to ask, I said, "What did you tell them? What's happening?"

"I just told them I understood their problem, and I was calling their president to inform him that the event he was hosting with the Ecuadorian national hero champion couldn't happen. They said that the cases would be through customs in an hour, and they would deliver them personally in two hours in their government trucks."

I asked how he had gotten the president's phone number. He said, "I don't even know his name." Pancho amazed me continuously like this for the next two decades.

In the days before the fight, we were taken to a special tourist attraction near Quito, el Mitad del Mundial, the Middle of the World. It's one of the two places where zero latitude meets zero longitude. The other is in the middle of an ocean. You can straddle the equator and zero longitude. There is a marker and a museum there and many tourist shops. At a large hat shop in the middle of the marketplace, many of us walked in including the Colonel and Carl King. Carl was constantly teasing the Colonel about being from Boston and testing him to get his responses on Black issues. Carl was very sensitive to any racist views. Inside the store, Carl spotted an African kufi hat. He suggested that it was perfect for the big Bostonian and said he should put it on. He picked up the African hat and put it on, the Colonel's eyes got big, he looked off to the sky, and exclaimed, "Carl, this is amazing. I understand now."

"Understand what, Colonel?" asked Carl.

"I understand everything now," he said, still wearing the hat. "I hate white people."

Everybody laughed except Carl.

Carl tried the Colonel again on Black issues after the Peter McNeeley versus Mike Tyson fight shortly after the OJ trial. Mark Furman, the police officer who was grilled about using the "N" was the subject of conversation. After the fight, the Colonel and I were walking through the old Betty Boop bar at the MGM at about 2 a.m. Carl and a few of his friends, who were all agitated about the trial, stopped the Colonel and asked, "Did you see the trial?

The Colonel answered that he hadn't. "I know you're from Boston, Colonel," Carl said. "Do you ever use the N-word?"

"No, Carl, I never ever say the N-word," quickly answered the Colonel. And then after a well-timed pause he added, "I do say n****r, probably daily." And everyone but Carl roared with laughter. The Colonel was as far from a racist as you could get. He's just a funny bastard. In his last two years of life, he "adopted" three young Black men as "sons," Dennis, Darrin, and Damon. They were inseparable.

In my second year with Don, it almost came to a screeching halt one night. I directed the world feed of the fight between Nigel Benn and Gerald McClellan at the London Arena on February 25, 1995. After a brutal fight, which should have ended in the first round after Benn was knocked out of the ring for more than ten seconds, the British Boxing Board not only suspended the rules, whereby a fighter out of the ring for ten seconds lost, but allowed him to fully recover before continuing. It absolutely would have been stopped in the second round by any non-British referee, because Benn was taking too much punishment without answering, but continued until McClellan suffered a subdural hematoma and needed brain surgery.

He was in a coma for two weeks and hasn't fully regained his speech, sight, or the ability to walk to this day. I had become very friendly with Gerald. He was a young man I wanted to hang out with. I believed he was the next superstar, and I wanted to be on the bandwagon. The catastrophic ending really shook me up. I announced to everyone that night that I was leaving DKP. Several people rallied to talk me out of it, from the Colonel to Don's head of boxing operations to several other staff. It affected me dramatically. I think about is constantly.

The Tyson era was now in full swing. I first met the champ when he was in prison in Indiana on a rape charge. I was sent to interview him with commentator Charles Bietry for Canal+, the French sports network. When I walked in with John Horne, Tyson's friend and co-manager, Mike looked at me and said to John, "Don got himself another one."

I asked John what he meant. "You're Jewish, aren't you?" asked Horne.

Mike surprisingly asked for, and received, books on French architecture from the Canal+ journalist who was there for the interview. I learned that Mike was much deeper than I thought. If he trusted you, as he did my friend Jody Heaps, a writer from Showtime, he would have deep discussions on a wide range of topics from philosophy to world affairs. You'd be surprised at how deep he is. I believe part of his aggressive nature derived from an insecurity about how his speech made him sound. So, he overcompensated.

I was with Don when Mike came out of prison. Don, me, Mike, and Mike's fiancée, Monica, made clandestine moves to avoid the press and took a private plane from Indiana back to Southington, Ohio, where Mike lived. I had a camera on my shoulder in the plane almost the entire time. Every time I tried to put it down, Mike said, "Keep shooting; I might do something funny." We were sequestered at Mike's huge house while Mike kept moving upstairs and downstairs in a new set of pajamas every few hours to sign contracts with Don King; executives from the MGM; Jay Larkin, head of boxing; and Showtime CEO Matt Blank.

Mike's personal cook fed everyone steaks, lobsters, ribs, and other fine seafood. All Mike's favorites. I walked outside occasionally in my leather Showtime Boxing Jacket to get air. The next morning, I read in Wally Matthews's column in the *New York Post* that Don King and the Showtime Boxing TV crew were thrown out of Mike's house because Mike was furious that Don ate shellfish in Mike's presence. Matthews reported that Tyson dumped Don and was going to fight for the Nation of Islam now that he was a Muslim. I

Don King, January 30, 2003. AP Images

showed the article to Don in Mike's kitchen and asked when that happened. He laughed from his belly.

Don did try to avoid confrontations with Louis Farrakhan's people. At a meal at Sylvia's in Harlem, I was seated between two Nation of Islam representatives across from Don. Don told them that he was very impressed with their dedication and commitment to Islam and that he was considering becoming a Muslim himself. Don's son, Carl, leaned over to his dad and said, "You'd have to give up ribs, Dad."

"Well, I guess that ain't happening," said Don. The shortest conversion ever.

My first mega-event was Tyson versus McNeeley. The lead-up to the event with press conferences, satellite media tours, and building a TV compound that included separate facilities for several other countries including France, Germany, Japan, England, and Mexico was bigger than any NBA or NHL playoff game I had produced. We created shows every day of the week for the pay-per-view.

The weigh-in show was tremendous. There was a red-carpet show the day of the fight. The non-pay-per-view preliminary fights were on TV, as well. Showtime had hundreds of people flown in from every department to participate. I had been living at the MGM for weeks, in the old emerald tower, which was really the worst part of the hotel, with corridors that were so long you felt like you had changed time zones. The Colonel was in rare form doing interviews that went all over the world, educating and entertaining boxing fans in a hundred countries.

My other two favorite Tyson stories happened around the Tyson versus Holyfield II Fight, the ear-bite fight. When the fight ended with that vicious ear bite, I was sick to my stomach seeing it in slow motion. I did, however, show the replay twenty times from every angle and even in extreme slow motion. I made the truck engineer open the TV truck door so I could get some air because I wanted to barf. But I showed it over and over, like a professional.

Weeks before the fight, I was in San Antonio with Don on an event when he held an impromptu press conference announcing the name of the upcoming Tyson versus Holyfield rematch. "We're calling the fight 'The Sound and the Fury,'" King announced to a few dozen reporters and a handful of cameras.

A San Antonio reporter asked, "Why the sound and the fury?"

"I'm glad you asked that question," Don replied, and many rolled their eyes at the embellished story they knew was coming. "I was lying in bed one night, and I got a vision and a call from the other side. When the other side calls, you gotta answer. Ernest Hemingway was standing at the foot of my bed, plain as day, and told me I had to name the fight The Sound and the Fury."

The literate reporter, who beamed broadly because he thought he could expose Don's mistake, said, "Uh, Don, *The Sound and the Fury* was written by William Faulkner, not Ernest Hemingway!"

"Everybody knows that," Don said, "that's exactly what Hemingway said. Name it after Faulkner's *The Sound and the Fury*."

6

ARUM AND KING
The Eighties

Seth Abraham, former president of HBO who worked with Arum for years, declared that "Bob is the most advanced thinker ever in the marriage of television and boxing. Don operated largely in the present, Bob was always thinking down the road."[1] That flies in the face of Don King having planned for, and obtaining, three of the four heavyweight belts while Mike was in prison to fight for upon his release.

On June 20, 1980, Sugar Ray Leonard (27-0), copromoted by Bob Arum, fought former undisputed lightweight champion Roberto Duran (71-1), promoted by Don King. Duran had been 8 and 0 since moving up to welterweight. Leonard, who was defending his welterweight belt, was almost the de facto promoter, working with copromoters Arum and King and negotiating finances. "He and Mike Trainer have done a great job," Bob Arum said with admiration for how the champion and his lawyer had arranged the finances for the June 20 fight at the Olympic Stadium in Montreal. Arum confidently predicted that it would be the biggest money-earning event in boxing history.[2]

"Even before the first closed-circuit money really rolled in," Arum said, "Ray had about $5 million in the bank." In the deal that Trainer worked out, Arum and King sold the live gate for $3.5 million to the Olympic Installations Board, which ran Olympic Stadium. All $3.5 million went to Leonard. If they sold all 77,000 seats—Arum predicted a crowd of about 60,000—the Montreal organizers could take in $8.6 million. Of the $3.5 million that Leonard received, he had to pay Duran $500,000, the only real "purse" connected with the fight. The rest of the money that the boxers earned would be from percentages of the closed-circuit and foreign television rights. This fight was only available on closed

Bob Arum in his New York office, April 21, 1978. AP Images

circuit, which ruled the day back then. This was evidence of the tremendous business savvy of Sugar Ray Leonard. He was one of boxing's best business-men. This continued after boxing as he became a real estate mogul, owning many properties in Hyattsville, Maryland, and elsewhere.

Duran was called "El Cholo" (of indigenous roots) and "Manos de Piedra" (hands of stone) due to his punching strength.[3] This first meeting between Leonard and Duran was dubbed the Brawl in Montreal. The fight took place in the Olympic Arena where Leonard had captured his gold medal four years ear-lier. Duran overcame a five-inch reach disadvantage by being the more aggres-sive fighter and captured a unanimous decision, although it was initially called a majority decision after a mistake in one judge's card was corrected. Arum said that Duran clearly got under Leonard's skin before the fight.

Duran had a spy watching Leonard's hotel to alert him if Leonard's wife, Juanita, was leaving the hotel. Then Duran jumped in a waiting car and drove next to her saying things to her that he knew would get back to Leonard. It drove Sugar Ray crazy and made him brawl, instead of boxing Roberto, and cost him the fight. Bob Arum said, "That caused Leonard to lose that fight. It's why he fought Duran the way he did during their first fight. Ray had to box to win that fight, and he knew it. And that's what he did in the rematch and their third fight. But Duran, he just had a way of getting under his opponent's skin."[4]

Leonard summed it up this way: "He pissed me off. He challenged my manhood, and I fell for it. His [verbal] attacks weren't calculated. It's just the way Duran was. He won through intimidation. I wasn't intimidated. I was mad. I wanted to kill him. I was twenty-four and I wasn't mature enough to respond to his trash. His wife gave my wife the finger. I didn't think it had to go that far."

The "No Mas" fight, officially Duran versus Leonard II, took place on November 25, 1980. Billed as "The Superfight," it took place in the Louisiana Superdome in New Orleans. The fight became famous after, in the eighth round, Duran turned to the referee and said, "No mas," Spanish for no more, in response to, as some experts concluded, Leonard's taunting and tactics. In the seventh round Leonard had swung his right hand around, advertising a "bolo punch," and then jabbed with his left. This antic infuriated Duran. It should be noted that Duran claimed that he never said "no mas'" to anyone. He suggested that Howard Cosell came up with that on ABC sports. He said he stopped due to stomach cramps.[5]

The early '80s was the height of the Arum–King rivalry. Arum would later remark that it helped keep him sharp. At the time, however, I don't think he appreciated King's dealings and manipulations. A good example of the friction between them in dealing with fights and fighters back then was the case of Roberto Duran. Roberto was made a centerpiece of a feud between the two promoters after he apparently tried to move from King to Arum in 1982.

On July 21, 1982, in a fit of anger that, by Duran's description, was purely impulsive, Duran signed a contract with Bob Arum's Top Rank to fight WBA champion Davey Moore on November 19. Duran said he was unaware at the time that he was under obligation to fight three more times under the banner of Don King Productions, while King insisted that Duran would, instead, fight Tony Ayala of San Antonio on November 19. The impression was that Roberto Duran, out of blind loyalty to Don King, would bypass the title shot that could resurrect the love and admiration of his countrymen that drowned in a sea of humiliation when he quit against Leonard, and instead fight the No. 3-ranked Ayala. The reality, as Arum suggested, was that "The whole thing, the pending Arum–King legal battle over rights to promote Duran, is to get King a piece of the Duran-Moore title fight promotion November 19."[6]

Duran tried to explain away this latest controversy at a news conference. The former champion sat at the head table in Larry Holmes's Round One Lounge. King had held exclusive rights to Duran in his glory years. However, King's interest in Duran appeared to diminish after the once-peerless champion quit against Leonard in New Orleans in November 1980. Duran said his decision to join forces with Arum was prompted by an item in the *New York Daily News* that quoted Carlos Eleta as saying he no longer was Duran's manager. He said he called Arum immediately, went to the promoter's New York apartment where he signed the contract, and accepted a check for $25,000 as a show of Arum's good faith.

"I was very upset because that was in the paper," Duran said through Luis Henriquez, his longtime friend and new manager. "Carlos criticized me as 'fat' and said that I should be in the 'heavyweight division.' I'd have personal problems with Carlos. I accept the problems. I accept them because some of it was my fault. But it was difficult to continue with him. I was very angry and upset. That's when I went to Arum. I was wrong. I have apologized to King." On Henriquez's advice, Duran returned a cashier's check for $25,000 to Arum. However, Arum said he refused to accept it. Contacted in his New York office, Arum insisted that Duran had no obligation to fight for King. "His contract is for one fight," Arum said, referring to a September 4 bout against Curtland Lane of England. "It's only for one fight, unless they think they can back-date the contract." Arum said he had no plan to interfere with Duran's September fight. However, Arum said that he would not stand by and permit Duran to fight in October, as Henriquez planned. "Duran signed a contract with me, and Duran is liable to me for damages," Arum said. "There's no way he'll fight in October because that's too close to the November date. He won't fight again. Ever."[7] Duran, of course, fought twenty-one years more, all the way up to 2001.

Bob Arum knew how to fill a big venue. The Orange Bowl in Miami was the setting for the massive Alexis Argüello versus Aaron Pryor mega-event on November 12, 1982. "The Battle of the Champions" would lead to the first ever four-weight division champion if Arguello prevailed. Dustin Hoffman pushed Arum for a better seat; Muhammad Ali was stumping in crowds in Coconut Grove with his shirt off showing his legendary moves. Vicki La Motta was dazzling crowds with talk of jabs, head feints, and staying power. This was the biggest south Florida event in boxing since 1964.

"This is the biggest Latin fight of all time. Anywhere, anytime, period," boasted Bob Arum. "This is becoming a Latin festival. I would say between 50 per cent and 60 per cent of the people in the Orange Bowl tonight will be Spanish-speaking people."[8]

HBO was carrying this broadcast, showing Pryor for the first time on their network. Pryor had been scheduled to fight Sugar Ray Leonard, but that fight was postponed when Leonard suffered a detached retina. The Pryor-Argüello fight was memorable for several reasons. Before the bout even started, a man with a gun tried to gain access to Argüello's dressing room. Alexis was hurried into and guarded in a shower room. The man was stopped, arrested, and re-moved with the help of spectators.[9]

From the start of the fight, the contrasting styles were evident. Pryor tried to push the pace aggressively, throwing numerous and reckless assaults while Arguello remained calm, throwing fewer but more effective punches. Pryor kept pushing the pace and won a few rounds in the middle of the fight before Argüello took charge and hurt him in the late rounds, especially the eleventh. The fight ended in the fourteenth as Pryor was able to do significant damage to Argüello, nearly knocking him out of the ring before referee Stanley Christo-doulou stopped it.

The biggest controversy in the bout surrounded Pryor's water bottle, which people noticed was changed by his trainer between rounds. The manager was caught on a mic saying, "give me the other bottle, the one I mixed." Pryor seemed to come out refreshed and re-invigorated after that exchange. Aaron's trainer was the notorious Panama Lewis, who was banished from boxing after the infamous scandal where he removed padding from his fighter Luis Resto's gloves before he fought Eddie Collins Jr. Pryor didn't take a drug test after the bout. Pryor won the rematch with Argüello, and both fighters retired after the bout.

* * *

Bob Arum's first broadcast partnership in 1983 was with a start-up broadcast outlet for sports that was called the Entertainment and Sports Programming Network, ESPN. Now, forty years later, Bob is back with ESPN as a partner. Top Rank and ESPN showcased new and up-and-coming fighters. Great content for the new network. The first Top Rank fight on ESPN was between middleweights Frank Fletcher and Ben Serrano from Atlantic City in 1980. When that first Top Rank–ESPN partnership ended in 1996, it was the longest running cable series and longest running weekly boxing series in history.

Bob quickly became prolific as a promoter. He had a natural talent at build-ing that shaky card table and convincing fighters to join him, venues to want his events, broadcasters that his events were going to attract viewers, and the public that they couldn't miss this fight. Bob's keen skill at making legendary matches is clear; over the years those included fights such as Ali versus Frazier, Leonard versus Duran, Foreman versus Frazier, Hagler versus Hearns, Corrales versus Castillo, De La Hoya versus Mosley, the Morales versus Barrera trilogy, the fights of Iran Barkley, Michael Carbajal, Floyd Mayweather, and the greatest fights of Manny Pacquiao.

Don King, by contrast, was more often a controversial mastermind in the handling of his fights and fighters, even his superstars.

In 1982, Muhammad Ali sued King for underpaying him $1.1 million for his fight with Larry Holmes. In the hospital with failing health, Ali signed off on a deal accepting a $50,000 cash settlement from King.[10]

The settlement for Ali was delivered by a friend of his. The friend took the suitcase and the agreement to the hospital where Ali was staying. Ali signed the agreement and took the money. The agreement also gave King the right to promote any future fights Ali would be in. The friend later admitted that he regretted helping King, not realizing how much the man had needed money. Ali's lawyer reportedly cried when he found out how the lawsuit had ended.[11]

Larry Holmes also sued King in June 1984, saying his promoter had taken $10 million over the years in earnings that were supposed to go to Holmes. In one instance, Holmes indicated he had received only $150,000 from a contract that guaranteed him $500,000. Later, Holmes would settle for a payment of $150,000 from Don King and sign an agreement that said Holmes would no longer say negative things about King in the press.

Muhammad Ali's longtime physician Ferdie Pacheco once suggested, "Think of Don King as a sledgehammer and Bob Arum as a stiletto." British promoter Mickey Duff remarked, "One's Black and one's white. That's the only difference."[12]

In 1984, the same year that Don King and his secretary, Constance Harper, were indicted on insurance fraud charges, King promoted the Victory Tour with Michael Jackson and his brothers across the United States and Canada. Don got a large up-front payment. Michael donated his proceeds mostly to charities such as the United Negro College Fund, Camp Good Times for terminally ill children, and his own foundation. It was the only tour with all six Jackson brothers, and it went from July to December 1984. It would also be the last time they appeared together, as the tour was plagued with ill will and tempers flaring among the brothers.

It was rumored that Michael only agreed to the tour to help his brothers who, unlike him in the aftermath of his *Thriller* album release, needed money. The fifty-five dates they performed, in front of nearly two million fans, were a financial success for the band and promoter Don King, although a financial disaster for the tour's backer and copromoter Chuck Sullivan, the forty-year-old son of New England Patriots owner Billy Sullivan. Billy Sullivan was forced to sell the Patriots, Foxboro Stadium, and Sullivan Arena in the aftermath of the concert tour that young Chuck backed when his debt was added to other debts the family was dealing with. The young Sullivan promised the Jacksons guaranteed payments that far exceeded industry standards.

Another interesting point about that tour is that Don King negotiated a deal with Pepsi, unbeknownst to the Jacksons, that forced them to break off negotiations for a Quaker Oats deal that was more lucrative. The Pepsi deal also required Michael to do two commercials for Pepsi, a product he didn't use. One of the commercials resulted in a bad accident as a pyro device malfunctioned, catching Michael's hair on fire. Some blame the incident for his starting to use prescription painkillers.[1314]

In his twentieth year as a promoter, in 1985, Bob Arum, who many had thought would be finished after Muhammad Ali retired, promoted a fight in Las Vegas that he regarded at the time as the greatest fight he had ever seen: Marvin Hagler versus Tommy Hearns. Bob said that it was the best middleweight fight possible at the time because Sugar Ray Leonard was recuperating from an eye injury. The fight was relatively easy to put together, he said, because he promoted Hagler and had a good relationship with his comanagers and trainers Goody and Pat Petronelli. Arum was also a friend of Hearns's trainer, Emanuel Steward. Bob carried out an unprecedented barnstorming tour to publicize the fight, stopping in twenty-four cities in two weeks.

Marvin Hagler versus Tommy Hearns, originally dubbed "The Fight," occurred on April 15, 1985, at Caesars Palace in Las Vegas. After it ended, many dubbed the three rounds of nonstop action "The War."[15] Hagler, the undisputed middleweight champion, had overcome a controversial draw in his fight with Vito Antuofermo and a riot after beating Alan Minter, the hometown favorite in England on his way to a title in September 1980. "Marvelous" Marvin Hagler successfully then defended his title ten times, nine by knockout. His only win by decision was against Roberto Duran after fifteen rounds in November 1983. Tommy "Hitman" Hearns was also one of the hardest punchers in boxing, scoring thirty knockouts in his first thirty-two fights. He had moved up from welterweight to junior middleweight to middleweight shortly before the match with Hagler. Hearns was trained by the legendary Emanuel Steward.

The first round was regarded by many, including HBO play-by-play announcer Barry Tompkins, as the best round in middleweight history. Round two and the beginning of round three also included nonstop heavy blows and blood as Marvin Hagler's forehead cut opened up again in the second round. The third round, after brutal blows, ended as a blood-soaked Hagler celebrated while referee Richard Steele held Tommy Hearns up after stopping the fight. *The Ring* regarded the fight as the fight of the year, despite it only lasting three rounds.

Bob Arum, talking about the Hagler–Hearns fight, said, "I've now promoted 655 world-championship fights. Hagler–Hearns was the greatest one of all.

This was a real fight, not a fight with defense, with any jabs. It was nothing other than two guys punching the shit out of each other at the highest level in boxing. I had never seen anything like it."[16]

Bob added, "I had great admiration for Tommy. He was one of my favorite fighters, a real warrior who gave 1,000 percent. There's nothing not to like about Tommy Hearns. But when you saw Marvin take Hearns' best punch and respond the way he did before that barrage that sent Tommy crashing back to the canvas in the third round, it spoke to Marvin's total determination and the total physical courage he had. Marvin might not have been the best boxer in the world, but he was a very tough, tough guy. The best fights for him were the ones he got pressed the most and the ones that became physical because he was just so strong."

In late July 1985, at a press conference at the Harley Hotel in Manhattan, Arum, alongside Hearns's trainer and manager, Emanuel Steward, was discussing a Hagler rematch. Tommy Hearns surprised them both by announcing that he was taking up drag racing. Arum thought quickly and said, "There is a clause in the rematch agreement barring drag racing," without missing a beat. Arum had created a doubleheader to keep both fighters on track for a lucrative rematch. Hagler would fight John "The Beast" Mugabi, and Hearns would take on James Shuler, who switched between southpaw and orthodox styles like Hagler, on November 14, 1985, at Caesars Palace.[17]

In the lead-up to the Hearns-Shuler fight, Bob Arum explained his marketing strategy. This explains how boxing used to advertise. "The first step," he explained, "is a nationwide tour with the boxers in September. These news conferences precede training camps." He hoped to generate press from boxing writers. The second step he said, "is to assign film crews to the training camps to get lots of footage of the two fighters in action. That footage will be edited and transmitted to TV stations and satellite television stations, especially 24-hour cable channels with voracious appetites."[18] Finally, Bob explained, there were the commercials he had created by Lou Volpicelli, a former ABC sports guy and now a freelancer.

The Hearns-Shuler fight was a sensation for Hearns, coming off his loss to Marvin Hagler, with his performance called a perfect ten by boxing writers. James "Black Gold" Shuler was 22–0 before meeting "The Hit Man." He was a standout amateur with Golden Gloves Championships two years running and had a place on the 1980 Olympic team, although Jimmy Carter would boycott the Russian games. Shuler came out with a high guard that allowed the "Motor City Cobra," another of Hearns's nicknames, to show off his devastating body work. When he lowered his guard to protect his body, Hearns unleashed a perfect right cross, dropping Shuler. The KO was a precursor to the Pacquiao KO of Ricky Hatton more than thirty years later. Tragically, a month later, with money he got from this fight, Shuler purchased a motorcycle and was killed in an accident in Philadelphia. He was only twenty-six.

* * *

For those of you who view all boxing promoters as heartless businessmen, ruthless barons of wealth accumulated on the backs of their workers, here is a little wake-up call. In March 1986, Bob Arum helped his fighter Richard "Richie" Sandoval after a brutal knockout and gave him a job with Top Rank on the condition that he stop boxing. Richie is an extremely good guy who performed well as a fighter, accumulating a 29–0 record as a twenty-five-year-old WBA bantamweight champion before meeting tough Texan Gaby Canizales at Caesars Palace on March 19, 1986. Sandoval was knocked down four times before finally losing by TKO at the end of the seventh round when Carlos Padilla stopped the bout. Many thought the fight should have been stopped sooner because Sandoval couldn't defend himself after the second knockdown. He might have suffered a seizure, which led to his exit from the ring on a stretcher and required a trip to the Valley Hospital. It took him nearly fifteen minutes to regain consciousness. As a result of the bout, Arum gave Sandoval a $25,000 bonus as compensation for his ordeal and a job as a consultant if he'd retire as a boxer.[19] When I joined Top Rank in 1999, Richie was still in the office almost daily at the desk next to mine.

Arum moved from New York to Las Vegas in 1986. He said that is the only reason he managed to enjoy the longevity he has. "I don't think I could still be doing what I'm doing if I'd stayed in New York," Arum said.[20]

For the record, Don King was also, completely without publicity, a generous businessman, donating food and support to thousands on an ongoing basis. He conducted his "Turkey Tour" annually and banned any press from the tradition.

* * *

In April 1987, Arum promoted one of his most controversial fights between "Marvelous" Marvin Hagler and "Sugar" Ray Leonard. Arum was in his prime, conducting the orchestra. At the weigh-in, Bob was standing beside Leonard, who was stripped down and on the scale. "Where is Marvin," screamed Arum. "Still in the medical exam," was the reply. "Screw the exam. Let them do it later; c'mon we're waiting."[21] Within minutes Hagler had climbed the platform, and Arum, in black sweater, light-blue slacks, and gold-rimmed glasses, perched over the champion as he removed his World War II baseball cap, his

T-shirt, jogging pants, socks, sneakers and, finally, his dark glasses. All that remained were his beard and kelly green briefs. Leonard weighed in at 158, and Hagler at 158 1/2. Arum, hooking his hands inside his waistband, allowed himself a smile. The captain is attentive on the bridge.

Hagler, at the time, was the long-reigning middleweight champion. Ray Leonard had retired twice since 1982 and fought only once in the previous four years.[22] In March 1986, Hagler fought John Mugabi. He won in the eleventh round but Leonard, who was ringside, thought Hagler looked beatable, so said he would come out of retirement for the potentially lucrative fight with Hagler. In the final accounting, Hagler earned approximately $20 million and Leonard $12 million. Leonard's camp insisted on a large ring, twelve rounds rather than fifteen, and ten-ounce gloves rather than eight-ounces. In exchange for accepting these conditions, Hagler received the richer purse.

The fight opened with Hagler abandoning his usual southpaw stance for a traditional one, losing the first two rounds. At the end of each round, Leonard would unleash a flurry of shots to "steal" the round. In the end, Leonard won on a controversial split decision. Two judges, Lou Filippo and Dave Moretti, scored the fight nearly even; a third judge, JoJo Guerra, gave Leonard an eight-round margin nobody else saw. Hagler wanted a rematch, but Leonard retired again. Hagler retired fourteen months later, becoming an actor in Italy. In 1990 Leonard finally offered Hagler a rematch but was turned down. Also notable after this fight was that longtime trainer Angelo Dundee refused to work with Leonard again after being paid less than he thought was fair from the $12 million purse.[23]

At the end of the Leonard-Hagler fight, another notable incident occurred between Bob Arum and Don King. They were bitter rivals back then and Don, who was just a spectator at the event, tried to get into the ring after the bout. As they were waiting for the decision, Don moved down press row and headed for the Leonard corner. Bob Arum grabbed Don from behind, tearing a pocket on his tuxedo and stopping him from climbing the ring stairs. Security separated them, and the scuffle ended without a blow. It was also reported, though I couldn't confirm it, that security relieved King of a handgun. In 2011, during the lead-up to Miguel Cotto versus Ricardo Mayorga, where I interviewed copromoters Bob Arum and Don King together in New York, the incident came up. They were joking with each other, almost playfully, about their rivalry when Bob mentioned that he had to stop Don from getting in the ring at his event at Caesars, ripping his jacket to do so. "Oh, you finally admit it," bellowed King, "now I can sue you!" A picture from that day is included in this book.

* * *

Don King also remained active in the eighties. Although thirty-eight-year-old Larry Holmes had been retired for two years, Don matched him up with his current mega champion, twenty-one-year-old Mike Tyson on January 22, 1988. Holmes had defended his heavyweight belt twenty times, more than anybody since Joe Louis. He accumulated a 48–0 record before losing two close—and some say, at least about the second split decision, controversial—losses to Michael Spinks in Nevada. Mike Tyson had unified the four heavyweight belts, and Don King thought a fight against Holmes was a dream match. Mike said that he wanted to beat Holmes to avenge Larry's win over Muhammed Ali. Critics of the fight say that Don King lured Larry Holmes out of retirement with the $3 million offer but didn't give the rusty Holmes adequate time to train.[24]

Holmes, fighting in the event dubbed "Heavyweight History," wanted to regain the title after two losses to Michael Spinks twenty months prior. Mike said it was his tribute to Muhammad Ali, seeking to beat the man who beat him, and invited Muhammad Ali to be ringside for the spectacle. Holmes was dropped three times in the fourth round in a lopsided fight stopped finally by referee Joe Cortez.

In the next year, when George Foreman met Bert Cooper at the Pride Pavilion in Phoenix on Thursday, June 1, 1989, nobody had any reason to believe anything was amiss in the match. Carried on USA Network, Foreman was a favorite, but the twenty-three-year-old Cooper, with twenty wins and only four losses, seemed like a fair opponent. After Foreman landed a few shots in the first two rounds, Bert Cooper refused to come out for the third round. The crowd booed loudly. So did the commission, which withheld his $17,500 purse. Cooper tested positive for cocaine after the match, blaming the infraction on a pair of twin sisters who he met a few days before the fight and partied with for days. He believed he was set up but didn't know by whom. Cooper could, when in shape to fight, be dangerous as an opponent. He sent Ray Mercer to the hospital and almost beat Evander Holyfield. The fight with Foreman proved to be expensive for him. After only receiving $2,500 of his $17,500 purse, he paid a lawyer $5,000 to sue and failed to secure any more.

Bob Arum's promotional savvy was on full display when he treated the boxing fans to the rematch of Sugar Ray Leonard and Tommy Hearns. On June 12, 1989, at Caesars Palace in Las Vegas, Hearns would get an opportunity for revenge after losing in a TKO to Leonard in their first match eight years earlier, despite being ahead on all three cards. Both Hearns and Leonard were five-division champions, a rare and impressive trophy for any boxing career. On the day of the bout, Hearns's younger brother, Henry, was arrested and charged with the murder of his girlfriend in a Detroit home that Tommy owned. Arum said he went by Hearns's hotel to check on him and he told reporters, "Tommy was angry at me for coming by and he said to me, This is not going to affect me. Look, I'm here to do a job—I've been waiting eight years to knock this guy out."[25]

On December 7, 1989, Sugar Ray Leonard entered the ring for a third time with Roberto Duran in a fight billed "Uno Mas," one more. On a night when Tommy Morrison and Ray Mercer also won their fights, Arum and matchmaker Bruce Trampler, one of boxing's best and still his senior matchmaker today, put on the event at the new Mirage Hotel and Casino, which had only been open for a month. The title, Uno Mas, was a reference to the end of the second meeting between these fighters when Duran apparently quit in the eighth round, telling the referee "no mas," no more. This fight was much more lopsided in Leonard's favor with wide margins on the judges' scorecard for the unanimous decision.

7

ARUM AND KING
The Nineties, Part I

In January 1990, George Foreman, in the third year of his comeback run, fought a serious contender for a heavyweight title for the first time. The fight was held at Caesars Palace. Unlike journeymen Foreman had been facing such as Bert Cooper and David Jaco, Gerry Cooney had beaten several notable heavyweights including Ken Norton, Ron Lyle, and Jimmy Young. He had also made a good showing in a loss to Larry Holmes several years earlier in 1982. His last fight with Michael Spinks wasn't successful because Spinks was too quick and elusive to get caught by Cooney's powerful left hand. He thought George Foreman might be a better target.

Cooney brought in veteran trainer Gil Clancy, Foreman's former trainer, to beef up his preparation. The main criticism of the fight had to do with the fighters' ages, although Gerry Cooney was only thirty-three at the time of the fight. The fight, called "The Preacher and the Puncher" by promoters Bob Arum and Frank Gelb, was nicknamed "The Geezers at Caesars" by a writer in Orlando.[1] Cooney caught Foreman with a left hand at the end of the first round that appeared to hurt him, a rare occurrence in Foreman's comeback. When asked about it, George said, "He hits harder than Joe Frazier with the left hook," pointing to a swollen right eye. "I didn't stumble in the first round. I was hit. I knew if I didn't do something quick it would have been me on the canvas."

The second round was all Foreman. George caught him with two uppercuts and several straight right-hand shots knocking him to the canvas. He beat the ten count but was rocked several times after that, and another left uppercut and a right cross led referee Joe Cortez to stop the fight, declaring Cooney unable to defend himself further.

Don King with Fred and Donald Trump, December 1987. AP Images

Just forty-two days later, on February 11, 1990, undefeated Mike Tyson lost to 42-1 underdog James "Buster" Douglas at the Tokyo Dome in Japan. Mike, the undisputed heavyweight champion had just knocked out Carl "The Truth" Williams in ninety-three seconds. This put to rest for many the idea that Mike's turbulent out-of-the-ring life would affect him. His marriage to Robin Givens, conflict between manager Bill Cayton and promoter Don King, and the aftermath of leaving trainer Kevin Rooney seemed not to affect the boxing world's most feared heavyweight. Evander Holyfield was ringside for the fight. Douglas was a good opponent, ranked seventh by *Ring* magazine, who had lost by TKO in his last title fight against Tony Tucker more than four years earlier. Unknown to many, Douglas had lost his mother less than a month earlier, and the mother of his son was suffering from a kidney ailment and had contracted the flu the day before the fight. Most experts expected another Tyson win inside of two minutes. Ed Schuyler, reporter for the Associated Press, when asked by custom officials how long he planned to work in Japan replied, "About ninety seconds."[2]

Singer Bobby Brown wrote in his autobiography that he met with Tyson in Tokyo, and the two partied extensively the night before the fight. Brown claims Tyson refused to go to sleep early for the fight, deeming Douglas "an amateur" he could beat "if I didn't sleep for five weeks."[3]

Sugar Ray Leonard, commentating ringside for HBO, was one of the first to observe Tyson's predicament in the ring in the early rounds as he took more shots from Douglas and failed to make Douglas fear him. "Tyson is having one of those occasional days in the ring where you just don't have it, things just don't click in." By the fifth round, Tyson's left eye began to swell. His corner hadn't brought an Enswell or ice packs, standard equipment for a corner, possibly because they thought Mike would end it quickly. At the end of the eighth round, Tyson landed a flush right uppercut that sent Douglas to the canvas. The ringside timekeeper started counting when he hit the canvas, but it was reported that the referee, Octavio Meyran, started two beats later. Douglas made it to his feet at the referee's count of nine, but the bell sounded right after. Don King, Tyson's promoter, later argued this in vain. By the end of the ninth round, Tyson's eye was closed completely. Douglas unloaded on Mike in the tenth round, forcing him back to the ropes. When Mike came forward, Douglas hit him with a four-punch combination including an uppercut that laid Mike out flat. He couldn't rise before the count.

When asked in the post-fight interview how he was able to get the win, Douglas said, "Because of my mother . . . God bless her heart."

Don King, and the rest of Mike Tyson's camp, protested the result due to the referee's possible long count. Initially the WBA and WBC agreed and didn't record the win. The IBF claimed Douglas the winner immediately.[4] After a public outcry and complaints from boxing commissions globally, the WBA and WBC relented and declared Douglas the winner four days later. Bob Arum testified in support of King at the lawsuit.

"The Battle of the Ages" is what the bout was called in April 1991. It could have also been called Boxing gets Trumped. Donald was unable to meet his obligations under the deal he made with Arum and Dan Duva to bring the bout to Atlantic City. Trump tried to renegotiate the deal, claiming an "act of war" clause brought on by the war in the Persian Gulf. He possibly couldn't make the contracted payments to Top Rank and Main Events due to his casinos' financial troubles. Arum negotiated with Caesars Palace to move the fight to Las Vegas. Ultimately, Trump made new promises, some of which he never kept, and the fight did happen in Atlantic City. The breached deal cost Arum and Deva more than $3 million. Bob and other promoters steered clear of Trump going forward.[5]

The participants, forty-two-year-old George Foreman and twenty-eight-year-old Evander "The Real Deal" Holyfield agreed to fight each other in the Atlantic City Convention Center on April 19, 1991. Promoters Top Rank and Main Events guaranteed Foreman $12.5 million and Evander $20 million.

Evander, now undisputed heavyweight champion, put off a potential Tyson fight to make this match with Foreman after he defeated James "Buster" Douglas. Foreman's popularity was at an all-time high, having gone 24–0 since ending his ten-year "retirement" in pursuit of the heavyweight belts. Main Events promoter Dan Duva made fun of Foreman's weight in the lead-up to the fight, saying that it should be called "The Real Deal" versus "The Big Meal." The fight surprised everyone by going the distance. Although a dynamic seventh round saw each man dominate, in turn staggering his opponent, neither succumbed, and the unanimous decision went to the younger Holyfield.

"Who would think George could go 12 with me at a furious pace," Holyfield would marvel after he'd left the ring with a unanimous decision, three versions of the heavyweight title, and some newfound respect for his elders. "He made me do things I didn't want to do, punch when I didn't want to punch. He cut off the ring. At 42, George is not dead."[6]

In the aftermath of the fight, Arum sued Main Event's Duva, Holyfield, and his adviser, Shelly Finkel, for $100 million, claiming their contract included a rematch where Foreman was guaranteed $12.5 million and 50 percent of the gate. Holyfield opted to pass up the rematch for a fight with Mike Tyson, a fight that ultimately would have to wait until Mike left prison. The November 8, 1991, date with Tyson was scrapped after Mike pulled out due to a rib injury.

Although Muhammad Ali reportedly told George he should stay far away from Mike Tyson, George thought he could handle the smaller Tyson and wanted to get in the ring with him. What George might not have known is that Mike wanted to steer clear of George. On June 16, 1990, Tyson and Foreman did appear on the same card in a co-main event. Tyson avenged his two 1984 Olympic trial losses to Henry Tillman by knocking him out in the first round and Foreman took out top-ten contender Adilson Rodrigues with a second-round knockout. ESPN had a few segments on the anticipated match between Tyson and Foreman. The public wanted it, and Foreman was on board. But journalist Frank Lotierzo once recounted a lunch he had with Don King's long-time matchmaker, Bobby Goodman, who told him that Mike Tyson was scared to death of George Foreman. He supposedly said to Don King, "I'm not fightin' that f****ng animal. If you love the motherf***er so much, you fight him!"[7] My friend Bobby Goodman passed away in March 2023.

March 20, 1992, was memorable for the rematch between Tommy Hearns and Iran Barkley. Barkley had defeated Hearns by KO in the third round in their first match four years earlier. In June 1991, Hearns upset Virgil Hill to capture the WBA light heavyweight title. He planned in his next fight to move up to cruiserweight, challenge Bobby Czyz, and become the first fighter with championships in six weight divisions. That fight didn't materialize, possibly due to Hearns's demand for $10 million. This fight was a classic because it was so close. Barkley scored the only knockdown, which probably was the cause of his narrow split decision win. Barkley's eyes were nearly shut by the end of the fight, and Hearns was almost unrecognizable due to the amount of swelling to his nose and eyes. They were one point apart on two scorecards and two points apart on the third. When asked after the fight, Hearns said, "This time it really could have gone either way."[8]

Six months after this fight, Bob Arum would be embroiled in a controversial fight cancellation with IBF super middleweight champion Iran Barkley. Barkley was supposed to fight Doug DeWitt in Beijing. Due to tendinitis of the left elbow, Barkley was unable to train and had to withdraw from the event. Arum stated that the cancellation had nothing to do with the lawsuit brought by a Chinese businessman, through a Vancouver law firm, claiming that the Chinese government had swindled him out of more than $3 million.

Bob Arum and Dan Duva would do it again on June 19, 1992, at Caesars Palace in Las Vegas. Larry Holmes at forty, would face off against Evander Holyfield, separated only by Mills Lane. Holmes, who had retired twice, was 5–0 in his newest comeback bid. Holmes lost a unanimous decision despite a good second round. Fans, and at least one *Sports Illustrated* reporter, Pat Putnam, were disappointed in the lackluster fight. The reporter said, "They invited two heavyweights to a title fight at Caesars Palace in Las Vegas last Friday night, and neither came."[9]

On February 20, 1993, Don King promoted a boxing event that has a record unbeaten to this day. That is the day Julio César Chávez, one of the greatest fighters of all time and one of the greatest sports heroes of his country, met Greg Haugen at Estadio Azteca in Mexico City in front of more than 150,000 in attendance. The paid attendance was 134,000, still a record today.[10] That crowd beat the previous record, 120,470 paid attendances, at the Philadelphia Sesquicentennial Stadium, to see Gene Tunney capture Jack Dempsey's heavyweight title.[11]

Jimmy Lennon Jr., the ring announcer for this and almost all Don King events, recalled, "Here you had this vast sea of people. I saw these little fires high up in the stands. People brought their own food and were cooking way up in the more distant seats. I remember thinking this was more of a mass celebration than just a sporting event. Whether or not a lot of people could really see much down in the ring, it certainly seemed that they were enjoying themselves. It was kind of like the huge crowd for Woodstock; just being there was a huge part of it."[12]

Haugen entered the ring to Bruce Springsteen's "Born in the USA," carrying an American flag. Mexican President Carlos Salinas de Gortari descended into the stadium on a helicopter to climb through the ropes and wish Chávez success. Julio took the cue and did what his adoring fans hoped: he demolished the skilled Haugen. Greg, a crafty trash-talker, made the mistake of insulting many Mexicans by claiming that Julio had padded his record by mostly fighting taxi drivers. Insulted at his attack on the common man, they were delighted when Julio came out blazing with both fists and knocked down Haugen twenty seconds into round one. Referee Joe Cortez finally stopped the one-sided match at 2:02 of the fifth round. When asked about his taxi driver comment after the match, Haugen said, "They must have been tough taxi drivers."

Don King created a remarkable event on this day. He pulled off what only a very small number of promoters could have accomplished. Overshadowed by Chávez, national pride, the attendance record, and the appearance of the country's president were the other great fighters on the card. Félix Trinidad, Jose Badillo, Gerald McClellan, and Michael Nunn also fought there on that day. Terry Norris beat Maurice Blocker with a second round TKO, and Azumah Nelson won a majority decision over Gabriel Ruelas. It was a truly amazing event.

In 1993, Oscar De La Hoya fought an amazing nine times—almost double the number of fights he had in each of his other sixteen years as a pro. Eight of his fights in 1993 he won by KO, TKO, or causing his opponent to quit. The only decision, which he won unanimously, was to Mike Grable in April of that year, despite Mike being down in the second, fourth, and last rounds. In the very next year, Oscar won the WBO super featherweight championship, his first title, against Jimmi Bredahl at the Olympic Auditorium in Los Angeles. In this, his twelfth fight against, also undefeated, Oscar won his first of six weight category titles by dominating from the start. Bredahl went down in the first and second rounds. He managed to stay on his feet until the fight was called by TKO in the tenth round.

De La Hoya won his second weight class championship, lightweight, four months later against Jorge Páez for the vacant WBO belt. Oscar didn't even have a warmup fight first. Oscar hurt Jorge with two left hooks in the second round and then dropped him with a third. Páez had only been down once in his sixty-three previous fights. De La Hoya added the IBF belt by beating Rafael Ruelas before heading up to junior welterweight.

On January 1, 1994, one of the greatest upsets in boxing history occurred. "The Surgeon" Frankie Randall won a split decision at the MGM Grand in Las Vegas over the legend Julio César Chávez, his first loss. Some historians had Randall a bigger winner than the judges did, possibly admitting that Chávez received "favorable" judging. In the eleventh round, for example, Chávez was knocked down and had a point deducted. Only one of the three judges awarded Frankie a 10–7 round, standard in such rounds. Chávez was definitely on top in the middle rounds, hurting Randall. But the Surgeon finished the fight strong and took the belt.

Also on this might, Don King put on a star-studded undercard with undefeated Felix Trinidad defending his welterweight title with a lopsided decision win over Hector "Macho" Camacho in the chief supporting bout. Simon Brown defended his 154-pound title with a majority decision win over Australia's Troy Waters. We saw Thomas Hearns in a cruiser bout against the hapless Dan Ward of Arkansas. Hearns, who got a great reception, won in the first round. Razor Ruddock, Meldrick Taylor, Italy's Olympic gold medalist Giovanni Parisi, and future bantam champ Tim Austin (having his fifth pro bout) all won by KO.[13] Christy Martin and Terron Millett rounded out this great card by Don King.

On September 17, 1994, Felix Trinidad met Luis "Yori Boy" Campas in the IBF welterweight championship. There were six world championships on that night, a remarkably rare occurrence in boxing. I haven't found evidence of it ever happening again. Don King was the only promoter I am aware of to have championships on a card that weren't even in the televised portion of the event. This couldn't happen today because the early fights are streamed on network apps and streaming channels.

Trinidad took care of business in the fourth round by snapping Campas's head back while he was against the ropes, so hard that I thought his neck had been broken. Campas, 56–0 with fifty KOs entering the fight, knocked Felix down in the second with a left hook. The barrage by Trinidad, including the right that snapped Campas's head back, caused referee Richard Steele to stop it in the fourth.

On November 5, 1994, Bob Arum copromoted George Foreman's fight with Michael Moorer. Kathy Duva was Moorer's promoter. Moorer, twenty-six-years-old with thirty-five wins and no losses, met a forty-five-year-old, 72–4 Foreman. George won the IBF and WBA heavyweight belts, which he tried to get from Evander Holyfield earlier, by knocking out Moorer in the tenth round. George was a few years into a comeback bid after ending his ten-year retirement. The fight almost didn't happen. The WBA didn't have Foreman in its top-ten ratings and refused to sanction the fight. Moorer and his promoters, Main Events, looked at other options for their fighter including Lennox Lewis. Bob Arum, the Harvard lawyer, filed a lawsuit arguing that the WBA was colluding with Moorer's promoter and other entities to discriminate against him. Arum demanded that Moorer not be allowed to enter a ring until he fulfilled the contract with Top Rank that he had signed. The Nevada judge ruled that the WBA acted "capriciously" and ordered that if Foreman passed the medicals he would have to be allowed to fight for the title.[14]

Gil Clancy took Foreman's place on the HBO broadcast where he was a color commentator. Foreman said that he wanted to lay the ghost of Zaire to rest in this fight, referring to Muhammad Ali's knockout of the previously undefeated Foreman twenty years earlier, Foreman's only KO loss. Toward that end he wore the same red trunks he had worn in Zaire and had Angelo Dundee, Ali's trainer in Zaire, in his corner to face Moorer.

The fight was well in Moorer's favor through nine rounds. Michael was ahead on all three judges' cards. Before the tenth round, Dundee warned George that he had to KO Moorer to win. Teddy Atlas, Moorer's trainer, reminded Moorer to stay away from George and make him come to Moorer so as not to get caught with a powerful inside shot from the still dangerous Foreman. Michael forgot the advice after George landed a few strong shots and ultimately landed a devastating right, flush on the champion's jaw, knocking down on his back. He was unable to get up in time to beat the ten count. Arum, Foreman's promoter, confirmed the synergy with the earlier reference after the fight when he said, "It was something that all of you who follow the sport will never forget. It'll go down in history comparable to when Ali knocked George down in Zaire 20 years ago."[15]

Early in my tenure with King I arranged everything for the TV productions, and produced and directed the fights. I also planned, wrote, and edited all the videos that we aired in the shows on one of the first nonlinear Avid editing systems. Don asked me to make a "banquet tape" for him to show when he accepted an award for being the first to promote forty-seven world championships in a single year. No other promoter had ever come close to that. I thought it would be a great thing if I could make a montage of all forty-seven fights. I created it moving backgrounds with multilayered moving elements and moving boxes that danced around each other as they came and went showing all the fights. I picked the best, most dramatic moments from each fight and timed the punches and motion of the boxes to synchronize with the music playing throughout the piece. Crescendos and punctuated movements in the music matched the fighters' motions and punches perfectly.

I selected Mozart's *Eine Kleine Nachtmusik* as the soundtrack. Besides being one of my favorite classical pieces, I thought it would give a dramatic counterpoint to the violence of boxing. I worked on it several hours a day for almost a week. When I brought it to Don's office the day before we left for the banquet to impress him with the four-minute piece, I was promptly shattered by his critique. "The fight stuff is good, but get rid of that 'Bee-toven' shit. Try the O'Jays instead, and remember we leave early tomorrow." I guessed that it wouldn't help to inform him it was Wolfgang, not Ludwig van. I had to work all night to change the soundtrack to the O'Jays, you've got to "Give the People What They Want," and re-edit the footage to hit the downbeats. Herr Mozart and I never collaborated on boxing videos again.

I attended another awards banquet at the First Baptist Church in Tusca-loosa, Alabama, in 1995. Don was being honored with a few others for their community service. Coretta Scott King was the honorary host. Larry Holmes was also there as a guest. I had my friend and cameraman Steve Greenbaum with me, another homie from the synagogue set. I believe we were the only white faces in this crowd of thousands. As Steve stood at the back of this very crowded church videotaping, members of the Nation of Islam approached him and asked, with a touch of what Steve thought was aggression, why a white cam-eraman was there recording the event. As I went back, Steve was explaining that we worked for Don King. He said, pointing to me, that I was Don's producer. I said I was and offered my card. "Why the hell would Don King have a white producer?" I was asked.

"So he can find us at events like this," I offered, and they left. Steve hasn't forgiven me to this day for that answer, noting that my lousy sense of humor could have gotten us hurt. It also happened to be Passover that night. I walked outside to call my mother who asked if I was at temple. "Not exactly," was my answer.

One reason we were at this event was because I wanted to interview Larry Holmes, whom I admired and thought would have been known as one of the greatest heavyweights of all time if he hadn't immediately followed Ali.

"Mr. Holmes, can we ask you a few questions?"

"Sure, ask away," he said graciously.

As Steve started recording, I told Larry, "I want to be up front with you from the start. We work for Don King Productions."

"Why are you telling me that?" Larry asked.

I said that I had heard rumors about bad blood between him and King and I didn't want to hide my association with Don.

"Are you rolling?" Larry said, pointing to the camera. He looked straight into the lens and started, "People keep telling me that I hate Don King. People tell me that Don robbed me, Don cheated me. Well, let me set it straight for you. I made more money working for Don King than any other time in my life. If he robbed me, I wish he'd come back and rob me some more."

It should also be noted that years earlier Larry Holmes was quoted as saying, "[King] looks black, lives white and thinks green."[16]

Any story almost always has two sides. People usually prefer to believe the worst. When the HBO movie *Don King: Only on America* starring Ving Rhames came out, based on the Jack Newfield book, everyone thought Don was finally exposed and that he must have hated it. The movie purports to show Don paying bribes, cheating fighters, turning on friends such as singer Lloyd Price, losing his mind at home one night smashing a LeRoy Neiman painting in an out-of-control rage. The movie retells many of the exaggerated, disputed, and purportedly one-sided stories in Newfield's book. People around me thought that Don would be furious. In fact, Don loved the movie and especially Ving Rhames's portrayal of him. He invited Mr. Rhames to the next pay-per-view and sat ringside with him. Carl King, Don's stepson, who is seen in the movie bringing a huge sum of cash to a fighter to pay him off, told me his dad laughed about most of the plot.

"Do you think my dad is going to hand me a fortune to take to anyone?" Carl asked me. "And do you think for one moment that my dad, cheap as he is, would smash an original LeRoy Neiman?"

* * *

I've worked boxing events in every size venue imaginable, from hotel banquet halls and bar or restaurant back rooms to soccer stadiums, from no spectators, in the bubble during the pandemic, to 90,000+ events in Australia, Mexico, and the United Kingdom. But, as I mentioned earlier, not all my international experiences were completely pleasant. When Francois Botha met Axel Schulz in December 1995 at the Hanns-Martin-Schleyer-Halle in Stuttgart, Germany, we were treated to a riot and death threats. Only six days before Bob Arum promoted Oscar De La Hoya versus Jesse James Leija at Madison Square Garden, I had to produce the King fight from ringside with special monitors and communications equipment because the production truck booked by the German promoter wasn't large enough to accommodate Don's producer: me. Probably not an oversight.

The fight was for the vacant IBF heavyweight championship belt. The fight came about after George Foreman vacated his title, refusing to rematch with Schulz after defeating him in a controversial decision. The IBF then ordered Schulz, No. 2 ranked heavyweight, to face its No. 1 contender, Francois Botha. Axel Schulz was the heavy favorite. Botha shocked the crowd by beating Axel handily for the first six rounds of the fight. Many of the fans were drinking champagne on the balcony, expecting their countryman to become the heavyweight champ. The next three rounds started to tip toward Schulz, and he absolutely pounded Botha in the last two rounds, nearly knocking him out. The German fans were celebrating Axel's victory a little too early, however. Botha was awarded a split-decision victory. The crowd was stunned. It was not, in my opinion, a bad decision.

Botha won all the early rounds, which the fans forgot because Schulz was winning handily at the end. Judges Harry Davis and Al DeVito had it four and six points in Botha's favor whereas Judge Henry Grant had Schulz up by two. The crowd erupted in chaos. They started throwing everything they could get their hands on. It escalated into a full-fledged riot. They were shouting "fix," "hinkriegan" in German, as if Don King could control the IBF judges on German soil. Champagne bottles were launched from the balcony, as were glasses, which is why such things are not put into the hands of patrons at boxing matches anymore. Chairs, which in the United States are usually cable-tied together, were flying everywhere. The Showtime announcer, Steve Albert, was underneath the table. Not our announcer, the Colonel. He was still on the air seated ringside, explaining what was happening and telling people how the scoring could explain Francois's victory. I told the Colonel that we better get off the air and seek cover, but he said, with his hand covering the microphone, "Mahti, I was in the 'Nam; I love this shit."

He was still on the air when, as I stood holding a towel over his back shielding him from flying glass, I was hit on the thigh by a two-pound champagne bottle thrown from the balcony. I went down like a sack of potatoes, and the Colonel hastily interrupted himself with, "That's it from Stuttgart, goodnight, everybody." He hovered over me, thinking I might be dead.

The Colonel said in military tone, "Let's go, grab my belt." I grabbed Francois's wife, who was next to us, she grabbed the Colonel's belt, I protected her back, and limped back to the dressing rooms. The police escorted us back to the Graf Zeppelin Hotel. We were told we couldn't go back to our rooms because of death threats against our party. We had to sit in the lobby under armed guard until our flights in the morning. We went to retrieve our belongings one at a time with a four-man guard escort.

I sat in that lobby for six hours next to my good friend Duke Durden. Duke was a classic boxing guy. Elbert John "Duke" Durden was a former baseball and basketball player for Southern University, sought by the Harlem Globetrotters, who became a first baseman in the Brooklyn Dodgers' organization. After a knee injury, he eventually became the first Black commissioner in the Nevada State Athletic Commission before becoming a vice president at Don King Productions. Part of Botha's group, I had known and considered him a friend for several years on the road. At one point, Duke, a proud Black man, said to me, "You know, all these guys with the guns here," pointing around the room at the police, "would love to string my black ass up."

"Duke," I said, "who do you think they'd string up next to you?"

"Yeah," Duke smiled and said, "they don't like your Jew-ass here neither. We'll be swinging together brother," and handed me a Budweiser.

Note: it was all for nothing, because Botha tested positive for a banned substance and was stripped of the win after a court case brought by Schulz's promoters, Cedric Kushner and Sauerland Promotions.

Another of Don King's big international fights was a lead-up to Mike Tyson's release from prison, included Oliver McCall trying to secure a belt for Mike to claim. When McCall fought Frank Bruno for the WBC belt in September 1995 in London, the interest was overwhelming. The fight was scheduled to take place on the hallowed ground of Wembley Stadium, and the winner would face Mike Tyson. I was almost tackled by an employee at Wembley on the site survey when I stepped onto the grass, more than twenty yards from the field, with sneakers on my feet. Rookie mistake.

A month before the fight a production meeting was held at Wembley to discuss broadcast arrangements. The meeting was hosted by Mike Allen, the director from SKY Sports for the event. Mike has one of the best senses of humor I've come across in TV. The fight generated a tremendous amount of interest in broadcasters around the world due to its significance in the heavyweight division.

Broadcasters from Teiken Sports in Japan, Sky in the United Kingdom, Showtime in the United States, Premiere World in Germany, Televisa in Mexico, TV 1000 Scandinavia, Telepiu in Italy, and Canal+ in France all came to this meeting. It was the largest site survey meeting for a boxing event I had ever seen. Mike gave everyone all the details for the production and an explanation of their coverage and introduced me into the conversation to explain what I would provide to all these foreign broadcasters and others who had the rights for the world feed in their territories.

When Mike opened it up for questions, Lewis Horne from Plaza Media, the production arm of Premiere World Germany, asked if Sky was providing live aerial camera shots during the event because it was an outdoor fight at Wembley, despite almost no aerial coverage being done live that long ago. "I think the Sky helicopter is in the shop just then," Mike said sarcastically. The Sky helicopter didn't exist.

"Well, we at Plaza Media have a new, experimental blimp with a camera mount that we could lend to the telecast if you like," Lewis offered. A revolutionary device at that early date.

Mike looked at the German broadcaster and without missing a beat said, "I think we've had enough of your airships over here!"

Jay Larkin of Showtime, seated next to me, almost fell off his chair laughing.

* * *

On November 1, 1995, Mike Tyson was sidelined by a broken right thumb in his plan to fight Buster Mathis Jr. On July 4, 1996, nine days before he was due to fight Bruce Seldon, Mike Tyson had bronchitis. The fight had to be postponed until September 7. (That rescheduled Tyson–Seldon fight in September 1996 is the date that Tupac Shakur was shot shortly after the fight, hours after he had an altercation with someone at the casino. He died six days later.) The losses to Don King caused by those late changes were likely millions of dollars. How many individuals at the helm of a small business can sustain losses like that and stay in business? This is a very high-risk industry.

Bob Arum suffered similar postponements with De La Hoya versus Miguel Ángel González due to Oscar's left shoulder tendonitis in September 1996 and Pacquiao versus Matthysse due to Ramadan in 2018.

Perhaps the most famous postponement of all time in boxing happened on September 17, 1974, when George Foreman suffered a cut over his left eye while sparring eight days prior to the scheduled Rumble in the Jungle in Kinshasa, Zaire. Don King, on behalf of the fight's promoters, Hemdale Films and Video Techniques, had to hold this massive event together. It also included a huge music festival with James Brown and B. B. King, negotiating with Zaire's dictator Mobutu Sese Seko and his principal financial backer, Muammar Gadhafi. More than money was at stake. The principals were not allowed to leave the country—making them wonder whether their freedom was ultimately at stake.

When Oscar De La Hoya met Julio César Chávez in June 1996, Bob Arum made history again. He rejected the now-traditional pay-per-view model to return to the old days of closed-circuit television, probably a revolt against cable operators he was not happy with. He wanted to bring back closed circuit's favorable, everybody-has-to-pay model. Cable operators had failed in their attempts to stop the use of "black boxes" to steal PPV events in the past. The fight was a disappointment to Arum, who only brought in approximately $14 million from a crowd of 750,000, and to fans who had to settle for four rounds. Chávez suffered a bad cut in the first round. By the fourth, it had deteriorated, and Joe Cortez gave Oscar a TKO victory. It was a bold move for Arum, the seasoned promoter, that didn't live up to his hopes.

On September 12, 1995, in Stuttgart, Germany, we met the owner of a detective agency and his partner from Turkey. Roland Simoneschi is an Italian whose family lived in Stuttgart. He did private detective work and was a bodyguard for celebrities. His partner, Savas Mentes, Sasha to his friends, is a proud Turk who partnered in the agency and would eventually marry Roland's sister. We met them in the hotel pub around the Axel Schulz versus Francois Botha fight that ended in a riot. Much more on that riot later. They were hired to be bodyguards for Botha.

They were immediately fascinated by the Colonel. Big boxing fans, they discussed the Joe Louis versus Max Schmeling fight in great detail. At one point the Colonel said, "If you boys are ever in Vegas look us up." Three months later, on Wednesday of fight week for the Tyson versus Bruno fight at the MGM in Las Vegas, I was on the stage of the Hollywood Theater where we were preparing to conduct a press conference. I heard my name called from the overcrowded audience in front of the stage. From the massive crowd assembled, I saw two men pushing their way to the front, calling me. It took me a minute to recognize them, but Roland and Sasha were smiling broadly, "We are here; where is the Colonel?"

They had flown from Stuttgart, with no hotel rooms, no tickets, no other contacts, because the Colonel said, "Look us up." This fight was sold out for months. Hotel rooms were also nonexistent. I couldn't believe they showed up, so I did my best to take care of them. They even talked their way into credentials, which was no small feat. They might have shown their detective credentials and indicated that they were hired for private security. All I know is that after the weigh-in, they were standing on either side of Mike, with phone earpieces in their ears, looking like security.

To this day, we have stayed in close touch. Roland even invited my wife and me to their family's villa in Terracina, Italy, near Naples, for a vacation. At the last-minute, Roland and Sasha couldn't be there because, unexpectedly, Turkey made it to the second round of the World Cup, and they did security for the Turkish National Football Team. His family drove us from Milan to Terracina, a seven-hour trip, and treated us like royalty for five days. The loveliest people you ever want to meet. They spoke no English but fluent Italian and German. They spoke to the locals in Italian and translated into German for me, which I translated to English for my wife. It was sketchy because my German, left over from high school, is lousy, but it got us through. I remember one late night while at a café bistro on the beach watching my wife and Roland's father "talking" for an hour about everything from politics to family without ever knowing the other's language. They communicated perfectly. For the past twenty-five years, Roland has never missed my birthday.

In the nineties, Don had a special relationship with Mexico. He was there almost weekly with fights in bullrings, stadiums, and even nightclubs. Julio César Chávez was as big a boxing name as there ever was in any country. He was known as "the Legend" while he was still fighting. After he fought Miguel Ángel González to a draw in the bullring in Mexico City, we had to escape a riot, my first of three riots in my boxing career, where the locals threw everything from beer, urine, and seat cushions to D batteries. I always wondered how they happened to be carrying D batteries to the fight.

To cover a fight in Merida, Mexico, I landed in Cancún and drove to Merida by rental car. Still a little new to the ways of Mexico, I didn't know that in Mexico your rental car doesn't necessarily come full of gas. I'd never rented a car that was almost on empty before.

It was 11 p.m., and the drive to Merida was about three and a half hours, with nothing in between. I mean nothing. There were absolutely no gas stations and almost no lights of any kind for the entire drive. I made it about an hour and a half, and was in total darkness, not having seen another car since leaving the outskirts of Cancún, when the car died. I assumed that it was mechanical failure. I assumed I'd have to wait in the car all night until somebody hopefully came by in the morning. About an hour later I saw a light in the distance coming toward me. I was relieved and then not when I saw that it was a military vehicle, and I remembered that my first-grade Spanish was probably not going to be good enough in this instance. The five young Federales with assault rifles surrounded my car and barked orders in Spanish. I believe they assumed I was transporting narcotics. Why else would a gringo be here by himself? I just stood speechless and offered my passport hoping that would explain everything. They nearly ripped the car apart looking for contraband, and it looked like I was clearly being arrested for being a jerk who would drive this desolate stretch at night alone.

After a long while, I decided to try my juvenile Spanish. "Yo amigo con Julio César Chávez," I tried. A poor attempt at saying I was a friend of Julio's. They became curious, so I slowly took out a picture of me with Julio and my business card that had a Don King logo on it from my briefcase in the car. I kept saying television and Julio César Chávez.

Suddenly, it was as if I won the jackpot in the Merida lottery. They smiled broadly, put away their guns, clapped me on the back, all the while chattering away in Spanish about something that allowed me to put my hands down. The leader barked orders to the others. One of them checked out my car. They ran back from their Jeep with a five-gallon can of gas and poured it all into my rental. As I left, they seemed like my best friends wishing me well, just excited to meet someone who had been close enough to have his picture taken with the legend.

8

ARUM AND KING
The Nineties, Part II

The last fight I directed outdoors at Caesars was the Larry Holmes versus Oliver McCall match on April 8, 1995. Don King brought this fight to Caesars Palace, one of the last fights at that outdoor pavilion. Felix Trinidad made short work of Roger Turner that night, and Bruce Seldon won the WBA heavyweight title against Tony Tucker. That title was stripped from George Foreman, who refused to fight Tucker.

The most notable fight of the night was when Terry Norris sent Luis Santana to the dressing room on a stretcher with the championship belt on his apparently unconscious corpse for the second time. Terry hit Luis a fraction of a second after the bell, and Santana flopped to the canvas like Buster Keaton. Santana pulled this stunt the first time on the undercard of Michael Carbajol versus Humberto Gonzales, a fight I directed the world feed for in the famous bullring, Plaza del Toros, in Mexico City. Terry hit Luis behind the head, and Santana went down. As Ferdie Pacheco, Muhammad Ali's former doctor, cornerman, and a color commentator on Showtime, stood up and screamed, "Get a doctor in there, the guy is dying," Santana's manager Elvis Grant Phillips, told Luis to stay down. Terry lost the belt, and a trilogy was born.

One of my biggest scares in boxing occurred the night before the Tyson versus Holyfield II event, June 27, 1997, the "ear-bite fight." I walked by the sports book at the MGM and ran into my good friend George Calvert from Christchurch, New Zealand. I asked George if he had seen the Colonel. I had some updated info to share with him on the next day's event. "No, Marty, he was here but he left looking for a doc. Said he had some chest pains."

Don King with Mike Tyson and Peter McNeeley, August 8, 1995. AP Images

"What?" I replied, alarmed. "George, you know he's a heart patient. Where did he go?"

"I don't know, Marty. I hope he's all right; he's like a bottle of blood to me," George stated, in the thickest New Zealand accent anyone has ever heard.

The Colonel had already had two serious heart attacks and a couple angioplasty surgeries.

I ran to the Betty Boop bar at the MGM, which boasted an animatronic figure of Foster Brooks and his drunk act, where I knew I'd find Pancho. "Pancho, we have to find the Colonel. He might be having a heart attack." Pancho immediately snapped his seven-foot, 450-pound frame, and genius mind into action.

I called several hospitals before calling Desert Springs and getting connected with the emergency room. "Do you have a patient, possibly with a heart issue, named Bob Sheridan?"

"Oh, you mean the Colonel," the nurse said calmly.

"Pancho, I found him." And we ran for my car.

The Colonel, who knew from experience he was having his third heart attack, had walked to the taxi line, told the front person in line that he was having a heart attack, and asked if they'd mind if he cut the line. He told the driver he needed a hospital with a good cardiac unit and then nearly passed out in the seat but stayed awake due to the pain. The driver took off like a NASCAR star. A cop saw him and told him to pull over. He gestured and yelled, heart attack, pointing to the Colonel and received a siren and light escort to Desert Springs.

While the nurse hooked him up to an IV and wheeled the gurney toward the ER, the Colonel told her, "Honey, I know it's Friday night, but I'm having a heart attack, so you better call a cardiologist in right away. Give me painkillers but cut them off around 2 a.m. because I'm calling the Tyson fight tomorrow night." She looked at him like he was an alien and told him to shut up and lie there because he wasn't going anywhere.

When Pancho and I got there, he had already had an emergency angioplasty to correct a 99 percent blockage, but he was stable. He would need at least two more procedures in the next week. While driving to the hospital I called Bruce Beck, a great boxing announcer, who I knew was at the event doing daily reports for his network but wasn't calling the actual fight. Bruce agreed to step in for his friend the Colonel. I thought this would be great news for Bob. Not only could he relax and recuperate, but his replacement also wasn't available to take his job after he recovered. As usual the Colonel surprised me. With tubes running everywhere in and out of his body, he told me to come closer. He grabbed my shirt and pulled me in, "Mahti, if you don't let me call this fight tomorrow, I'm gonna kill you. Maybe not this week, but someday when you don't expect it. This week I might just wing ya."

With Pancho present, I asked the Colonel's cardiologist, Dr. Ram Singh, what we could do to try and keep the Colonel alive. I knew he was serious about doing the fight.

"Well," the five foot five Dr. Singh said, "you must have a doctor on standby. You might also have a defibrillator standing by and make sure he does not get excited."

Can you imagine a more stressful day back at work after a heart attack than being ringside for the Tyson–Holyfield II ear-bite fight and the riot that came after?

"Doc," Pancho asked, looking down at Dr. Singh who he towered over, "what time can I pick you up tomorrow?"

"Oh, no," the doctor said, "that is impossible. I am very busy, and I do not like boxing."

The next day, I took Dr. Singh to Andy Olsen, the head of Magna Media, who provided event credentials with photographs embedded for the MGM. He laughed at me, because all credentials had been cut off weeks earlier due to the huge demand, but after telling the story, I got the doctor credentialed, sat him ringside next to the Colonel, with a defibrillator I rented under the ring, an ambulance waiting outside to bring the Colonel and Dr. Singh back to Desert Springs, Pancho sitting right behind the Colonel protecting the perimeter, and Bruce Beck on the other side of Bob, allowing the Colonel not to have to do all the talking, a concession I demanded.

When the fight ended abruptly, and the riot began, I told Pancho to get him out of there. Pancho raised his arms and elbows, battering through the melee with the Colonel holding his belt and Dr. Singh holding the Colonel's belt. Once back in the ambulance and his IV reconnected to the femoral tube still inserted, he waited to depart. My graphics person, Jonae Taylor, who loved and worried about her Colonel, rushed to the open ambulance to make sure he was OK. "Come closer, darling," the Colonel said weakly. "Closer. Listen, sweetheart, I need your help. The doctor said that I need to keep my heart rate and pulse slightly elevated if I want to stay alive. I'm going to need sex right now, dahling."

Jonae swung at the scoundrel and departed shouting, "You're OK. I can stop worrying."

At about this time, I was dealing with a metropolitan police lieutenant back in my truck who was demanding the tapes of the fight as evidence since Mike swung at the police in the ring. I told him he'd have to wait because we were still on the air, showing a fight recorded in the afternoon as the end of our telecast. He got impatient and went to the Showtime truck, where they negotiated for hours with lawyers to prevent giving up the tapes that they knew they'd never get back.

When we recorded that afternoon fight, seven hours before the ear bite, I told the Colonel to say good-bye and end the telecast after the fight because this would air after the Tyson fight. I also did that so he wouldn't have to wait around and could get back to the hospital. We really didn't notice it at the time but were floored when it played back. The Colonel's voice, recorded seven hours earlier, ended the world feed of Tyson–Holyfield II with, "That will do it for our telecast of this historic event. What a great night. I know you'll agree that you're glad you caught it live. Who would have believed what happened in that main event? I bet we'll probably never see that again. Goodnight, everybody."

Another I-wouldn't-have-believed-it-if-I-hadn't-seen-it-myself moment that I had with Mr. King happened before the 1998 Evander Holyfield fight with Vaughn Bean at the Georgia Dome in Atlanta. It was the first time Evander was fighting in his hometown. Both Don King and Showtime wanted to make it a big event. Evander was recently born again and wanted to show his new strong faith and connection with his church by involving the church youth in the event.

A month or two before the fight, I was in a meeting with Jay Larkin of Showtime in Don's conference room adjacent to his office. King was explaining to Jay about the great idea he had for Evander's ring walk that included dozens of the church youth holding signs with Evander's logo. Jay asked what kind of signs Don was talking about and he said, "Just a minute; I'll show you." And he disappeared into his office for a minute. When he returned, he was carrying *The Pictorial History of the Third Reich*. He thumbed through the pages excitedly as Jay looked at me with an "is he kidding" look. Don found the page he was looking for. He held up a giant glossy picture of hundreds of Hitler Youth carrying banners on signs with swastikas on them. "Forget the Nazi shit," Don said, "but the signs would be great, don't you think?"

Jay didn't know what to say. Don had no idea how offensive it was just putting that book in front of him. Don continued, "I'm not saying Adolf was a good guy or anything, you understand. But he was a hell of a sign man, don't you think?"

At that meeting Don also brought out from his office a Zippo lighter that was engraved "Adolf Hitler," saying it was Hitler's personal lighter, a genuine artifact that he had purchased for six figures.

Don was serious. He wasn't saying that the Nazis were good people, but he admired what they did. That Albert Speer guy could really build a great building, and Goebbels really was a great PR guy. I experienced this again on the day of the Crown Heights "Stop the Violence" rally where Don King and Al Sharpton teamed up with Rabbi Shea Hecht of the Hasidic community after a young Hasidic boy and a Black boy were killed. After the march, we went to Juniors deli in Brooklyn to eat. Back then it didn't get much better than Juniors for Jewish kosher-style food. I was seated next to a Holocaust survivor from the temple, and Don sat across. About twenty people from the Black and Hasidic communities were at the table. Don told me to order for everyone: "You know this Hebrew soul food, right, Marty?"

While eating. Don tried to strike up a conversation with the elderly Holocaust survivor by talking about his trip to Germany. "I saw some of the buildings these guys made. Man that, what's his name, Marty? Speer? What an architect. And those generals; they would do anything that man said. He could organize anything. What loyalty, and the production he ramped up was really something. I heard he even had help from Henry Ford. I don't know how they lost."

Finally, the Holocaust survivor looked at me and said, "Is he for real? Is he kidding? Does he even know what happened in the war?" Then he excused himself and left. Don didn't really understand that subject and how offensive his admiration for the Third Reich was.

When I first went to the Hasidic compound, for the event that I just mentioned, the person answering the door asked what I wanted. I said I was there with Don King for the march. They let me in and told Rabbi Hecht. He asked who I was, and I handed him my card identifying myself as the VP of television for Don King Productions. He looked at me with curiosity and finally asked,

"Are you a landsman?" Am I Jewish. I said yes, and he asked if I was bar mitzvah. When I replied in the affirmative again, he grabbed my wrist and dragged me quickly to his office. I asked if there was a problem, but he just started taking out a leather tefillin set, used to say prayers. He applied the leather straps and boxes to my wrist and forehead and helped me recite the appropriate prayer in Hebrew. When finished he explained that doing so was a mitzvah, or good deed. I said thank you, and he quickly replied, "Not for you." Lesson learned.

On a night in Atlanta after several difficult shows in a row, I was itching to get back to Maryland and my kids, who I promised a visit. We went to a banquet at the Atlanta Marriott given by one of the boxing commissions. About 11 p.m., Don's son, Carl, was describing to his dad the famous shoe store in Atlanta that all the NBA players went to because it specialized in big sizes and high-end shoes. Carl asked me, "Don't you know that store, Marty? You traveled as a director in the NBA, right?"

"Yes, Carl," I said, "I know Friedman shoes on Mitchell Street. We always stopped there when the team landed in Atlanta. They'd always send vans for us. Great place, and the owner, Bruce Teilhaber, is a great guy."

"OK," Don said, "we'll go in the morning."

"C'mon, Marty, we gotta take him," Carl said.

"I can't," I protested, "I have an early flight." Because I had promised my kids that I'd be home to see them.

Don asked Carl, "What did Marty say?"

"He said he has to change his flight so he can take you shoe shopping, Dad."

Then, realizing I was saved, I said, "Actually, Friedman's is closed tomorrow morning. It's Sunday."

"What's the owner's name? We'll call him," Don added.

I did have Bruce's number in my phone book because we had become friends over my ten years covering the Bullets, but I was sure I was right about them being closed. When I called him near midnight, apologizing profusely, I explained that Don was staring at me across the table. "Do you think it would be worth my while?" he asked.

Defeated, I replied, "Yes, I'm sure it would."

He opened the store just for Don at 9 a.m. King was escorted to the third floor "skin room" and set up in a chair that resembled a throne. Shoes were paraded in front of him made from the finest leather, lizard, ostrich, crocodile, Argentinian carpincho, snake, shark, and caiman. Each shoe style came in a choice of colors, and all were available in sizes up to 20 and widths up to 4E.

Don was in heaven. There were shoes everywhere around the man. At one point, Don's flip phone rang, and he told the other party he was coming to see him but wanted to bring him some shoes. He handed the phone to the owner. "Just ask his size." The owner listened for a few seconds and looked at me and mouthed the words, "Mike Tyson?" I nodded yes.

In ninety minutes, Don had purchased 110 pairs of shoes for a total of $56,000. The owner pulled me aside and told me to get any three pairs I wanted, no charge. I picked some nice, inexpensive shoes, which he took from me and directed me back to the skin room. I picked out some skins for a grand each, $800 more than I had ever spent on a pair of shoes. The owner told me it was his best day in the shoe business in his thirty years, thanks to just one customer!

Don was indicted for wire fraud in the fall of 1994. The real claim was that he committed contract fraud, but because he sent the contract by FAX machine, they tried him for the more severe felony of wire fraud. Don was acquitted; and as he had done once before, he invited the jury to a thank-you vacation. The first time he took them to London. This time it was to the Atlantis Casino and Hotel on Paradise Island in the Bahamas. I was one of the few staff who went along. Eleven of the twelve jurors accepted the invitation. The holdout, one juror told me, decided it was unethical. The holiday went very well and was uneventful up to the fourth day. Don was holding court near a pool when I spotted a guy with a cameraman alongside, hiding in the bushes and filming him. I bent over behind him and whispered, "What's going on?"

"That's Don King the boxing promoter," he told me. "Unless I'm mistaken, that is the jury from the court case that just ended, and they are here with Don." Then he dropped the other shoe: "I'm with CNN."

I carefully walked around the group and, when I thought I wasn't being observed, told Don about the CNN crew. "Bring them over here," Don said loudly. "I'll give them an interview. Maybe they want a piña colada and some shrimp."

I went back to the reporter and introduced myself. When I told him that Don would be happy to give him an interview, he looked at me silently for a couple minutes and then walked with me. "CNN everybody," Don bellowed. "C'mon, give us a little space; I'm going to be interviewed by this great reporter. You should have told me you were coming; I would have picked up your room, too. You've missed some of the party already."

The reporter, still uncertain how to proceed with this unexpected interview, got right to the point. "Is this the jury from your fraud trial?"

"You're a smart fellow. That's exactly right," Don said. "Why you hiding in the bushes? I'm not doing anything wrong. The case is over; this ain't no jury tampering."

I don't think the reporter got in another question. Don went on for at least fifteen minutes about the "Jewish-prudence" system, how people are out to get him because he's a successful Black man, and about the judge. His most memorable quote came when he explained why, for the second time in his life, he brought a jury on vacation after being acquitted. "What I want your viewers, and everybody in America, to know, is that," now looking directly into the camera, "if you find yourself in a courtroom, looking across a bunch of dark mahogany, at a n****r that looks like me, this could be you." Case closed.

Don King has always been able to bend to whichever wind seemed to favor him at the moment. That is how he chose to support men such as George W. Bush and Donald Trump despite being a rare Black man to do so. He also supported Venezuelan dictator Hugo Chavez. At the press conference for Hopkins versus Cloud after returning from Panama, King said, "I was so saddened to hear about the death of my dear friend, *mi hermano*, Hugo Chavez last night. I first met Chavez when he was a lieutenant in the Venezuelan army in 1971. He was my security when we opened the Poliedro de Caracas!"[1]

One thing very few people know about Don King, outside of those he has helped, is that he has always been very charitable. Remember, he started in boxing by working with Muhammad Ali on an exhibition for charity, saving a Cleveland hospital. He and his family made charity a regular event and never invited the press or sought publicity for it, at least as far as I observed. Don arranged what we staff called "the turkey tour" every November before Thanksgiving. Don would buy several tractor trailer truckloads of frozen turkeys and hire the staff to transport them. He would contact community centers, churches, mosques, and missions and arrange for them to have needy families and individuals be at a given spot on a certain day. We would show up and hand out the turkeys to very grateful people who blessed Don for making it a happy holiday. The turkey tour usually visited several cities in three or four days. By the end of it we were frozen and exhausted.

My first turkey tour included three memorable incidents. First, when I arrived at the initial meeting point in New York City, Don told me to get into a white Chevrolet Impala with three imposing-looking gentlemen. All three had cannons posing as handguns on their belts. The guy next to me in the back saw my face and started to laugh. He tapped the driver and said, "Marty is a little nervous about the guns; he didn't know we were cops." Don had a very strong relationship with the police in New York, and later, Florida. He always paid off-duty police to guard his homes and buildings and gave them well-paid assignments on all his press and fight events.

The second incident happened as we went up to Harlem. I was in the back of the limo with Don, and his personal assistant, Isadore "Izzy" Bolton, was at the wheel. I was born in the Bronx and grew up near the city line on Long Island. I worked at Nathan's in Times Square after I turned fifteen and had no fear of traveling throughout the city. As we drove up past 125th Street heading north, Don asked if I had been there often. "No," I said, "I didn't spend much time this far up into Harlem."

"Izzy," Don said, "is it my imagination, or is Marty getting whiter?"

At Muhammad's mosque number seven, a grand palace of worship that had been a synagogue until the 1960s, we were asked to wait in the small foyer because we weren't members and weren't allowed inside. Having drunk several cups of coffee already, I needed to use the restroom in a slightly urgent manner. I asked our host if I could just enter for a moment. He replied in the negative. Mike Marley, Don's press agent, asked if bathroom segregation wasn't, in fact, over.

Finally, we were in a stretch limo heading for the airport in Newark to pick up Don. I was seated behind the driver next to the chief of police, his captain was in the front, and both were in plainclothes. On a bridge packed with cars, not moving at all, the chief told the driver, also a policeman, to drive on the shoulder to get around the traffic. A driver ahead, who must have seen us in his rearview mirror approaching on the shoulder, jumped out onto the shoulder and braked to stop us from proceeding. This big man was screaming profanities as he came. He pounded on the captain's window to get it opened, said he was a policeman, and berated us for driving illegally. The captain calmly said, "Talk to the man behind me."

The man standing outside the car screamed, neck veins bulging, "I don't give a f*** who you're driving; you're all going to jail."

The police chief slowly lowered his window, called the irate man over, and opened his leather badge folder to show him the gold badge inside. "Come see me in my office in the morning," the chief told him. "He's on a desk in the traffic department, not even an officer on a beat, and it's his day off," said the chief. That guy was about to get a new opening somewhere. As Mark Twain said, "Good decisions come from experience. And most of that comes from bad decisions."

Near the end of my DKP years, I was doing an event in Shreveport, Louisiana. One of the "good ole" local boys asked me with a heavy drawl, "Where you from, boy?"

I answered, "The South, the Deep South, Boca Raton."

"That ain't no damn South," he bellowed.

"It's south of here," and I walked away briskly while he thought about it.

Another bad decision. He wasn't amused.

Down near the bottom of that card was Frankie Randall, scheduled to fight with an opponent yet to be named. Frankie, who passed away in 2021, was a tremendous champion, known best for being the first man to defeat Julio César Chávez, previously deemed unbeatable. Frankie was near the end of his career at this point and was listed on the card as Randall versus TBA. To Be Announced appeared on every bout sheet until an opponent could be confirmed. On Wednesday, three days before the fight, Frankie asked me in the hotel bar if I knew who his opponent was. Being a confirmed smart-ass, I said, "Yeah, I saw on the bout sheet you're fighting a guy named 'Ta-bah, Tee-bah, Ti-buh,'" pretending that I knew the guy but couldn't pronounce it.

"Do you know this guy?" Frankie asked.

"Yeah, I've seen him on a lot of bout sheets. But I wouldn't worry about him. He's obviously chicken because he usually drops out right before the fight. And he seems to keep going up and down in weight."

Carl King, Frankie's friend, leaned over to me and whispered, "Are you sure you want to f*** with a world champion?"

"Point taken," and I never did again.

I've produced events in the famous El Foro Antiguo Palacio Jai Alai fronton in Tijuana, built in the 1940s. I saw the Rosarito Castle on Baja California that was rumored to be built by Jack Dempsey for his pal Al Capone during Prohibition as a fun hideaway. I got to drink what was easily some of the best tequila ever made at the home of Roberto González Barrera, the founder and owner of Maseca flour, and one of the richest men in Mexico.

Although a few of us from Don King Productions were invited to his home prior to the Chávez versus Tony Lopez fight in Monterrey, Señor Barrera was showing Don, Carl, and I his precious bottle of rare tequila made for him by a distinguished tequila maker. Don looked at the sealed crystal bottle and said, "I don't drink this stuff, but Carl and Marty like it," and handed the bottle to Carl, who, without an invitation, opened it and started pouring it into soda glasses. I was horrified because the look on Señor Barrera's face clearly indicated that he hadn't intended it to be opened. Once the indiscretion had taken place, I decided not to pass up the rare opportunity.

I was privileged to produce fights in Juan-les-Pins and Antibes, France, on the Riviera. Don King asked me to meet with French promoters, the Acaries brothers. I had brought an associate from Don King Productions who was from Quebec and fluent in French to help with production arrangements for the event. After speaking in English and having my associate translate in French several times, Michel Acaries stopped us and said, "Please, Marty, let's just use English."

I was surprised and said, "I thought you'd prefer French, which is why I brought my friend to translate."

"No, Marty, it is more difficult. She doesn't speak French, she speaks Canadian."

Lesson learned. In that meeting, we called Don in Florida when there was a question he needed to answer. Don said that we should hold on so he could get his lawyer, Charlie Lomax, on the line. Michel said, "Marty, this is bullshit. We have lawyers in France, too, but we don't take them to the bathroom."

I produced fights in Berlin, Cardiff, Macau, Amsterdam, Glasgow, and all over England—all in front of amazing fans. One of my most memorable international fights was one I didn't produce but just attended with Frank Warren, Don King's partner in the United Kingdom. The event was a rematch between "The Celtic Warrior" Steve Collins and Chris Eubank at Páirc Uí Chaoimh, Cork, Ireland, on September 9, 1995.

I had done a fight for Don in London the week before. The following week we had another fight in Europe. With a week off, Frank invited me to Cork. I spent most of the week at Benny McCabe's pub talking about Tyson, because the young owner and his customers couldn't hear enough about him and kept buying me pints. To them I was a celebrity just for having been near him. They told me about the citizens of Cork once electing the town drunk as mayor. Weeks into his term, he traveled to San Francisco with other Irish mayors. He opened an empty suitcase he had brought at their welcome reception and told the American hosts they could fill it up with cash, and he'd be grateful. He was recalled shortly after.

When I arrived in Dublin by plane from London, I realized that it was colder there than I expected. Before driving to Cork, I bought a beautiful Guinness sweatshirt to be prepared. On the day of the fight, I arrived at the outdoor venue in Páirc Uí Chaoimh and was greeted by Frank. He introduced me to his lead sponsor, the owner of the prestigious Cork brewery Beamish, famous for Irish stout. Don't get ahead of me. The man was extremely nice but started to laugh at me when he saw the sweatshirt. It was the equivalent of wearing a Miller Lite sweatshirt to a Bud Light event. Frank was horrified, asking me how I could wear that. The owner of the Beamish brewery said something to his assistant, who came back with a beautiful Beamish sweatshirt, hat, and T-shirt. I said, "Do you know a better way to get Beamish gear than showing up to their event wearing Guinness rags?"

After the event, Frank told me that his driver would drive me back to Dublin—three hours—so I could catch my flight. Also in the Rolls would be Wilfried Sauerland and his business partner. Sauerland and Don King were bitter enemies. Sauerland asked me to sit in front so he and his partner could speak on the drive. Knowing that I worked for Don, Sauerland spoke for three hours in German to his partner. He was very angry about Don beating him on a deal and, in his words, stealing a fight from him.

Wilfried was unaware that I had taken seven years of German, from fifth grade to my senior year in high school. The German teacher in our district in New York, Herr Hank Schloboëm, was a particular favorite of mine, so, after ALM German levels 1 through 3, I kept taking his classes in conversational German and German literature. I even took a year of Russian from him in my senior year. After listening to Sauerland call Don horrible names and denigrating his family and eating habits, we arrived in Dublin. Herr Sauerland apologized nicely to me as we got out of the car at the airport that he had to speak business in German the whole trip. I smiled and said, "Überhaupt kein problem. Ich verstehen vollkommen, dass geschäft geschäft ist." (Translation: No problem at all. I understand completely; business is business.) He walked away with his mouth open, trying to remember what he had said for the previous three hours.

I will never forget a fight in Lyon between Mike "The Body Snatcher" McCallum and Fabrice Tiozzo. After covering thousands of boxers, The Body Snatcher is still my favorite boxer handle. Don had a new arrangement with Tiozzo's promoters, Sebastien and Michel Acaries. Some writers thought he had set Mike up to lose his title on that night.

It was June 16, 1995, and Mike was brought to France very late. The Palais des Sports de Gerland in Lyon had no air-conditioning. It was a stifling 90+ degrees in the arena. Mike, a much older fighter, ran out of gas and lost his title. Don King was accused of helping Tiozzo get the belt by bringing his fighter, Mike McCallum, to France so late.

In Tijuana, from 1996 through 1998, at a night club named Las Pulgas, the Flea, I had to do some small fights. They were building a back room for club fights. They could hold weekly boxing events there with three hundred paying customers. They asked me to help with the lighting. I consulted my good friend Bill McManus, who was the best lighting guy in boxing. He also had a long and illustrious career in concert production. He helped me deliver a plan for an inexpensive, small, easy-to-install, easy-to-operate, light system that only cost about US$3,000.

Some was used gear sourced locally and came with diagrams, instructions, and a good deal of backup information to make the purchase and installation easy. Two months later when I returned for the inaugural event in this new boxing venue, he had a surprise for me. The owner ignored what I gave him completely. He purchased a giant scoop security light, intended for hanging high over a parking lot, and hung it from the ceiling twelve feet above the ring. It was bright enough to light up a football field from one hundred feet high. It shone a blinding light straight down, making it impossible to see the people standing in the ring because it had a UFO effect of drowning in light. The shadows would have made a silent movie director proud. I asked the owner why he did that, and he told me it only cost him 75 bucks. Bienvenido a Mexico. I had to scramble to a local TV station and get lights on poles I could aim at the ring for the event.

Some shows I've worked on in other countries were among the best productions I've been involved with. Some spent a great deal of money, and others got very creative.

Bob Arum was also no stranger to working his magic to maintain the star of his stable. April 12, 1997, was notable for the fight that put Oscar De La Hoya on top of the pound for pound list. Pernell Whitaker, Oscar's opponent, was the four-year reigning WBC welterweight champion and one of boxing's greatest defensive boxers, the former undisputed and lineal lightweight champion. He would eventually become a four-weight division champion. De La Hoya, a three-division champion already was twenty-four and undefeated. He left the super lightweight ranks after defeating the legendary Julio César Chávez the previous year. The fight seemed to favor Whitaker, who landed many more punches than De La Hoya and scored the only knockdown in the fight's ninth round. But, when the scores were tallied, Oscar got the unanimous decision, perhaps because of his advantage in power punches. Pernell, sure he won decisively, cried foul after the fight, demanding a rematch. But Bob Arum decided it wouldn't make sense from a business perspective.[2]

"It may have seemed like an exciting fight, but that was because of the buildup," Arum said, his face a bright shade of rouge. "But my opinion is it was a dull, stinking fight. I don't want to see it again. I want to see Oscar fight people who fight, for Pete's sake. I've always hated to watch Whitaker fight. He can't even sell out a 1,200-seat ballroom in Atlantic City. I'm not going to lose my money on a rematch. If these two guys were from my gym, the crowd would've been booing them—because there was no action."[3]

Boxing has had more than its share of crowd incidents. I suppose that as a violent sport, temperaments might lead to overstimulated fans letting their excitement boil over. In most venues the chairs, if not fixed to the floor, must be zip-tied together so fans can't use them as projectiles. That change was made because fans did exactly that in several events in the past. In 2012, a chair-throwing riot broke out in Buenos Aires because the Argentine fighter, Luis Lazarte, was KO'd by Filipino John Riel Casimero. In 2018 at the Essex Arena, a riot in the stands had chairs and punches thrown for half an hour before order could be restored and the event could continue. In July 2021 in West Yorkshire at the Al-Hikmah Centre, fans threw chairs, impatient while the judges tallied scores.

There have been a few notable riots at U.S. boxing events, too. In July 1996 at Madison Square Garden, Riddick Bowe faced Andrew Golota. After Bowe won the fight because Golota was disqualified for repeated low blows, members of Bowe's team attacked Golota. Jason Harris hit Golota with a walkie-talkie, causing a wound that needed eleven stiches. Ringside, George Foreman got into the action trying to protect Jim Lampley and Larry Merchant. Lou Duva, Golota's manager, had to be taken out on a stretcher after he suffered chest pains and fell to the canvas. Eight police officers were injured, 10 persons were arrested, and nine spectators were injured.

Riddick Bowe was at another mini riot when he faced Evander Holyfield outdoors at Caesars Palace. The infamous Fan Man incident occurred on November 6, 1993, when a parachutist with a "paramotor" tried to land in the ring at the fight. He came close but hit a rope and fell ringside into the laps of some very unhappy members of Bowe's security team. They knocked James "Fan Man" Miller unconscious. It occurred in the beginning of the seventh round, and Evander Holyfield just stopped boxing. Bowe, confused and with his back to the intruder, later said, "I saw the look on Evander's face. I thought he saw King Kong." Bowe's pregnant wife fainted and was removed via stretcher. Miller was arrested three more times for flying over the LA Coliseum during an NFL playoff game, flying over an Arsenal Football match in England, and finally for landing atop Buckingham Palace. In 2002, he committed suicide in Alaska.

To date, I've been in three riots. After Francois Botha won a decision over Axel Schulz in Stuttgart, Germany, on December 9, 1995, the entire arena erupted in a brawl. Glass bottles from wine sales were thrown toward the ring. This was the event where I was hit in the thigh with a two-pound champagne bottle thrown from the balcony, which dropped me to the floor.

My second riot was at Tyson versus Holyfield II on June 28, 1997. After the ear bite, MGM security and the police entered the ring. Mike took a swing at a couple of them, and pandemonium ensued. The audience erupted in skirmishes everywhere.

My third riot was when Julio César Chávez met Ángel González in the bullring in Mexico City, on March 7, 1998, and the fight ended in a draw. The Mexican fans were so angry that they pelted the ring and anyone close with seat cushions, bottles, urine-filled cups, D batteries, and anything else they could grab.

On September 18, 1999, two great Hall of Fame boxers met at the Mandalay Bay event center in Las Vegas. The fight would unify the WBC and IBF welterweight belts. Félix Trinidad defeated the favored Oscar De La Hoya with a majority decision. King attempted to pry De La Hoya away from Arum by whispering to him in the ring moments after he lost a controversial decision to Trinidad, "If I was your promoter, you'd have won this fight."[4]

My departure from Don King Productions was due to me helping a friend with an urgent need for a director on a Top Rank fight. I directed an Oscar De La Hoya fight in 1999 for Top Rank after the company lost its director due to an illness or injury on fight week. I said I'd do it as long as we kept it to ourselves, because I knew Don wouldn't like it. Someone at Don King Productions heard that I directed a fight for Top Rank, and I was fired by one of his subordinates without notice on the week of a fight in New York.

I arrived at a press conference for the fight and was asked by a DKP staffer what I was doing there. Confused I said, "For the fight, of course." I was told that Don had decided he was "going in a new direction" with his producer and director for the event. We didn't speak again for ten years.

There couldn't possibly have been a more fortunate firing. Don's business went steadily downhill after that, and my twenty-five years and counting with Top Rank have seen Bob's company flourish and grow. I'm not saying that's because of me, but . . .

9

TYSON PUNCHES IN

Mike Tyson is a multifaceted man who is much deeper and much more interesting than most people know. In his peak boxing days, Mike repelled people with his aggressive antisocial appearance, which, in my opinion, masked his pain and insecurities. I witnessed Mike having deep conversations with people he trusted that most people would find hard to believe were in his repertoire. While in prison in Indiana for his rape conviction, I was there when Mike got books on French architecture from Charles Bietry, a reporter from Canal+ France. During the week of a Showtime event, I was there when Mike engaged in a philosophical conversation with, Jody Heaps, a writer for Showtime who he trusted, an intellectual, gentle, vegan man, quite the opposite of Mike. I learned watching Mike talk to Jody Heaps that there was much more to the man than I suspected.

Mike had as hard an upbringing as you can imagine. Born Michael Gerard Tyson on June 30, 1966, in Fort Greene, Brooklyn, he was moved by his family from Bed-Stuy to Brownsville, Brooklyn, when he was ten.[1] His older brother was Rodney, born in 1961; and his sister, Denise, was born in 1965. Denise died at age twenty-four of a heart attack.[2] Mike's mother, Lorna Mae Smith Tyson, of Charlottesville, often raised them alone.[3] Mike's father, Purcell Tyson, a cabdriver, was from Jamaica.[4] He was gone shortly after Mike was conceived. Mike considered his father to be Jimmy Kirkpatrick, a street hustler.[5] Kirkpatrick left when Mike was a baby and died in 1992. Mike regretted that his mother had a hard and unhappy life. She died when Mike was sixteen and never really saw him succeed, never reaped the benefit of his accomplishments.[6]

Marty Corwin with "Iron" Mike Tyson right before the McNeeley fight. Marty Corwin

Mike had been arrested thirty-eight times by the age of thirteen.[7] His first fight was with a kid who killed one of his pigeons. As a young teenager he lived in the Tryon School for boys in Johnstown, New York. While there, Bobby Stewart, a counselor and former boxer, noticed Mike's potential as a fighter and told Cus D'Amato about him. After his mother passed, Mike was given to D'Amato, who became his legal guardian. Kevin Rooney became Mike's first trainer along with assistant Teddy Atlas.[8] Cus fired Teddy after he threatened a fifteen-year-old Mike, allegedly over an incident involving Teddy's wife.[9]

Mike's amateur career was impressive. He won gold medals in 1981 and 1982 in the Junior Olympics. He beat Joe Cortez in 1981. In 1984 he won gold at the Golden Gloves. Before the 1984 Olympics, Henry Tillman beat him twice on points. Tillman went on to win gold in LA.[10]

Mike's pro debut was on March 6, 1985, against Hector Mercedes. He KO'd Mercedes in the first round in Albany, New York. He had a remarkable fifteen bouts in his first year as a pro. His first nineteen bouts were won by knockout, twelve in the first round.[11] His career KO percentage was a staggering 88 percent.

Cus D'Amato died in November 1985 when Mike was nineteen. Many believe this changed Mike overnight, making him lose his compass and feel bitter about his lifelong circumstances of loss and difficulties.

Mike's first televised bout was on February 16, 1986, against Jesse Ferguson. Mike broke his nose on ABC.[12]

Mike won his first belt on November 22, 1986, against Trevor Berbick. This WBC belt Mike won at twenty years, four months, and twenty-two days made him the youngest heavyweight champion in history.[13] He added the WBA belt from James Smith and the IBF belt from Tony Tucker in 1987.[14] He became the first heavyweight to hold all three belts.[15]

His fastest KO came against Marvis Frazier in thirty seconds. Mike's early style was described as strength, speed, and timing learned from Cus D'Amato. Cus taught Mike to avoid counterattacks while timing his one-of-a-kind power punch. His use of the right to the body followed by a right uppercut finished several opponents.[16]

In 1987 Nintendo approached Mike to launch a video game; Mike Tyson's Punch Out sold millions of games.

Mike beat Larry Holmes with a fourth round KO on January 22, 1988, the only KO loss for Holmes in seventy-five bouts.[17] He became the "lineal champ" when he beat Michael Spinks in a stunning first-round KO on June 27, 1988.[18] The lineal champ is a coveted title that reflects the first heavyweight champion, Jim Corbett, followed by the man who beat him, and the man who beat him, and so on down the line. The current lineal champion is Tyson Fury.

In late 1988, Mike left Bill Cayton and trainer Kevin Rooney to sign with Don King and Don King Productions.[19][20]

After joining King, Mike continued his winning ways, defeating Frank Bruno with a fifth round KO and Carl "The Truth" Williams with a knockout in the first. But he would soon start to show the effects of his marriage to Robin Givens. The marriage was failing due to incompatibility and the interference of Robin's mother, according to Mike. Robin trashed Mike, with him sitting next to her, on Oprah Winfrey's show on national television. They divorced in 1990, and Mike seemed to lose focus.[21]

On February 11, 1990, Mike suffered the worst loss of his career in Tokyo. James "Buster" Douglas, a 42-to-1 underdog, beat Mike by knocking him down for the first time in his career and knocking him out in the tenth round.[22] Many have speculated that Mike didn't train seriously for Douglas—he expected to beat him easily—and that his cornermen were inadequately prepared to assist him. They forgot the Enswell, a hemostasis device to reduce swelling, applied to facial contusions.[23][24] Tyson said the loss was a good thing. He said, "It was needed."[25][26]

Bob Arum defended Don King in the aftermath to this fight. Arum was called to testify in the lawsuit brought by Douglas; his manager, John Johnson; Golden Nugget Inc., and its subsidiary, the Mirage Casino. Douglas et al. claimed that King was in breach of contract for his behavior, screaming to stop the fight, when Mike knocked down Douglas in the eighth round. The referee was behind the timekeeper in his count. King's exhortation to stop the fight was, Arum said, the wrong remedy, but he insisted that it was understandable. "In the heat of combat," Arum testified, "we all say crazy things that we are not accountable for."

On cross-examination by the Mirage's attorney, John Sharer, Arum said that boxing protocol permitted King to lodge a protest. "A protest is the correct procedure," Arum said. "You yell your head off; otherwise nobody pays attention."[27]

King was furious with Steve Wynn. King was sued by Buster Douglas and Wynn, an action that sought to break the promotional exclusivity clause King had with Douglas for future fights. King countered the next week with a suit of his own.

"Buster Douglas is being led astray," King said from his home near Cleveland. "Before he can enjoy being heavyweight champion, before he can enjoy the wealth of being the heavyweight champion, the first thing he discovers is, he's embroiled in a lawsuit."

King also said that Tyson had already begun doing roadwork at Catskill, New York, when his sister, Denise Anderson, died in New York. Tyson left upstate New York to attend her funeral in Brooklyn.

King described himself as "still in shock" over Tyson's being knocked out by a 42–1 underdog. "We were all put into shock," he said. "No one could believe what they were seeing, yet it was happening right in front of our eyes."

After the upset, King went into closed-door meetings with leaders of the governing bodies, suggesting to many present that he was trying to arrange a reversal of the outcome. "There was a perception out there, a smoke screen, that I was trying to change the outcome, like I was the perpetrator of some sort of evil scenario, and I wasn't," he said. "I didn't even file a protest. But people jumped on that misperception, and I guess I have to accept that."[28]

King attacked Wynn, who had signed Douglas to a $25 million contract for a September fight with Evander Holyfield, providing King's contract could be broken in court. To get the Tyson fight, Douglas signed a contract designating King as his promoter, should he defeat Tyson, for virtually the rest of his career.

"Steve Wynn has a total disregard for the law," King said. "He told me categorically he would take my [legal] rights from me. He said to me, 'It doesn't work like that anymore, for guys like you and Arum. You're dinosaurs, extinct.' Then he [backtracked] and offered me two or three million dollars, and I told him I'd never work for him.

"I promoted Buster Douglas for years, I developed him, I nurtured him. I didn't even give up on him when he lost a title fight [to Tony Tucker] in 1987. Now, after investing all that time and money in Buster Douglas, and now that all of a sudden he's the heavyweight champion, you want me to make him a free agent?"[29]

In his next fight Tyson avenged his loss as an amateur by easily beating Henry Tillman.[30] He followed that by a win over Alex Stewart. On March 18, 1991, Mike beat Donovan "Razor" Ruddick in a controversial stoppage in the seventh round by referee Richard Steele. They met again on June 28, and Mike got a unanimous decision after knocking Donovan down twice.[3132]

Mike was due to fight Evander Holyfield next. The meeting was postponed when Mike suffered a rib injury while training. On July 19, 1991, Mike was arrested and charged with the rape of Desiree Washington, Miss Black Rhode Island, after he attended the pageant rehearsal.[33] The trial was widely criticized because witnesses who observed Miss Washington embracing Mike passionately before heading to his hotel room in the middle of the night were not allowed to testify.[34] During the trial a fire broke out in the Indianapolis athletic club where the jurors were sequestered. A hotel guest and two firemen were killed in the blaze. Mike was sentenced by Judge Patricia Gifford to ten years but was paroled after four.[35] He served his incarceration at the Indiana Youth Center, now the Plainfield Correction Facility, which is where I met him for the first time.

After more than ten years covering 110 games a year for the Washington Bullets, Washington Capitals, and Baltimore Orioles for a Paramount station owned by Viacom in Washington, D.C., I had entered the boxing world as Don King's VP of television production. One of my first assignments in boxing was to head into Mike's prison with Charles Bietry, a sports reporter from Canal+ France for an interview. Mike's manager, friend John Horne, was there as well. Mike was introduced to me by John and immediately responded to John, "Don got himself another one." I asked what he meant, and John asked me if I wasn't Jewish, like Don's other producer, and I knew a lot more about Mike. I was Don's second producer. His first, David Fox, a British Jew who came from CBS Sports, was the other. David would ultimately be beaten and hospitalized near death after being attacked in the men's room of the MGM in Las Vegas. The attack likely had nothing to do with Don King and everything to do with robbery.

In this first meeting with Mike I was surprised by his passion for books, his interest in unexpected subjects, and his calm demeanor with this reporter he considered a friend. While in prison Mike met regularly with members of the nation of Islam and converted to Islam. He took the name Malik Abdul Aziz. Some reports said the name was Malik Shabazz.[3637] He left prison in March of 1995. I had a cameraman outside the prison with hundreds of cameramen and reporters waiting for a glimpse of the release. I also had a camera, which back then was a bulky device with heavy batteries.

When Mike did exit, a bodyguard opened his coat to hide Mike as he got in the car. Don shouted, "What the hell are you doing that for. Let 'em see him." There was a secret plan for Mike's departure, to avoid paparazzi and reporters, to whisk Mike back to his home in Southington, Ohio, on a private plane. Four people were on the plane, Mike; his fiancée, Monica Turner; Don King; and me. Monica, who went to medical school, is the sister of Michael Steele, former head of the Republican National Committee and CNN analyst for Republican affairs. Mike and Monica were married from April 1997 to January 2003.

I was shooting Mike's cheerful departure from Indianapolis, a place he referred to as the birthplace of the Ku Klux Klan. Every time I tried to put the camera down, Mike said, "Keep shooting; I might say something funny." Mike asked Don if he had the "toy bag." Don dropped a small duffel bag at Mike's feet. He opened it and pulled out rubber-banded stacks of money, likely $20,000 per bundle, that he called footballs. He and Don proceeded to throw them around the plane. More cash than I had ever seen.

We arrived back at Mike's Southington home, where he had a family room with an immense Zebra print carpet and the largest projection TV I had ever seen in a house. His private chef had prepared a feast for his return, which included shrimp, lobster, and amazing steak. While there, Mike disappeared with Monica most of the time, coming downstairs in fresh pajamas when called to sign contracts. The contracts were with MGM, Showtime, and Don King. Mike was guaranteed $30 million a fight for a minimum of six fights.

I was exhausted by the long negotiations and wandered outside for air occasionally. Wearing a leather Showtime "baseball" jacket, I was mistaken by the press as a Showtime crew member. The press, fifty yards away behind an iron fence, could only look through long lenses at the house and occasionally, at me. Wally Matthews wrote an article the next morning in the *New York Post* saying that Mike threw Don King out of the house along with the "Showtime crew"—me—me, because he was now a devout Muslim who was outraged that Don served him shellfish on his return and would be fighting for the Nation of Islam. The meal was prepared for Mike by his chef. I asked Don, while reading the article in Mike's dining room, if he remembered being thrown out, and his belly laugh said no.

While Mike was in prison, Don King lined up McNeeley and Buster Mathis as warmups and the belts Mike sought right behind. Bruce Seldon had the WBA belt, the WBC belt would be the subject of a bout in London at Wembley Stadium between Oliver McCall and Frank Bruno, and the IBF belt was in the hands of Michael Moorer and later, Evander Holyfield. Much more about the Wembley fight later—a great story. It was during one of my four interviews at Don King Productions that Don put me on the conference call with boxing beat writers to announce a Peter McNeeley fight near St. Patrick's Day in Worcester, Massachusetts, against Francois Botha. Peter, son of Tom McNeeley, who challenged Floyd Patterson and later became commissioner for Massachusetts boxing, would later face several arrests after the Tyson fight for assault, petty theft, and larceny.

Mike's triumphant return to the ring, titled simply "He's Back," drew the biggest anticipatory attention ever for a boxer, selling a record 1.6 million buys, grossing more than $96 million worldwide, as he blew Peter McNeeley away less than ninety seconds into the first round.[38] Although I had seen basketball, hockey, and baseball playoff games and All-Star games with huge crowds and media attention, I had never seen a spectacle like this World Championship boxing pay-per-view at the MGM Grand Garden in Las Vegas. The excitement was infectious even though it wasn't even a championship.

As head of television for Don, I oversaw the foreign broadcasters and their facilities, in addition to producing and directing the world feed going to a record number of viewers worldwide. Showtime fed the U.S. market; I had the other 120 countries. I had to take care of eighty announcers speaking six languages ringside. More than a dozen TV trucks and a dozen more satellite trucks were in the TV compound. More celebrities were there than I had ever seen, which was a bit of a pain. Cameras and crew had great difficulty moving around. Mike's win made the past disappear. He was looking forward, with Don King behind his shoulder, to getting the belts and regaining the undisputed heavyweight championship.

Mike next faced Buster Mathis. What happened behind the scenes of this fight is even more impressive than the fight. A week prior to the fight, which was scheduled for Atlantic City and sponsored by Bally's, Don King called me into his office to alert me that the fight was moving to the Spectrum in Philadelphia instead. I was dismissed with that little information, and my mind started racing. All arrangements had to be moved in less than a week to another state for a big event—a Tyson event. The fight was also being broadcast by Fox, not Showtime, for the first time, and as fate would have it, the last time. I didn't yet know the Fox Sports people who would have to help me with this herculean task. Then a bell went off in my head: *Oh, my God*, I thought, *please tell me there is no Flyers hockey at the Spectrum on Friday night.* I quickly called my friend Randy Seidman at Spectrum Vision TV and got the news I was dreading. Not only were the Flyers at home, but it was a Rangers game, making it even more chaotic. A big event such as a Tyson fight sets up on Thursday and Friday because of the huge lighting, audio, television technology, and logistics involved. The arena needs a day and a half just to set up the chairs, tables, vendors, and security accommodations. All of this wouldn't be able to begin until 4 a.m. on fight day, Saturday, December 16, 1995. My second Tyson fight.

I remember that the light truss, normally set up in the rafters, focused and checked for malfunctions by Thursday evening, was a couple feet off the floor twenty minutes before I was supposed to walk the first fight of the preliminaries. It was literally raised as I walked the blue corner into my radio. The lights were tweaked and focused while the first four fights were going on.

My world feed includes the same fights the U.S. network carries and several of the undercard fights as preliminary bouts or as fill content, delayed broadcast from earlier recordings of non-televised bouts. I try to fill the show with fight action and avoid long gaps or "talking heads" filling airtime with often boring analysis. The Fox broadcast, like a Showtime broadcast—this time produced and directed by David Dinkins Jr., son of former New York Mayor David Dinkins, and Bob Dunphy, son of legendary boxing announcer Don Dunphy, would only show the scheduled bouts. They wouldn't improvise to include other fights if their fights went short. On this night, their two fights both ended in the first round. So, they showed two rounds of boxing in a two-hour show, with commentary all around. My world feed showed five fights and highlights of another. I'm not picking on Fox. Showtime and HBO did exactly the same thing on many shows. In my thirty years in boxing, many of the foreign broadcasters I've served have appreciated our "bonus coverage" when a short fight could have resulted in a very long wait for the next fight. Showtime, HBO, and ESPN have excellent announcers who provide the best analysis and feature content during their "studio" segments as they go on camera at a sports desk. The world feed can't do that because many countries use their own announcers rather than taking our show in English. I need to provide them with solid video content they can talk over and analyze themselves.

Mike's first heavyweight belt after prison came from Frank Bruno. The rematch with Bruno came on March 16, 1996. The fight, my second at the Grand Garden in Las Vegas, only lasted three rounds. My joke at the time was that Frank Bruno lost during the instructions. He looked very nervous from the start. Mike became only the sixth fighter in history to regain the heavyweight championship title.[39]

In 1996, Lennox Lewis turned down $13.5 million to fight Mike. He took $4 million from Don King as "step-aside" money instead.[40] At Don King Productions, I received a letter from a boxing fan with an offer to Don King. The fan said it was disgraceful that Lewis got $4 million not to fight Mike. Don shouldn't have paid that much. He, the fan, would agree not to fight Mike for the bargain basement price of $1 million. He went on to list other Don King fighters by name that he would agree not to fight for a few thousand up to six figures. Don passed the letter around the office staff.

Don King's plans were for Mike to fight Bruce Seldon next, once Lennox Lewis was paid to step aside. The winner, presumably Mike, would fight Lennox in a massive, immensely profitable event. But a week before his July 13, 1996, fight with Seldon, Mike was diagnosed with bronchitis, confirmed by Dr. Robert Voy, the former chief medical officer of the U.S. Olympic Committee. The fight would be rescheduled for September.[41] When the fight did happen on the night of September 7, 1996, there was controversy and tragedy. Mike won the WBA belt that night by knocking Seldon out in less than two minutes of the first round. The crowd shouted "fix," and Showtime's Jim Gray even asked Seldon in his post-fight interview what he had to say about that charge. "I didn't train twelve weeks to come in here and take a dive."

The tragedy of the night happened after the fight. Rapper Tupac Shakur, who attended the fight and was seen arguing with Orlando Tive "Baby Lane" Anderson in the MGM, was shot on a Las Vegas street and died six days later. Mike said he felt responsible for the tragedy because he had asked Tupac to attend.[42]

After a 1994 loss to Michael Moorer, Holyfield was next for Tyson. Don King might have thought he was a "done" fighter, past his prime. This would be Mike's fourth comeback fight.[43, 44] The fight, dubbed "Finally," occurred on November 9, 1996, five years and one day after the two were originally scheduled to meet. Mike's prison term was the main reason for the delay. I vividly remember the night as the last time I bet on boxing at a sports book. I spent $100 on a six-fight parlay ticket, which included my winning a couple upset fights before the main event. If Mike won his fight, and he was a huge 25–1 favorite, I'd cash in thousands. When the main event ended, while I showed replays and recapped the fight, I tore my ticket into tiny pieces and threw it across the TV truck. In the twenty-six years since, I have not bet on a single fight.

The fight shocked Mike's fans. Evander took Mike's shots but didn't go down, lose his composure, or seem scared. The post-fight analysis suggested that Evander "stood up to the bully," and the bully was beatable. That sounds easy, but to do it you had to stand up to Mike's power. Evander seemed like the first who could. The fight was stopped by referee Mitch Halpern in the eleventh round.

Tyson claimed that he lost due to Holyfield's intentional head butts. But after hitting Evander with a clean shot in the first round, making people assume the fight was over, Holyfield stayed in the fight and dominated almost every round. In the sixth, he knocked Mike down, and the ending seemed inevitable from that point forward. At the end of the tenth, Mike barely made it to the bell and was quickly finished at the start of the eleventh.[45]

Two months after marrying Monica Turner,[46] Mike was scheduled to rematch Evander Holyfield on June 28, 1997. Dubbed "The Sound and the Fury," Mike was expected to get revenge. Mitch Halpern was replaced as referee by Mills Lane because Don King and Mike suggested that Halpern let Evander head butt in the first fight. [47]

The fight sold 1.99 million buys and paid $30 million to Mike, $35 million to Holyfield.[48] However, "The Sound and the Fury" would be called forever more "The Ear Bite Fight." The fight, stopped at the end of the third round, was the first heavyweight championship ending in a disqualification in fifty years.[49, 50]

This night was one of the most memorable in my life for many reasons, none of them good. The night before the fight my best friend and play-by-play announcer, Colonel Bob Sheridan, suffered a moderate heart attack, and I thought he'd die. The ear bite led to a riot in the ring, one of the three I'd experienced, when Mike punched a police officer, and the brass of the Metro police came into my truck to seize the tapes as evidence. I truly believed that my boxing career was over, and I might have to start again looking for a gig because Mike and King were likely through. I remember being physically ill as I played the slo-mo replay of the ear bite over many times, asking the engineer to open the door of the truck so I could get some air.

On July 9, the Nevada State Athletic Commission suspended Mike's license. He was also fined $3 million, both by unanimous vote.[51] It would only take fifteen months for his license to be restored by a 4–1 vote on October 18, 1998.[52] Tyson accused Holyfield of intentional head butts, as he did after their first fight, but that didn't stop the suspension. After eighteen months, Mike fought twice more in Las Vegas, beating Francois Botha in January 1999 and getting a no decision against Orlin Norris nine months later. In between the two fights, Mike went back to prison for four months after being convicted of assaulting two motorists in Indiana. His one-year sentence was reduced to four months for good behavior.

Tyson ended up suing King for $100 million in 1998, although he eventually settled out of court for $14 million. "I found out that someone I believed was my surrogate father, my brother, my blood figure turns out to be the true Uncle Tom, the true n*, the true sellout," Tyson said later. "He did more bad to Black fighters than any white promoter ever in the history of boxing."[53]

After separating from King, Mike took an offer from WrestleMania. At WrestleMania XIV, Mike was a guest enforcer. He was reportedly paid $3.5 million for his appearance. He learned that his contract to King required him to share that payday.

Because Showtime did air the Tyson fights after he left Don King, I was extremely fortunate that my friends there allowed me to continue with the franchise. I was also doing Top Rank shows at this point, but it wasn't a conflict as far as they were concerned. I now owned my own production company, so I also did work for other clients in MMA, boxing, international soccer, volleyball, motor sports, and even entertainment events such as an annual beauty pageant.

In January 1999 Mike's next boxing event was against the white South African heavyweight Francois Botha in Las Vegas. Prior to the match he said that he would knock Botha out cold and expected him to die. He got a TKO against Botha in the fifth round when Richard Steele stopped the fight.[54] After the fight Jim Gray, the interviewer for Showtime, asked Mike about his violent comment. Mike turned on him, claiming that he wouldn't talk to anyone because they reported on him so negatively. Less than a month later, Mike was back in prison after a conviction for assaulting two motorists in August 1998.[55] He was incarcerated for nine months, fined $5,000, and ordered to serve two hundred hours of community service.[56]

In October 1999, Mike fought Orlin Norris, brother of Terry Norris, trained by Orlin Norris Sr., at the MGM Grand Garden. Orlin Norris, a former Don King fighter, had been a top contender before a dispute with King lowered him to a number six contender slot in the WBA. After winning a court decision, Orlin was granted an eliminator fight with Henry Akinwande, which he lost. He considered the Tyson fight an opportunity for redemption. The fight with Tyson ended in controversy when Mike hit Orlin after the bell ending the second round, causing Orlin to go down and hurt his knee. When he couldn't continue, the fight was declared a no decision. Mike's corner had to restrain him when he wanted to go after Orlin. Mike knocked down Orlin after the bell of the first round. Orlin injured his knee as he fell, and the fight was ruled no contest.[57]

After this bout, Mike headed overseas. First up was Julius Francis at the MEN (*Manchester Evening News*) arena in Manchester. This was Mike's first fight overseas since his loss to Buster Douglas. The British were questioning

Mike's admittance to England because of his criminal record. Jack Straw, the home secretary, said Mike was allowed in for the fight because he didn't want to hurt Manchester businesses or disappoint the crowds who wanted to see the fight.[58] When Mike arrived, he was faced with protesters, including the women's group Justice for Women; Mike called them frustrated women who wanted to be men.[59] The fight also had an odd footnote from one of Julius Francis's sponsors. *The Mirror* paid Julius £20,000 to wear their logo on the bottom of his boxing shorts, anticipating that he would be knocked down and the spectators would see it. They weren't disappointed, as Julius was knocked down five times in the first two rounds of the fight before the fight was called. Piers Morgan was editor at *The Mirror* at the time and was suggested as the one who came up with the idea. Julius also made £350,000 as his purse, his biggest payday. New to Manchester, I made the nearly fatal mistake of praising Manchester United Football Club in the wrong pub. The locals, all fans of Manchester City FC, straightened me out as I bought a round to make friends.

In June 2000, Mike faced Lou Savarese in Glasgow. I have always loved Scotland and took a side trip to the Necropolis and Kelvingrove Art Gallery and Museum with a Van Gogh and a Salvador Dali. The local Scottish television technicians weren't very happy with Showtime, which brought many of their technical staff from London. The techs were people they had used for years and were familiar with their show, but the Scots considered it a grave insult and didn't try to hide their contempt for the Brits.

The most memorable thing for me about this fight in Scotland was the weather. It poured all week as we set up, and it poured all morning of the fight and into some of the undercard. Although the ring was covered and dry, our announcers and some equipment were under umbrellas. I made a terrible joke in my terrible Scottish accent on show day as a tiny hole appeared in the clouds, and a ray of sunshine broke through: "Mummy, what is that bright yellow, shiny thing in the sky? I'm frightened." I regretted it immediately as my crew didn't think it was amusing at all.

Mike made short work of Lou Savarese with a KO in thirty-eight seconds of round one when they fought outdoors at the Hampden Park in Glasgow.[60] It's a good thing he wasn't paid by the round. Mike knocked him down with his first punch of the fight, a left jab. After Lou got up, he was assaulted with a barrage from Tyson causing the referee, John Coyle, to try to step in to stop it, only to get knocked down himself. Tyson's corner jumped in, and Mike calmed down, receiving his second shortest TKO victory. After the fight, Mike said during his in-ring interview that he wanted to eat Lennox Lewis's children. Lennox's mom said when she heard it that Lennox has no kids.[61] Later in the book, I'll tell you what happened when the Colonel, Bob Sheridan, saw Mike at the Glasgow airport in the morning. During the fight, my announcers, the Colonel, and color commentator Glen McCrory called the entire show huddled under golf umbrellas a few rows back from the ring in a torrential downpour.

Back in the United States, at The Palace of Auburn Hills in Detroit, Michigan, Mike Tyson faced Andrew Golota. The fight, dubbed the Showdown in Motown, occurred on October 20, 2000. Golota, dubbed the "Foul Pole" due to his heritage and propensity to use low blows in his arsenal, regrouped after a first-round knockdown and appeared to be making a fight out of it. He suffered a cut over his eye he blamed on a head butt from Mike. The crowd was stunned when Golota refused to come out for the third round, and Mike charged his corner wanting to hit anybody in his way because of Golota's refusal. The crowd pelted Andrew with beer cups on his way back to the dressing room. A trip to the hospital revealed that Golota had suffered a concussion, fractured cheek bone, and a herniated disc in his neck.[6263] The fight was later changed to a no contest after Mike failed a drug test. He tested positive for marijuana.[64] I'm not aware of anyone who considered marijuana a performance-enhancing drug for athletes. The Michigan State Athletic Commission barred Mike for three months. The Nevada Commission upheld the ban.

After Golata, Mike and I took a trip to Copenhagen in the fall of 2001, where he met and beat Brian Nielsen in a full six rounds. Mike and Lennox Lewis had been slated to meet in Memphis, Tennessee, after the state agreed to license the fight. It originally was slated for Las Vegas, but Mike was suspended again by the Nevada State Athletic Commission after he bit Lennox on the leg during a brawl at a press conference for the fight. Several other states also refused to grant Mike a license.

Originally, Mike was supposed to face David Izon. Showtime was hoping, however, for a mega-event with Hasim Rahman, who then held the WBC and IBF belts. This would have been Mike's first title shot since losing to Holyfield. Rahman, it turned out, rematched with Lennox Lewis, so an alternate plan needed to be made.[65] Danish fighter Nielsen (62-1), who had beaten Larry Holmes at the end of his career, was an impressive challenger. Nielson called Mike an "Abekat" during the press conference, a Danish word meaning someone who acts foolishly. Mistranslated for Mike as monkey man, Mike said he would punish him for that racial slur.[66]

Nielsen was a tough challenger who, despite taking tremendous blows for several rounds, including a flagrant low blow at the end of the third, made it through six rounds before being unable to continue. This was Mike's longest fight since his first with Evander Holyfield.[67]

Following this fight, Mike had his sights on Lennox Lewis for the showdown he had sought for many years. The fight was scheduled for April 6, 2002, in Las Vegas. But Mike made that impossible during a press conference with Lewis the previous January. The fighters were on platforms on the right and left of the stage with spotlights. Without warning, Mike stepped off his platform and approached Lewis. Lewis's security guys stepped forward, and Mike threw a left hook. Everyone jumped in with Mike and Lennox in the middle. Lennox shouted, "Hey, he's biting my leg," and they fairly quickly managed to separate the two and stop the minute-long melee.[68] The incident cost Mike $335,000.[69]

The press conference also meant that the fight would need to be moved after the Nevada State Athletic Commission called for another suspension. Several states declined, as the practice was to honor Nevada's suspensions. Tennessee was not inclined to miss the potential revenue and bid $12 million for the event.[70] The fight was scheduled for The Pyramid, an event arena in Memphis, now a Bass Pro Shop fishing and hunting store.

This fight was the first historic joint broadcast between HBO and Showtime. I never thought I'd see that day. Both companies had their own trucks and crews and would both control the PPV and delayed broadcasts on their premium channels. There would only be one world feed, and I was fortunate to be approved by both HBO and Showtime to provide that feed. Sky also had a unilateral broadcast for the event. Showtime, Mike's broadcast network, and HBO, Lewis's broadcast network, would put out a single PPV feed live, and both had delayed broadcast rights separately. The consequences for me were also a first. Both Showtime and HBO had to choose and agree to the producer/director for the world feed to more than 150 countries. I was honored that they both agreed that I should be the man. I also worked with Sky Sports, which had a unilateral feed for its fighter, Lennox Lewis.

The funniest thing that happened on show day was when I received a call from a stadium manager about a military unit that wanted access to the event. He called me only because he knew me from event meetings and had my cell number. I got to the main gate and was confronted with twenty uniformed men seeking to enter the event without tickets, as they claimed they always did in Memphis. They told me that they were representatives of the Tennessee Navy. I asked why landlocked Tennessee needed a navy and was given a Civil War river battle history that included a verbal map of the Cumberland River. I told the manager, who had no reason to ask me in the first place, to call the Pentagon to sort it out, or just ask the promoter. I wasn't sure whether Memphis fought for the Union or Confederacy. I think their plans eventually were sunk.

Mike, after winning the first round, was frustrated with Lewis's holding, which referee Eddie Cotton warned him about. Tyson took a few hard shots in the fourth causing him to go down, although it was called a slip. Beginning in the fifth round Mike started throwing fewer punches, Lewis was warned about pushing, and started to dominate the action. In the sixth round Lewis controlled Mike with jabs. For the rest of the fight, it was all Lewis. Lewis knocked Mike out in the eighth round. Mike didn't make any serious attempt to get back up. The fight, which to that point was the largest pay-per-view event of all time, grossed $106.9 million.[71] I feel very fortunate to have been a part of these historic mega-events.

On February 22, 2003, Mike faced Clifford Etienne in the Pyramid of Memphis once again. Etienne was a standout linebacker in his Louisiana high school who then served a ten-year prison sentence for armed robbery. While in prison he became a standout boxer with a 30-0 record. He won the state prison boxing championship.[72] The fight was canceled only days before it was supposed to happen because Mike's trainer, Freddie Roach, had suggested to Mike that he call it off because he hadn't trained adequately. But the unpredictable Mike showed up in Memphis the next day and declared that the fight was on. Etienne said that his team left when he heard of the cancellation. Then he decided the fight was on anyway and called his guys back because he feared not getting the payday. It was before this fight that Mike got his famous face tattoo.

Tyson made short work of Clifford Etienne. The fight only took forty-nine seconds. Both fighters missed more punches than they landed, but when Mike hit Etienne with the last right, he made no attempt to get up. This was Mike's fiftieth win and the last of his career.[73] In August 2005, Etienne was arrested for armed robbery, kidnapping, and attempted murder of a police officer. While allegedly high on cocaine, he robbed a business, hijacked two vehicles, and tried to shoot a police officer only to have the gun jam.[74]

In August 2003, Mike filed for bankruptcy, claiming approximately $23 million in debt. He had earned approximately $300 million as a fighter.[75][76][77]

An August 2003 fight with Bob Sapp in Japan failed to happen. Mike couldn't get a visa to visit there.[78] In July 2004, he lost to Danny Williams in Louisville in the fourth round by TKO.[79] Mike tore a knee ligament in the first round and needed surgery four days later.[80] In June 2005, he lost to Kevin McBride, quitting after the sixth round. He announced his retirement after that fight.[81]

In 2006, Mike announced a world exhibition tour. His first bout was to be with Corey Sanders, wearing head gear, in Youngstown, Ohio. The tour idea was not well received and was canceled. [82]

In August 2007, Mike pled guilty to drug possession and DUI.[83][84]

On May 25, 2009, tragedy struck Mike's life again. His four-year-old daughter, Exodus, was accidentally hanged from a treadmill power cord.[85] One month later, on June 9, 2009, Mike married his third, and current, wife, Lakiha "Kiki" Spicer.

On June 12, 2011, the International Boxing Hall of Fame in Canastota, New York, inducted Mike Tyson. He was inducted alongside Julio César Chávez, Kosta Tszyu, Ignacio Beristáin, Joe Cortez, and Sylvester Stallone for his movie *Rocky*.[86] Mike spoke about Cus D'Amato, emotionally pausing for long periods until the gathered fans encouraged him to continue. He credited Cus with taking a kid who only knew how to rob people and making him a man with strong potential.

After boxing Mike kept busy with high-profile projects. In 2009, he appeared as himself in the movie *The Hangover*. In August 2012, his one-man show, *Undisputed Truth*, landed on Broadway backed by Spike Lee.[87] In October 2012, Mike started the Mike Tyson Cares Foundation to help children from broken homes.[88]

In August 2013, my path and Mike's crossed again. Mike became a boxing promoter with a company called Iron Mike Productions. The company had offices in Anthem, a community in Henderson, Nevada. The financial backer was a Floridian whose name I can't recall. Mike's people contacted me and said they needed me to be their producer/director again. Because I had been the producer/director for Bob Arum's Top Rank organization since 1999, I decided to ask permission. I asked Bob, who was always like an uncle to me, if he'd mind if I helped Mike out with this project. He thanked me for asking and gave me the go-ahead.

We did several shows, beginning with a show in Miami in July with the main event between Argenis Mendez rematching Rances Barthelemy. It was the IBF junior lightweight championship. The first fight ended in controversy after Barthelemy landed a couple blows after the bell, and Mendez was counted out. He protested to the Minnesota authorities, and the fight was declared a no contest. In their rematch in Miami for Iron Mike Productions, Barthelemy earned a unanimous decision against Argenis. Another of my memorable fights with Iron Mike Productions was in Pittsburgh at the Consol Energy Center between Sammy Vasquez Jr. and James Stevenson. This IBF and USBA (United States Boxing Association) welterweight championship between undefeated fighters was a great main event between Vasquez Jr., a southpaw from Pittsburgh, and the Baltimore native, Stevenson. Vasquez Jr. beat Stevenson in an action-packed slugfest in the ninth on our broadcast on FS1. Stevenson never quit and made this a tremendous brawl. Mike seemed to lose interest after a few fights in a couple years, and the project was suspended.

On November 28, 2020, Mike had an exhibition bout with Roy Jones Jr. After the time out of the spotlight, the crowds were eager to see Mike again. Roy Jones was also a fan favorite. I was a fan of his as well, despite Roy Jones Promotions not paying me for the fight I directed for him at the Cox Pavilion on the campus at UNLV in Las Vegas. But that's another story. The two battled to a draw determined by fight celebrity judges. Christy Martin, who fought regularly on Tyson undercards for Don King, picked Mike. Vinny Pazienza picked Roy. Chad Dawson, former World Boxing Council, WBC, light heavyweight champ, called it a 76–76 draw.[89, 90]

Currently, Mike is doing very well with his cannabis brand, "Undisputed Cannabis." His company Tyson 2.0 expanded to more than five markets in July 2022 with its best-selling product, an edible shaped like an ear with a piece missing called "Mike Bites."[91]

Mike has also become a notable trainer. He trained Francis Ngannou, MMA heavyweight, for his bout with Tyson Fury in Riyadh, Saudi Arabia.

Regardless of your feelings about Mike, his demeaner, his outbursts, antics, legal tribulations, and his opinions, you cannot fail to include him as one of the top heavyweights of all time for his sheer power and ferocity. Mike was also a great boxing historian with a tremendous knowledge and understanding of fighters and fighting that was the most impressive I've encountered. He knows more about boxing than almost anyone I've ever met.

10

BOXING PAY-PER-VIEW
HEAVEN (2000–2010)

Boxing has become a spectacle. Great promoters such as Top Rank, Golden Boy, Matchroom, Queensbury Promotions, Premier Boxing, and others put on a big show, especially on pay-per-view events, with dramatic and beautiful lighting, DJs, spectacular ring walks, and even guest musical performances. Meatloaf performed before that Botha versus Schulz main event in Germany, Tom Jones at a Ricky Hatton fight, and Jamie Foxx sang at the Mayweather versus Pacquiao event.

The show is the thing. Adding graphics, screens, lighting, music, and special effects raises the production value of the show and lets the fan know it is a special, quality, event. The fight is why they came, but the quality of the production is what makes them enjoy the show. You don't need all the trash talk, aggressive announcers, and a ring announcer who is barking like a surreal psychotic.

The ring walks really separate the men from the boys. ESPN does a good job with graphics, videos, and animations in LED walls as main event fighters walk to special pyro effects. Showtime always excelled at ring walks, such as the great Crawford versus Spence walks that included Eminem escorting Terence Crawford. I have always felt that Sky Sports in the United Kingdom created some of the best ring walks of all time. The creativity of their Nigel Benn and Lennox Lewis ring walks and the imagination they used for Prince Naseem's walks were truly a cut above.

The prince came into Newcastle Arena in June 1996 on a palanquin, a litter carried by large men supporting poles, with maidens tossing rose petals. In another entrance, perhaps the best walk I've ever seen, the lights dimmed, the music started to build, and highlight video of the prince was projected onto a previously

Bob Arum with special Manny Pacquiao/Miguel Cotto Belt, September 12, 2009.
AP Images

dark gray screen on the balcony. As the music reached a crescendo, the screen went black. Then the live shadow of the prince was seen shadowboxing in the screen lit from behind, revealing that the screen was translucent. As the music hit another crescendo, the screen—which turned out to be flash paper—burst into flames and immediately disappeared. The prince stood there in a single spotlight and was lowered to the floor. The crowd went wild. He has also come in on a flying carpet, as the phantom of the opera organist in a "Thriller" gravesite Halloween entrance, in an old Cadillac convertible through a trio of "imposter" princes, and through an exploding wall versus Augie Sanchez.

* * *

The U.S. boxing fans, and I'm sure I'll take heat for this, are not great boxing fans compared to many other countries. Many U.S. boxing fans, egged on by U.S. boxing writers and bloggers with an agenda, many of whom seem determined to bring down the sport by preferring to write about scandals and conspiracy theories rather than support the sport, want only to see fighters they know knock out anybody they don't. The U.S. fans, with some exceptions, see name recognition and size as the only incentives to get interested in a fight. The exceptions are Latin and transplanted immigrant boxing fans residing in the United States who know and love the sport more than their native counterparts.

Most of the greatest fights I have seen are in the featherweight through the middleweight divisions. Fury versus Wilder III and Norton versus Holmes are clear exceptions. Of the fighters I've watched live, my all-time favorite boxers are Oscar De La Hoya, Julio César Chávez Sr., Ricardo Lopez, Félix Trinidad, Manny Pacquiao, Teofimo Lopez Jr., Shakur Stevenson, and Terence Crawford. The current group of favorites includes Tyson Fury, Canelo Álverez, Zander Zayas, Artur Beterbiev, Emanuel Navarrete, Naoya Inoue, Vasiliy Lomachenko, Oleksandr Usyk, Jermell Charlo, Edgar Berlanga, Errol Spence Jr., Josh Taylor, and Keyshawn Davis.

A successful promoter needs a star to make the kind of profits that prolong their reign. When Don King came to Jamaica in 1973, he was accompanying Joe Frazier fresh off his defeat of previously undefeated Muhammad Ali. Frazier's win over Ali made him a 3–1 favorite against Foreman. When King witnessed Foreman's total destruction of Frazier in the Sunshine Showdown, he seized the moment, stepping over Joe Frazier and leaving with George Foreman. Soon after, he pitted Foreman against Ali in the Rumble of the Jungle in Zaire, the most remarkable boxing event of its time. In April 2001 Hasim Rahman, a 20–1 underdog, shocked the heavyweight division by scoring a TKO victory over Lennox Lewis in South Africa. Rahman, who had been managed by Stan Hoffman and promoted by Cedric Kushner, was wooed by King with a $5 million contract a month after the fight. A judge allowed Rahman out of the contract in December 2005. The rumor was that King picked up Rahman at the airport in a limo and dropped a duffel bag at his feet holding more cash than Hasim had ever seen.

Bob Arum also knew how to draw a crowd before the main events. One of the most popular and successful boxers in Top Rank's long history was Eric "Butterbean" Esch. Esch, born in Atlanta and living in Jasper, Alabama, became the "King of the Four Rounders." Butterbean had humble beginnings in tough man contests, but he ultimately racked up a record of 77–10 with fifty-eight KOs as a boxer for Top Rank. Butterbean was a real crowd pleaser. He was a five foot eleven guy who looked shorter because of his huge girth. He looked like a guy you'd like to have a beer with in a pub but packed a wallop that took down giants in less than four rounds on a regular basis. Years later when Andy Ruiz, the first heavyweight champion of Mexican descent, started fighting for Top Rank, I noticed a similarity with Butterbean. Andy was strong and very fast for a man with a large, less-than-chiseled physique. With his permission, I started calling him Pinto Bean.

Although no one would call them staunch feminists, Bob Arum and Don King both began promoting women's boxing more than thirty years ago. Top Rank had Dutch superstar Lucia Rijker, and Don King had Christy Martin. Both were serious, great athletes—real boxers who deserved the attention they received. They never faced each other for the same reason most great matchups don't happen: promoter politics and protecting an asset.

Boxing has always been driven by big events. That is why it was the originator and is still world champion of pay-per-view. Smaller events and championship fights are the regular fodder of the real fans, but the mega-events bring out viewers who only watch when the hype hits 11. All the way back to Sullivan versus Corbett, big events get the media buzzing—and that brings even casual observers out to watch the "big fight." And unlike a baseball game or a football match where the score can be retrieved late for satisfaction, a mega boxing event must be caught live. The atmosphere of "you never know what might happen" permeates the air. You want to be able to tell officemates on Monday that you saw it live.

At the very beginning of my boxing career, I had the privilege of participating in some amazing mega-events. I was doing Chávez events right off the bat. Soon I was producing and directing Tyson's return to the ring after his three years in prison in Indiana.

Big events had a very different feel. The number of people requesting press access went from a dozen to thousands. The fighters were scheduled for grand arrivals, press conferences, satellite media tours, weigh-ins, one-on-one interviews with prominent broadcasters, including the primary U.S. rights holder, and a massive number of training and field shoots leading up to the big day. Bob Arum and Don King were totally in their element giving hundreds of interviews and tirelessly attending all the functions and hyping the importance of the event. They were always on—and always on message. I watched Arum, in his eighties, go from interview to interview and field questions from young reporters until a thirty-year-old would have cried uncle.

In February 2000 Arum promoted the first fight of what was to become one of the greatest boxing trilogies of all time. Erik "El Terrible" Morales met Marco Antonio "The Baby-Faced Assassin" Barrera at the Mandalay Bay Hotel and Casino in Las Vegas. Barrera was the WBO super bantamweight champion. Morales was the undefeated WBC champion and the only person to have knocked out Daniel Zaragoza in the process. After twelve action-packed rounds, Morales was declared the winner by a slim split decision. *Ring* magazine called it the fight of the year and later the best fight of all time.[1]

In June 2000, Top Rank's reigning star, Oscar De La Hoya, met undefeated Shane Mosley, a fighter with some of the fastest hands I've seen in my career, for the WBC welterweight championship. De La Hoya had lost that title to Félix Trinidad the previous year. Oscar got it back with a win over Derrell Coley, with Trinidad vacating the title to move up to middleweight to face David Reid at Caesars Palace.[2] Mosley, the underdog with only two prior welterweight fights, scored a narrow split decision win over De La Hoya. Oscar, feeling that he won, demanded an immediate rematch. No rematch was agreed to, and it would be three more years until they faced each other again on September 13, 2003. This would be one of the last fights before Oscar started his own promotion company, Golden Boy Promotions, in 2002.

In 2002 Bob was in a plane heading for a press conference in Big Bear, California, to promote the upcoming Oscar De La Hoya versus Fernando Vargas fight scheduled for September 12. The Cessna Citation 550 piloted by Joseph Tophan and copilot Craig Terry, carried Bob and a couple reporters, Kevin Iole and Royce Feour, from the *Las Vegas Review-Journal*. The other passengers were Scott Voeller and H. C. Rowe of the Mandalay Bay Hotel and Casino.

At 11:15 a.m., the plane crashed while landing. All the passengers seemed OK, but Kevin Iole saw the wings on fire after Scott Voeller sounded the alarm to get off the plane immediately. The copilot had to kick open the door, which had been damaged in the crash. The passengers made it off the plane seemingly unhurt except Royce Feour, who needed assistance. Royce fell about ten feet from the plane after exiting. Arum and Voeller were the last ones off. Fire trucks arrived almost immediately, and the firefighters shouted for all five passengers and two pilots to rush away from the plane just before the gas tank exploded.

"I remember shouting to Royce to move, to get off the plane," Arum said. "And when we got off, you remember we were standing right there by the plane. I had seen the flames. I knew we needed to get away from it. Feour was taken to the hospital where he was treated and released.

"We ran away, and I think we could have beaten [Olympic sprint champion Usain] Bolt that day. We couldn't panic and we had to get out of there."[3]

In April 2011, I was on a small private plane with Bob Arum flying to Big Bear from Las Vegas. We were headed to a press event at Shane Mosley's house where he was training for his upcoming fight with Manny Pacquiao. Four of us were on the plane besides the pilots. As we started our descent to the runway, Bob looked at me and said, "I can't f****** believe I'm doing this again."

Bob has faced his share of adversity through the years. In 2003 the FBI launched an exhaustive investigation into Arum and Top Rank that would end in complete vindication for Top Rank. After a twenty-month FBI sting operation, a raid of the Top Rank Boxing Organization offices in Las Vegas, and a subsequent investigation that lasted nearly 2 1/2 years, federal law enforcement officials dropped the probe of Arum's operation without handing down any indictments.

"I'm gratified, ecstatic," Arum said. "I understand that the government has to investigate when there are allegations, but I knew from the get-go that we had done nothing wrong. A great weight is off my back."[4]

Of course, Don King was no stranger to controversy either. In 2005, King decided to sue ESPN for $2.5 billion for defamation. The suit was over a documentary saying King had killed two men, which is common knowledge. The court ruled that ESPN had not knowingly made false statements and did not owe King money.[5]

Erik Morales met Marco Antonio Barrera for the third and final time on November 27, 2004. The fight, called "Once and For All," turned out to be one of their closest and did not disappoint. Barrera, the reigning WBC super featherweight champion, won by a razor thin majority decision that could have gone the other way with only one round changing in the minds of the judges. What made the fight especially exciting was the changing tides of the battle. Barrera won five of the first six rounds on most cards. Morales came back strong in the seventh and eighth rounds. The last two rounds of the fight were some of the best ever, with nonstop back-and-forth action. When it was over, and Marco Antonio had his hand raised for the second time in the trilogy, *Ring* magazine named it the fight of the year for 2004.

This wouldn't be Erik Morales's last relationship with a trilogy. Only four months later, on March 19, 2005, his first of three fights with Manny Pacquiao was held at the MGM in Las Vegas. This would be another close fight for Morales. All three judges scored it 115–113 for the eventual unanimous winner Erik Morales. This, Manny's first fight at 130 pounds, had him as the favorite, despite Morales's edge of nearly $1 million in the purse. Pacquiao's promoter, Murad Muhammed, had agreed to Morales's terms for the bout, including Morales determining the brand of gloves used. Morales, occasionally accused of brittle hands, chose Winning gloves, a Japanese brand that trainer Freddie Roach called "pillows." Pacquiao's gloves of choice would have been Cleto, a puncher's glove. Pacquiao also said after the fight that he felt drained and weak leading up to the fight for unknown reasons. A year and a half later, in November 2006, Manny Pacquiao would sign a four-year deal with Bob Arum and Top Rank.

Pacquiao signing with Top Rank was surprising because he had first signed a contract with Oscar De La Hoya's Golden Boy Promotions and received a $500,000 signing bonus. According to Arum, a master contract lawyer, Pacquiao retained the right to negotiate and make a deal up to January 2007.[6]

On January 21, 2006, the pair rematched in the Thomas & Mack Center on the campus of UNLV. This time, Pacquiao at his best, scored a TKO of Morales in the tenth round.

The November 18, 2006, third fight, his first with Top Rank, solidified the trilogy as one of the best of all time. It was back at the Thomas & Mack Center in Las Vegas and was Pacquiao's most devastating victory up to that time. He knocked Morales down three times leading up to a third-round KO. The winner was supposed to fight mandatory challenger Marco Antonio Barrera, but Top Rank and Golden Boy couldn't come to terms.

On April 8, 2006, six months before the end of the Pacquiao–Morales trilogy, Floyd Mayweather met Zab Judah at the Thomas & Mack. The fight was notable as one of the few times in the decade that Bob Arum and Don King copromoted. Judah, the IBF welterweight champion, was Don King's fighter; Mayweather, a three-division champion, at least for the moment, was a Top Rank protégé. Judah had recently lost to Carlos Baldomir, but the IBF title wasn't on the line because they chose not to pay the IBF sanctioning fee. (This is an example, as I mentioned earlier in the book, of avoiding a commission when it suited the promoters.)

The fight was most memorable for a regrettable battle that included the corners and not the principal combatants. In the tenth round, with Mayweather ahead on the cards, Judah landed an illegal low blow followed by a punch to the back of Mayweather's head. Mayweather leaped around the ring in apparent pain. Referee Richard Steele gave Floyd time to recover. Floyd's uncle and trainer, Roger Mayweather, entered the ring and confronted Judah. Judah's father and cornerman, Yoel Judah, responded and threw a punch toward Roger Mayweather. Both corners and a dozen police and security officers entered the ring. It took a while for the melee to be contained and the fight resumed. Roger Mayweather was ejected. The Nevada commission fined him $200,000 and took away his license for a year. Yoel Judah, Mayweather cornerman Leonard Ellerbe, and Zab Judah also received fines and suspensions.[7]

Sixteen months before meeting Manny Pacquiao and receiving one of the most brutal knockouts I've ever witnessed, Ricky Hatton met Floyd Mayweather at the MGM in Las Vegas. The December 8, 2007, meeting was titled "undefeated." Floyd, the reigning WBC welterweight champ, was facing light welterweight challenger Ricky Hatton, moving up for this contest. The British crowd was rowdy as always, singing "Hatton Wonderland" and booing any Mayweather supporter. After Tom Jones sang "God Save the Queen," the Brits booed the "Star Spangled Banner," drawing huge criticism in the press. Hatton tried to compete early, catching Mayweather in the first round with a left jab that knocked Floyd off balance. The fight was mostly one sided, however, ending with Floyd winning by TKO in the tenth round.

"The Dream Match" between Oscar De La Hoya and Manny Pacquiao took place on December 6, 2008. This copromotion between Top Rank and Oscar's Golden Boy Promotions took place at the MGM Grand Garden in Las Vegas. This fight represented a rare pay-per-view, carried on HBO PPV, without a title on the line. It managed to propel Pacquiao into stardom after he scored a TKO when Oscar chose not to return to the ring following the eighth round. It was as if he was passing the Top Rank torch to Manny.

Pacquiao, who was the reigning lightweight champion, moved up two weight divisions to meet De La Hoya. He, in turn, came down one division to meet Pacquiao at welterweight. The buildup was intense. Oscar and Floyd Mayweather had generated the top gate when they met the previous year. Although De La Hoya was considered past his prime, few thought Manny could beat him moving up two weight divisions to try. Oscar's experience, coupled with his height and weight advantage, was considered a formidable challenge for the rising Filipino star. Oscar assembled an amazing team to help him prepare including Angelo Dundee and "Nacho" Beristáin. Edwin Valero also helped him train.

Pacquiao showed great elusiveness in the early rounds, frustrating De La Hoya, who could only land a punch occasionally. In the fifth round Manny unleashed a barrage of punches that caught Oscar off guard. Manny outpunched Oscar 2–1 in the next few rounds and landed two four-punch combinations in the sixth and seventh rounds. Manny was ahead on all cards before Oscar's corner threw in the towel.

The gate was second to Mayweather versus De La Hoya and sold 1.25 million PPV buys. This was the fourth non-heavyweight bout with more than a million buys and the only non-title fight with that honor.

The year 2009 was a very big one for Top Rank and its star, Manny Pacquiao. The Pac Man scored one of the most devastating knockouts I've ever seen. On May 2, 2009, Pacquiao and Manchester's favorite son, Ricky Hatton, met at the MGM in Las Vegas. It was a copromotion between Arum's Top Rank and De La Hoya's Golden Boy Promotions. I'd seen several amazing British boxing fan assemblies in my time, but this one was special. On May 1, at the weigh-in, the MGM Grand Garden—an unusually large venue for a weigh-in—was overflowing. According to a friend of mine who was a manager there, the Grand Garden ran out of beer for the first time in its history. The fight was anticipated to be unusually raucous with the loudest contingent in the stands rooting for the underdog from England and singing "Sweet Caroline" loudly, vigorously, and off key. (Why this Neil Diamond song is sung at every UK sporting event is still a mystery to me.)

Another notable event for me at this fight occurred right before the bout began. The first fighter, Ricky Hatton, walked into the ring to tumultuous cheering. Tom Jones was standing in the ring ready to sing "God Save the Queen" before the Philippine and U.S. anthems. The crowd eagerly awaited Manny Pacquiao's entrance. One of Hatton's cornermen was having a meltdown in the ring. He observed my announcers, Colonel Bob Sheridan and his color commentator, along with my stage manager seated on the ring apron in their blue corner. Immediately behind the Colonel was seven-foot Pancho Limon acting as security, an immovable force and friend of the Colonel's. The cornerman, who might have been the cut man, I don't remember, was used to fights in Manchester, UK, where there was only one broadcaster, Sky, in the neutral corner, so he would sit right on the ring apron where my announcers were stationed to do the world feed, something he knew nothing about.

He was literally screaming to security that those people, pointing to our announcers who had been on the air for several hours, had to move because it was where he always works. He swore loudly that if they didn't move, there would "be no fight." I could hear this through the Colonel's mic while I directed because he was so loud. I asked the stage manager to hold up the stick mic lying in front of her so I could listen in on a pre-fade setting that wouldn't go out to air. I could see on a camera monitor that everyone in that corner, including Tom Jones, took him seriously and were very concerned. He screamed at Las Vegas Metro police, who got MGM security involved. They called the head of MGM security, there at the Garden because of the huge attention of this huge, world-wide event.

At that time, I was in charge of the ringside setup for Top Rank. I told my assistant director to fly the plane while I scrambled to ringside because my announcers and Pancho were getting concerned as they were the target of his attack. A few Top Rank execs in the ring were also concerned. HBO was asking about the holdup in the ring walk; their backstage manager Tami Cotel, a lifelong friend, told them it looked like some big problem in the ring with Hatton's corner. As I approached the corner, the head of MGM security, now flanked by a sea of police and security, told the Hatton corner that he would straighten it out by getting the man responsible for the setup. As he saw me coming, he exclaimed, "Oh good, there he is now, Marty, can you help us."

The cornerman screamed the problem to me and said the fight would be off if the announce position wasn't moved. I said calmly, "OK, I'll let Mr. Arum know that you are not allowing Ricky Hatton's participation in the event because these people, working where they always do on a worldwide event, can't be moved." The security chief asked me if the announcers in that position were in the right place, and I answered in the affirmative. He told the complainer that unless he had the authority to take responsibility for pulling out of the event, he should go to the seat he was assigned. Wouldn't it be nice if life was always like that? Keep Calm and Carry On.

Manny dominated from the start, and in the second round, achieved what Floyd Mayweather couldn't: he recorded a brutal knockout that *Ring* magazine quickly dubbed the KO of the year. I've watched it literally dozens of times and still believe that Ricky was out, while horizontal, before he hit the canvas. It was also noteworthy that Ricky Hatton's trainer was Floyd Mayweather Sr., hired after he fired longtime trainer Billy Graham following his loss to Floyd Mayweather.

Six months later Manny Pacquiao took on an opponent he wasn't expected to meet. Not only was Miguel Cotto a very dangerous opponent for Manny, but he was another of Top Rank's breadwinners. Arum was unlikely to take a chance with one of these blue-chip talents. Ross Greenburg, president of HBO Sports, said it was the biggest boxing event since Tyson versus Lewis. He said he hadn't seen the level of anticipation the fight generated: "This seems like a can't miss."[8]

Pacquiao was faster and a southpaw, Cotto was bigger and more powerful. Both had excellent training habits and were never unprepared. After all the anticipation, on November 14, 2009, "Firepower," the match between two Top Rank stars, took place. The first three rounds were slow as each fighter felt out the other. Pacquiao knocked Cotto down in the third and fourth rounds and dominated in all but one of the remaining rounds. The fight could have stopped in the ninth, but a bloody Cotto fought on as his wife departed the arena. Ultimately the TKO came in the twelfth round after fifty-five seconds. Manny Pacquiao became the first fighter in history to achieve seven world championships in seven weight divisions. Arum said, "Pacquiao is the greatest boxer I've ever seen, and I've seen them all, including Ali, Hagler and Sugar Ray Leonard."[9]

The most tragic thing Arum has had to face was the loss of his son, John, in August 2010. John, also a lawyer, was a mountain-climbing expert. He was in the process of climbing one hundred peaks in the Northwest United States when the tragedy occurred. Bob was a few days away from a spectacular event between Manny Pacquiao and Antonio Margarito at the huge new Dallas Cowboys stadium when his wife got the call from the park service that John was missing. He was discovered a short while later, confirming the accident.

"When you lose a child, I don't care what anybody tells you, you lose part of yourself," Arum said after getting the news. "It does not get easier over time."[10]

On November 13, 2010, six months after I was promoted to director of TV production for Top Rank, Manny Pacquiao faced Antonio Margarito in the massive Dallas Cowboy Stadium in Arlington, Texas. The fight came about after terms could not be agreed to for a fight between Pacquiao and Mayweather. Floyd knew better than to face Manny in his prime. Manny gave up almost six inches and nearly twenty pounds to Margarito. Manny was extremely dominant in this fight. His speed and superior technique over-whelmed Antonio. Margarito was cut badly in the fight. Pacquiao seemed to hold back on Margarito after he seemed unable to properly defend himself. It turned out that Margarito had suffered a right eye orbital bone fracture injury. When asked in the post-fight press conference if he was "taking it easy" on his opponent after he was injured, Manny said, "Boxing is not for killing. I didn't want to damage him permanently."[11] More proof of the outstanding character Manny Pacquiao possessed.

People outside of the TV industry would be surprised how many people are needed for a boxing broadcast. There are different levels of telecasts from the high-quality shows by ESPN, Showtime, DAZN, Fox, formerly HBO, and the cheaper telecasts on regional channels or internet streams. The high-quality shows, which the most people watch, have between 80 and 150 crew members on a standard or pay-per-view telecast. The crew positions are divided in above the line (ATL) and below the line (BTL). ATL includes producers, directors, assistant producers, assistant directors, and executive producers.

The heart of the telecast crew is made up of BTL positions that include the EIC, engineer in charge, technical directors, also known as video switchers, audio mixers, from the master A1 to the A2 and A3 positions that handle audio setup throughout the venue, comms, communications lines, camera people, video technicians, transmission engineers, power technicians, graphics techni-cians, replay technicians, editors, utility technicians who do the cabling, moni-tor placement, and trouble shooting. There are also jib operators, robotic cam-era operators, lighting technicians, in-arena audio mixers, wireless technicians, DJs, and in-arena digital media technicians feeding LED screens and enhancing the experience for the audience. There are also the announcers, reporters, ring announcer, and translators.

Back at the network feeding the consumer is an army of technicians and transmission people receiving the broadcast, scheduling the time slot, selling and inserting commercial and sponsor content, running the master control op-erations, and librarying the content. So, to bring you that Saturday night fight, hundreds of people are involved. Bob Arum and Don King both needed this army of TV people for their product. Neither micro-managed my work putting all this together. To their credit, they let the TV execs they put in charge do their jobs. I always admired Don and Bob for this decision and never disrespected their trust.

Many times over the years I've been asked what the boxing producer, boxing director, and executive producer for boxing do. The best analogy I have come up with is a restaurant. The executive producer, producer, and director can be equated to the owner, manager, and chef.

The executive producer is responsible for the money decisions concerning talent, equipment, and crew. He is ultimately in charge of the budget and approves expenses like the owner of a restaurant would. He also has the last say in who is chosen as the producer, director, and talent like a restaurant owner is responsible for hiring the managers and the chef. Therefore, the executive producer is the top person in charge of the production. This is often not the case in other entertainment projects such as scripted TV shows and movies where executive producer credits are handed out like party favors and rarely indicate the person in charge of the production. Ultimately, Bob Arum and Don King were the true executive producers. They had the authority to replace anyone in the chain and were the only ones who, in the end, approved the budgets. Todd duBoef holds that position for Top Rank now.

The producer is like the restaurant manager. He creates and maintains the show format that dictates what content will be included in the show. He also manages the show in progress, talking to talent about content alerts, making decisions about changing the format if time considerations require it, and being responsible for instantaneous changes when required in a live show to keep the broadcast smooth, exciting, informative, and technically appealing. This compares to the restaurant manager who decides how the restaurant looks and feels, where the tables and chairs are placed, what is on the menu, supervising the chef's presentations, staffing, and a smooth operation. If Bob Arum or Don King didn't like what the announcers said, or if a fighter wasn't promoted properly in a telecast, they, in their role as executive producer, would let the producer know about it.

The director is most like the chef. A director puts the elements together, the video, audio, graphics, music, commentary, commercials, sponsor elements, special effects, and transitions. The director is responsible for delivering the producer and executive producer's preferences for the look and feel of the broadcast. Like a chef, only certain people have the proper demeanor, temperament, skill set, and stamina for the very stressful concentration required of a live sports director. The control room monitor wall has dozens of images competing for the director's attention, and he has to keep in his head all the graphics, special effects, switcher wipes, transitions, and videotape segments needed to complete the soup that is the program feed.

Directing is my favorite job. I love the adrenaline of live sports directing. You can't watch the program monitor, which is what the viewers are getting, because that is where you've been. You must look at the other fifty-seven monitors to determine where you are going next. I've directed NBA, NHL, NFL, MLB, boxing, soccer, Muay Thai, MMA, beauty pageants, telethons, and entertainment shows. The most fun I ever had was directing the 2002 Super Bowl for an interactive feed to Mexico and Brazil for DirecTV Latin America. I had all fifty cameras from Fox and NFL Films but no communication to the operators and no tallies, which let the camera operator know he is on the air. Essentially, this was playing "danger-cam" for four hours. I was cutting cameras that could swish pan or snap zoom without notice. The telecast went beautifully, and I was on a cloud when it was over. Directing boxing is all about camera angles. Because the fighters move constantly, turning and changing their height as they box, which camera sees the action best can be a challenge. Add the movement of the referee, sometimes seeming like an intentional block to the camera view, and it becomes a ballet of changing angles. The director also needs to balance the desire to see the fighters' faces in a tight shot that allows the viewer to see their facial expressions with the wider view that shows their footwork and movement, sometimes the most important indicator of the fight's progress. The director's ability to blend in replays to complete the picture is also crucial. The best directors tell the story of the fight objectively, regardless of their preconceived notions of how it might play out.

For almost all my career I have functioned as a producer/director. That means I fulfill both roles. Working for promoters such as Don King and Bob Arum, this was a cost-saving decision. The right person can be a producer and director, wearing many hats, to save expenses.

Boxing isn't the hardest sport to direct, but it is one of the most rewarding. The story of a boxer's journey to the ring is often memorable TV. Football is one of the easiest sports to tell the story as a director because of the format, play, replay, play, replay, commercial.

When asked, I surprise many people by choosing baseball as the hardest game to direct. The speed of the game makes people assume it is easier than hockey, for example. The pace of the game is part of the problem. Long stretches of no action interrupted by a sudden burst of activity is a recipe for many directors to miss the crucial play live, forced to only show it properly on replay. The main reason I say that baseball is the hardest sport to direct is because it's the only sport, in my opinion, that the director needs to know the game like a manager. In basketball, following the ball can give you a basic result. But in baseball, when the batter makes contact with the ball, do you follow the ball to the outfield or cover the runner tagging? The action often isn't always with the ball. And the reason the director needs to know baseball like a manager has to do with situational awareness. Will the man on second try to steal third? In *this situation* will the man on second try to steal third? In *this situation* will that *particular* man on second try to steal third? Unless you can answer the last question, you'll probably miss it.

When I started in television, there were the four networks: CBS, ABC, NBC, and the fledgling newcomer Fox. CBS was known for boxing, and occasionally so was ABC. There were a few local independent stations in major markets, the cable giant ESPN, and a new upstart cable network called The Superstation owned by Ted Turner. TBS, the Turner Broadcasting System, was years ahead of its time. The future that Ted Turner saw was absolutely accurate. The cable world we have seen expand for thirty years and the new direct-to-consumer digital video distribution networks are a direct result of his pioneering vision. Cable was just starting; ESPN had as many viewers as showed up to an NFL stadium on a Sunday.

In 2023, I produced and directed two boxing events at Madison Square Garden, Berlanga versus Angulo and Beterbiev versus Joe Smith Jr. Earlier in the week I had produced and directed a world feed of an event in Japan, Naoya Inoue versus Nonito Donaire II, from a studio in Manhattan. My Garden fights always remind me of my start in that venerable building nearly forty years ago. My first foray into the Garden was in the early eighties with the Washington Bullets there to play the New York Knicks. I got hopelessly lost trying to find the control room, which was on floor 4½, under the arena floor. The "helpful" Garden employees kept misdirecting me for amusement. I wandered through kitchens, storage rooms, and a bowling alley that used to exist on the second floor. The current employees are skeptical when I tell them about the twenty-four lanes that used to exist here.

When I broadcast Bullets games at MSG as the visitor in the eighties, the "A Control Room" on the floor below the court level had a long table with the switcher at the far-left end and the Knicks broadcast team next to that with the visiting producer/director, me, at the far-right end. The Knicks TD had to cut our visiting show on one of the mix-effects banks of his switcher. But, of course, the Knicks show was his priority. On a typical game, I remember the Knicks switcher, technical director Rick Phillips—later a director for Showtime—and others, at the switcher; Bobby Brown, the Knicks' director next to him; Howie Singer, producer next; an AD, assistant director next to him; a phone AD next to him; and then, on a flimsy flip-up piece of wood at the far end, me. As a break approached, I leaned forward and called to the left, "wide shot to Washington." I wasn't heard, so I repeated it twice more in the ten seconds remaining. Before Mr. Phillips could change our feed, I got Marv Albert, the Knicks' play-by-play announcer on my telecast. Rick reached under his switcher, picked up a family size jar of Vaseline, handed it to Bobby, who handed it to Howie, who handed to the AD, who handed it to the phone AD, who put it in front of me. Rick, leaning in my direction, said, "It'll help."

My good friend from those days, John Gallagher, manager at MSG Networks, made me repeat that story to someone this week and told me to "put it in the book."

Bob Arum and Don King absorbed the many changes in television equipment and transmission paths as they lived through the revolutions in broadcasting. Prior to the 1980s, all big events in boxing were handled by closed circuit. This all but went away after pay-per-view television came about, with the exception of Arum going retro on the De La Hoya versus Chávez event in 1996. Lou Falcigno, the biggest closed-circuit pioneer back then, would line up three hundred venues or so in the metropolitan area for a big fight (four hundred for Ali-Frazier I in 1971). There wasn't enough equipment to do more back then. The phone lines were used to bring the signals to venues prior to satellite availability. When satellites became available, C-band uplinks and space were limited. Things changed remarkably when Ku-Band came about, increasing availability while also lowering costs. That number blossomed up to more than seven hundred for the Hagler versus Hearns fight in 1985. Pay-per-view TV would soon end this lucrative strategy.[12]

Boxing announcers are divided into play-by-play, analyst (or color commentators), and reporters. The play-by-play announcer's job is to tell you what happened, without just describing what you just saw. His experience allows him to tell you what you might not have noticed. His trained eye can see that the fighter used a left jab to set up the right to the body, for example, because his opponent had his left hand too high. You knew it was a good punch that hurt him but weren't as quick to catch the entire sequence.

The analyst, or color commentator, often a fighter or trainer, tells the viewer why it happened. His experience told him that the last straight right from the champion made the opponent hold his left too high. He notices things you might not see: for instance, the fighter starting to fight flat-footed, a sign that his training was incapable of giving him endurance. A good analyst can also predict what happens next. He or she predicts that a fighter's open mouth means he is out of gas, breathing harder, and might not make it through the next round.

The analyst also knows sooner than the viewer when a fighter is hurt or when the advantage switches.

The reporter gets the viewers' background information to make the fight more interesting with details about the fighters, camps, families, and history. During the fight, a good reporter hears what the corner is telling the fighter and lets the viewer in on the inside information.

I've had the pleasure of bringing along several ex-fighters who went on to become great analysts. As the producer/director for the world feed, owned by the promoter rather than a network broadcaster, I was able to start off many who became network professionals. We were their training ground. Raul Marquez worked with me for several years before he became a star for Showtime. Tim Bradley started with me before becoming a leader on the ESPN telecast.

I have produced shows in Mexico, China, England, Wales, Scotland, Ireland, France, Germany, Italy, the Netherlands, Japan, Kuala Lumpur, Singapore, Monaco, Argentina, Brazil, Costa Rico, Russia, Canada, Nigeria, Australia, New Zealand, Jamaica, Nassau, Macau, and the United States. I'm several passports down the road, some surrendered because they had no more spaces for stamps.

I've come to believe that boxing fans in countries other than the United States—England, Ireland, Japan, etc., know the sport better, like the sport more, support the sport more, and are less subject to boxing writers who spend more time tearing it down than building it up.

11

BOB ARUM CHANGES
WITH THE TIMES

"Digital is going to change everything," Bob Arum said. "Pay per view, as we know it, won't exist in three years. You'll be able to watch a fight on your phone, on your tablet, anywhere in the world. And you won't pay as much. Maybe 10, 20 bucks." Arum said because more people will be able to watch, fighters still will get paid big money. But the biggest challenge for boxing is to continue to develop stars and give people a reason to watch.[1]

Throughout Don King and Bob Arum's careers, they had to adapt and adjust to a myriad of changing factors. Boxing changed, fighters and their attitudes changed, the fans' attitude about boxing changed, venues interest in boxing changed, and broadcasting changed most of all. From the early days of closed-circuit through the current streaming landscape, there have been ups and downs to deal with. Pay-per-view eventually replaced closed circuit after fans got used to it and was a big step up in revenue for promoters. Broadcast television almost deserted boxing in the last decade of the twentieth century but has returned in a big way, again giving fans more boxing on free TV than ever before. In 1991, only one boxing event, Riddick Bowe versus Tyrell Biggs, was on network TV (ABC) in the first quarter. A few years earlier, there might have been a dozen by March on three networks. CBS produced seven boxing shows the year before and had talked of increasing that to a dozen in 1991. It decided to do as few as six and did none in the first quarter. ABC, long recognized for fights on *Wide World of Sports*, reduced the size of boxing's portion of its universe by cutting back from sixteen live shows to three.

"The short-term future of boxing is grim," Arum said. "Really grim. Network TV has always kept it in front of the people, but this year, who knows if

Tyson Fury with Bob Arum, January 28, 2023. AP Images

there will be more than three fights on regular TV? Even cable is having problems. SportsChannel America may shut down. Prime Ticket is cutting back. And it'll be worse in six or eight months."[2]

So, what do great promoters like Arum and King do? They change with the times. The willow bends but doesn't break when the wind blows hard from the other way. Network TV deals went to cable deals, went to pay-per-view deals, went to premium cable TV deals, went to free cable sports deals, and now, to streaming deals. Next, perhaps, augmented-reality deals. When a door closes a window opens.

Throughout his career Bob Arum was willing to try new things. It was Arum who put the first women's bout on network TV on April 17, 1977. OK, it was a little embarrassing when Lavonne Ludian began crying in the ring after being hit by Theresa "Princess Red Star" Kibby, probably for the last time until Oliver McCall followed suit two decades later.

Sometimes necessity is the mother of invention.

On March 12, 2020, I was in a TV truck on Eighth Avenue outside Madison Square Garden when it was announced that our event, scheduled for the fourteenth, was canceled due to COVID-19. That shaky leg brought the table down to the floor with a thud. There wouldn't be another boxing event for Top Rank until June when Bob Arum's genius for promoting led to thirty-two straight events "in the bubble" at the MGM in Las Vegas, without audiences, helping ESPN, which had almost no other live sports content to rely on; and helping fighters, who needed to work, not to mention TV producers, directors, and technicians who also had mortgages.

Promotions have changed considerably over the years. Once television entered the picture, replacing all the great radio broadcasts of fights including Joe Louis versus Max Baer, Tunney versus Dempsey, Louis versus Schmeling, and thousands more. Initially, broadcasters such as CBS put fights on their networks with sponsors like Gillette paying the way. Then ABC paid hefty rights fees for big events like those of Muhammad Ali. Pay-per-view was first conceived as closed circuit. A movie theater, for example, might get a satellite feed that allowed it to offer a live viewing projected on a big screen. As television became more sophisticated, viewers could see the live satellite feed in their homes through their cable provider.

High-definition television was a game changer. In 1995 at Madison Square Garden, I broadcast my Don King show from a new high-definition truck that blew my mind. The giant monitors in the truck, showing a wide shot from a camera at one end of the Garden, looked like windshields to me. It seemed like I was looking through glass instead of a TV screen. The long lens zoomed all the way into a figure hundreds of feet away, and I thought I could see dandruff on the shoulder. It was an amazing thing to experience two decades after starting in television. The first time I saw high-def was in the press room for the 1985 NBA All-Star game. Sony was showing video of a sumo match it had captured. It seemed like something very far off.

Boxing was a very innovative sport, however, because no commission had to be persuaded to embrace the new technology. We used a Nokia 360 VR camera at a Pacquiao fight and added AR elements to it long before I saw this on other sports. HBO also tried heat signature cameras to determine whether they could detect accurately how much force a punch possessed. We expect 5G to make new innovations possible very soon. Top Rank and ESPN will likely lead the way. They are both very aggressive innovators.

The boxing TV landscape has made earth-shattering changes in the past few years. First, HBO, boxing's leader in broadcasting big fights, abruptly announced that it would be leaving the sport. Ownership changes at the network made unexpected seismic shifts in the status quo. In late 2023, Showtime, the other boxing TV giant, announced that it would also change its game plan moving forward and abandon boxing and other sports programming. These changes would be devastating to boxing fans if not for the shift to direct live streaming networks. It might well turn out that there is more boxing than ever with ESPN, Prime, DAZN, and others picking up the slack. Direct-to-consumer pay-per-view events are much easier and more cost-effective to deliver.

Now, and for the foreseeable future, viewers will get a live feed directly over the internet from the promoter, allowing them to bypass the cable operators who took 50 percent of the purchase for providing the highway.

The success or failure of future promoters and promotions depends on the promoter's ability to attract viewers, facing more and more choices, in an ever-increasing cacophony of sports broadcasts.

In 2017, I attended a press conference at Madison Square Garden when the Garden presented Bob with a plaque commemorating his fifty years of boxing at MSG. The unprecedented nature of the accomplishment really caught my attention, like the record for longevity celebrated by Cal Ripken, passing Lou Gehrig, a record nobody thought could be broken. I find it extremely unlikely that anyone will catch Bob Arum. This is a sport that eats people alive. Bob has had to face off against rival promoters, fighters, the media, and the public to make it as far as he has. Very few people could do that for even a short while, never mind over fifty years and still counting. In 2023, BoxREC listed Bob Arum's promoting career at 1,685 events. That is approximately thirty events a year for fifty-seven years. By comparison, Don King is listed with 423 events.

In 2019, a reporter from a law publication asked Bob about his work as a promoter, and he responded, "Work? I am having fun," which is about as healthy a perspective as one can have about their career.[3]

It is much harder now to create the boxing empire Bob Arum did in the way he did it. The print media is especially difficult for Bob to count on. "The newspapers that say we're not going to cover boxing because it's a niche sport don't know what they're talking about," Arum said. Arum slammed the "elitist" attitudes of newspaper sports editors who don't make an effort to cover boxing.

"The *Daily News* has always covered boxing because they know it is something that pleases the readers," Arum said. "If newspapers don't wake up and start writing about things that people want to read, they're going to go out of business."[4]

Promoters are attacked daily by the media, other promoters, and even by their own fighters. There is no coalition of same-party politicians to watch your back. The risks of financial and legal pitfalls are all on you alone. The possibility of long-lasting success is so remote as to be miraculous. Bob Arum is truly unique in his accomplishments.

Seth Abraham, former president of HBO, said, "Bob Arum is one of the 10 smartest people I've ever met, not one of the 10 smartest boxing people I've met.

He combines, which is extra formidable, traditional book smarts with street smarts, common sense, and experience. You put those things together and he is truly brilliant." [5]

Arum and Top Rank saw television broadcasting go from giant hulking cameras with huge cables running everywhere in the old NTSC format, the original U.S. TV standard, through PAL TV in the United Kingdom and elsewhere, Secam III-B in Russia and parts of Africa, the advent of stereo, the addition of quality slow-motion replays, and eventually super slow-motion replays and every advancement in picture quality, from NTSC 535 lines per frame in the sixties up to four thousand HDTV lines per frame in new 4K video. Shotgun mics and superior audio devices have added tremendous quality to the product.

Top Rank has tried every innovation imaginable, including heat sensor cameras fifteen years ago, which, it was hoped, would show the difference between a mere touch of a glove on an opponent and "effective aggression," which would be seen in a significant change in the heat signature. It didn't. In the Pacquiao era we were the first to shoot boxing with a 360 camera and virtual and augmented reality added. The Nokia OZO camera was mounted on a ring post, giving the viewer the closest seat possible to the action and a fully immersive experience watching the fight or looking up, down, and behind you so you feel like you are right next to the boxers. I'm sure that next year we'll broadcast with AI technology.

On June 5, 2010, Bob Arum returned to Yankee Stadium as promised. It just took him thirty-five years to do it. Miguel Cotto would face Yuri Foreman. Foreman was an orthodox fighter. I don't mean he wasn't a southpaw. I mean he couldn't fight from sundown Friday until Sundown Saturday. Foreman, an orthodox Jew studying to be a rabbi, couldn't even leave his hotel room until sundown on fight night. The brand-new Yankee Stadium would be the setting for the fight. Arum hadn't graced Yankee Stadium with a major fight since Ken Norton faced Muhammad Ali in the Bronx in September 1976. This was Miguel Cotto's first fight with trainer Emanuel Steward. Cotto pressured from the start. Foreman held his own and pressured back occasionally. In the seventh, Yuri went down from a slip, reinjuring his braced right knee. After a few more falls, his knee giving out, Foreman's trainer threw in a towel to call the fight. The ring filled with people. Referee Arthur Mercante Jr. asked Foreman if he wanted to continue, because a corner technically cannot "throw in the towel." Only the referee, or a doctor in California, can call the fight. Foreman said he did want to continue. They cleared the confused assembly in the ring after a couple minutes and continued the eighth round of the fight. Cotto landed a hard left hook to the body, sending Foreman down again forty-two seconds into the ninth round, and Mercante called the fight.

HBO said it was their highest rated event of the year with just under two million viewers. This fight was part of Bob Arum's "fights at big venues" strategy, which also included Cowboys Stadium. "It's important to show the brand of boxing, the enthusiasm for boxing," Arum said. "The way you do that is in big, known venues. That's why we have the fight [on Saturday] at Cowboys Stadium and the fight in June at Yankee Stadium. I think you do a disservice to the sport if you bring all big fights to Las Vegas. You make it insular. This is the template for what our plans will be."[6]

Bob Arum was always an innovator. Occasionally that meant stepping back. In June of 1996, Arum tried a bit of nostalgia, selling the Oscar De La Hoya versus Julio César Chávez bout, dubbed "Ultimate Glory" on closed circuit, turning his back temporarily on the pay-per-view model that had become the norm. Cable companies had problems with viewers stealing their events with "black boxes." Equally troubling for promoters was that a single PPV buy resulted in a room full of viewers seeing the event rather than paying individually. Also commercial establishments were purchasing events as less expensive individuals rather than paying the commercial rates for a full bar or restaurant. Policing this practice was difficult and expensive. Lou Falcigno, a major closed-circuit entrepreneur who had left the business eight years earlier, joined the effort and lined up many venues. The fight brought in approximately $14 million and got a $7 million site fee from Caesars Palace. The fighters were guaranteed $18 million, so, after expenses it was not a financial triumph for Top Rank.[7]

Arum has always been open to new broadcast partners as well. In addition to his great success on ESPN, HBO, and his own PPV efforts, he has also created specialty Mexican and Filipino events called Latin Fury and Pinoy Power. Bob made agreements with Spanish language channels from his earliest days in boxing. He also worked with nontraditional boxing channels.

By 2010, Don King hadn't promoted a major fight in more than ten years. He said he was semiretired but claimed he was still looking for the best fighters to promote. "You can call me semiretired," he said. "But I just got to find the right fighter that really wants to fight. The sport is not the same. These guys are not dedicated and committed to the sport like the older guys were. They all want to read the headlines, and when you go out and extol them virtuously and say things about them, they believe the things to the extent they don't have to do nothing. They believe it's going to be like osmosis, it's going to fall from the sky."[8]

One thing boxing promoters must deal with that most executives don't is the uncertainty of the outcome of their business plans. There might be a chance that a catastrophic event or an "act of God" might surprise a CEO, but it is rare and usually unavoidable. In boxing, the promoters negotiate for and put forth their best plans and hopes for success with an understanding that things just might not go their way. A star in their stable might get upset at an event, causing millions of dollars in consequences. Bob Arum admits he didn't know how several of his events would come out.

Imagine that you, as the head of a Fortune 500 company, had to create business plan after business plan with no idea whether you would be successful. Boxing is a tough business. That is why any long-term success like Bob Arum has achieved is worthy of so much respect.

A perfect example of the ability to adapt, and thus survive in boxing, is the reaction of Arum and Top Rank to the pandemic. Top Rank was thrown a curve on March 17, 2020, when they learned that their event, scheduled for three days later at Madison Square Garden would be canceled. First reports, later changed, said the event would happen without spectators. As I said, I was in my TV truck on Eighth Avenue outside MSG readying equipment for the event when the news came in. After three months of no events, Top Rank and ESPN, who were desperate for live sports content, launched a plethora of fights from the bubble at the MGM in Las Vegas.

In the convention area of the MGM in Las Vegas they commandeered a series of ballrooms and meeting rooms to launch more than thirty fights in a few months. A large ballroom was outfitted for the fights with a ring, fighter walk, lights, special effects, facilities for medical staff and the Nevada State Athletic Commission, and a multitude of LED screens around the ring to take the place of the spectators who were not permitted to attend. Other ballrooms were used as dressing rooms, a commissary for fighters, trainers, staff, and TV crew to eat, exercise and training areas, recreation areas, and offices. Everyone involved, once screened and tested rigorously, couldn't leave the bubble (quarantine) area. The MGM cordoned off a secure floor for the sequestered staff and athletes to live on. ESPN built a TV compound that became semipermanent for the half year it would remain in place, including a large temporary building structure above the compound to shield it from the oppressive Las Vegas sun.

From March 9, 2020, starting with a bout between Shakur Stevenson and Felix Caraballo, to February 20, 2021, when Oscar Valdez faced Miguel Berchelt in the WBC super featherweight championship, Top Rank held thirty events in this manner. These fights were major events including boxing superstars such as Terence Crawford, Jessie Magdaleno, José Pedraza, Andrew and Jason Moloney, Xander Zayas, Nico Ali Walsh, Mikaela Mayer, Félix Verdejo, Edgar Berlanga, Joe Smith Jr., José Ramírez, Jamel Herring, Egidijus Kavaliauskas, Richard Comey, Efe Ajagba, Gabe Flores Jr., Emanuel Navarrete, Naoyo Inoue, and most notably Vasiliy Lomachenko taking on Teofimo Lopez in the undisputed Lightweight Championship.

This was not only a demonstration of clever contingency planning; it was a masterstroke of innovative company planning in the face of a potentially disastrous "act of God."

Unlike other businesses, plans in promoting might change dramatically without warning. As a promoter, even huge events might suffer late catastrophic issues that require quick thinking—for example, Don King got mad at Ballys a week before the Tyson versus Mathis fight and moved the event from Atlantic City to Philadelphia on six days' notice.

Arum is unmatched as a career promoter in boxing. Any promoter's career would have been complete with Muhammad Ali or Oscar De La Hoya. Arum's Top Rank list of boxing champions includes Ali and De La Hoya plus Joe Frazier, Roberto Duran, Alexis Argüello, Carlos Monzón, Thomas Hearns, Sugar Ray Leonard, Marvin Hagler, Julio César Chávez, Paulie Ayala, Ray "Boom Boom" Mancini, Iran Barkley, James Toney, Erik Morales, Miguel Cotto, Floyd Mayweather Jr., Nonito Donaire, Manny Pacquiao, Terence Crawford, Vasiliy Lomachenko, and Tyson Fury. Very few great champions have not fought for Top Rank. As of this writing, Top Rank also has the most promising stars of the future, including Shakur Stevenson, Teofimo Lopez, Naoya Inoue, and Artur Beterbiev.

Bob has recently been considering his mortality, and, at his age, that's completely natural. He told a journalist from *Business Insider* magazine that he had recently signed a baby-faced assassin called Xander Zayas, a seventeen-year-old phenom from Puerto Rico, and Arum openly wonders whether his "clock will run out" by the time Zayas wins a world title.

"I would hate to be gone when that happens," he told *Business Insider*. "As I sign younger kids and I get older, the idea that I'll be there jumping in the ring when he wins a world title becomes less realistic."[9]

Although other promoters have enjoyed the heights of the profession with great champions, none have the accumulated collection of Hall of Fame champions that Bob Arum can brag about. From Bob's first card at the Maple Leaf Gardens in Toronto, Canada, where Muhammad Ali met George Chuvalo for the WBC/WBA heavyweight championships and Jimmy Ellis was the co-main feature, to the dozens of event dates at the MGM in Las Vegas in the summer of

2020, where Bob adapted to no audiences and still gave fans a great show with state-of-the-art high-tech screens providing graphics and video action that enhanced the experience, Bob Arum has adapted, innovated, overcome obstacles, and remained the greatest showman in the sport.

People have asked me why Don King Productions has declined over the past decade while Top Rank has flourished. I believe the main reason is Don King. Don always handled the business personally and completely. Bob Arum, on the other hand, gave people in the company the authority to act on his behalf. In contrast, Don had his hand in every aspect of every event. Nobody was as smart or as good at multitasking as Don King. His mental capability and photographic memory, which probably also made him an excellent street hustler, made him a superb executive, even if his moral compass was suspect. Bob Arum didn't try to do everything himself. He had matchmakers, boxing operations people, lawyers, event operations people, marketing people, and accountants he trusted to handle business decisions.

I believe that the time Don started winding down the operation was after his wife, Henrietta, passed away in December 2010. Henrietta was a great lady. The people closest to her in the organization called her "the General." Although she was married to Don for fifty years, many people, even hardcore boxing people, couldn't identify her if they had to. She avoided the media, and even when she attended an event, she was rarely close to Don when cameras were present. She was as smart and strong as Don was, and I believe she kept him playing the game.

In my opinion, after she passed Don appeared to lose some of the energy and desire that motivated him to keep up the fight and play the game. I met her on a few occasions at their home in Windsor, Ohio, and immediately saw her intelligence and her strength. "That is an unfillable void," he said. "That woman stood by me, man, and any success that I attained is because of her. She never tried to change me or do nothing but enhance and strengthen my spirit. She may have vacated the house she rented here on earth, but to me, spiritually, she never died."[10]

During the COVID-19 pandemic, we were covering boxing but without an audience. I wasn't traveling at all, which was a shocking readjustment for someone who was at airports twice a week for more than thirty years. Those ten months, after a two-month layoff during the initial lockdown, saw Top Rank and ESPN produce thirty-two events at the MGM Convention Center. Some of Top Rank's international boxers stayed active at home. Michael Conlon from Belfast, for example, fought in Northern Ireland, and the fight was transmitted to ESPN in Bristol, Connecticut, to produce.

I've heard that boxing was dead more times than I'd care to recall. The truth is quite the opposite. Boxing has more coverage than ever. More bouts are on the air weekly now than at any time in history. I've also read a hundred articles on why MMA is taking over boxing. It is my belief that MMA has garnered more of its audience from potential wrestling viewers and gamers on fighting games than boxing. They have a similar production feel, and the sinister cage is an old theme stolen from wrestling.

Arum started in boxing with none of the technology that promoters use today. Bob got the word out through press events and contact with boxing writers who promoted the sport. Now anyone with a cell phone can spread info on social networks and blog the world, whether or not they know what they're talking about. Bob had to rely on newspapers and press conferences to disseminate information about fights and fighters.

"We'd invite the writers up to camp where Ali trained, and they'd stay for a few days," Arum said. "They'd write their stories, and that's how you built up interest in a fight. We did the same thing when Ray fought Duran and Tommy and Marvin, and when Marvin and Tommy fought each other. Today, very few newspapers even have a boxing writer. You've got all these websites, and everything is up in a matter of seconds, but you don't know what's accurate or not. There's no accountability. There's no screening. And that's a problem for the public, because they have to try to determine what's true and what isn't."[11]

The written coverage of boxing has gone downhill in many ways. Few good papers even cover the sport anymore. Whether it's budgets or the editor's choice, the result is bad for boxing. Now, anyone with a Web page, regardless of knowledge, writing skill, or ethics, can write about boxing and boxers without consequences. These "journalists," and I couldn't use the term more loosely, never hesitate to give opinion as fact without a shred of truth in their blathering.

Since January 2020, Top Rank and its partner, ESPN, have begun to employ this streaming strategy for their world-wide networks. Top Rank's digital and social teams feed daily, as does ESPN on its websites and ESPN+ the new channel for live and archived content. OTT streaming is not just an alternative to traditional methods; it is a significant improvement on the old model. The consumer gets more content faster, and the provider feeds the consumer directly, avoiding costly fees to the cable or terrestrial broadcast providers. Traditional outlets would never feed a training session live or a press conference that was called on short notice because of liability issues that plague live uncontrolled sessions, as well as programming issues with changing broadcast schedules on short notice.

The Top Rank deal with ESPN was brilliant in the way it embraced the changes in TV technology while helping preserve the legacy of boxing. In August 2017, ESPN and Top Rank announced they were entering into a four-year deal. The first fight of this exclusive partnership was on September 22 of that year when Óscar Valdez and Gilberto "Zurdo" Ramirez defended their titles at the Tucson Arena. Valdez met Genesis Servania and Ramirez faced undefeated Jesse Hart. Valdez had an easier time with Servania despite being knocked down in the fourth. Ramirez's battle with Hart was reported as a "barn burner" with the close result going in Zurdo's favor. ESPN had long-range plans for boxing when it signed up with Top Rank, paving the way for its streaming platform ESPN+, which would launch the next year. The network was already the most successful sports broadcaster of all time. It wanted to line up solid content for the new streaming service as well.

In April 2018, ESPN+ was launched. The app followed the new model of a subscription pay service with the distinct advantage of a massive amount of desirable live and on-demand content behind it.

"ESPN is thrilled with this new long-term agreement with Top Rank, which represents the most innovative and comprehensive relationship in the world of boxing today," said Jimmy Pitaro, ESPN president and the cochairman of Disney Media Networks.[12]

Only one year into the new four-year deal between ESPN and Top Rank, they jointly announced a newer seven-year deal that would replace the three remaining years in their existing deal. The new deal called for fifty-four events a year on ESPN through 2025.

With Top Rank, boxing fans have learned to expect such live feeds from its partner ESPN because they are easy and inexpensive to provide and help promote the events they benefit from. This delivery method also allows Top Rank and ESPN to track the success of their feeds by determining how many viewers clicked on the feed and how long they watched.

The model for success in promoting boxing when I began in the industry required pay-per-view events to make any real profit. Having smaller events carried on a channel or pay platform helped cover the rent, but the pay-per-views made you rich. That hasn't changed even today. What *did* change is the way promoters can distribute pay-per-view events. Instead of giving up 40 to 60 percent of the profit to the guys who own the highway, like InDemand, now the promoter can distribute the event OTT, over the top, and keep the profit. There are still supplemental costs such as advertising, marketing, internet distribution, and safeguarding your copyright, but it's a big win for the promoters.

Internet streaming is also much cheaper and more secure than the satellite distribution that used to rule the day. On a Tyson PPV event in the nineties, for example, we had as many as eight uplinks carrying Ku and C-Band signals around the world. That was just on-site. The signals were also downlinked and re-uplinked in certain places to make longer "hops" to get to the most distant regions. A "second hop" was required for transmission to Asia, for example.

Now post-2020, internet streams mean that a promoter can upload the live stream that can be taken down anywhere internet is available. Now, that creates other problems, including reliability, security, and bandwidth availability on the receivers' end. Assuming you don't want to give your event away free to everyone, you need a system that has authentication protocols so that only authorized users can receive it. The potential problems of internet transmission became all too real for me on March 26, 2022, at Resorts World in Las Vegas when the venue briefly lost power. The event lights and TV production trucks were on a generator so the audience was never even aware of the short lapses of power in the arena, but the internet also went out and wouldn't be reset for a long while.

One tremendous benefit from internet transmission of an event that goes directly to the end consumer is instantaneous ratings. If the event is available on your website, you know exactly how many people accessed the stream, for how long, and where. These ratings make it much easier to charge your sponsors based on HUTs—homes using television—and PUTs—persons using television.

Traditional ratings were based on formulas extrapolated from their paid users to represent the entire potential pool of viewers. Those ratings were always attacked as being unreliable, especially because they really reflected the preferences of people who were inclined to become paid users for the ratings companies. People who never signed up for anything weren't counted. People who watched on a mobile device certainly weren't counted.

Now, twenty years later, we can do the same project, better, more graphically dramatic, with new toys such as drones, wire cams, virtual reality and augmented reality, with better images, better sound, and grander technical special effects, cheaper. Everything in live sports broadcasting has become more amazing and cheaper, unless you expand the use of new technologies to intentionally make it more expensive.

ESPN+, HBO Max, Disney+, Hulu, YouTube, Amazon Prime, CBS All Access, Netflix, and a hundred more by the time you read this, are the products of this revolution. There is no going back. Another aspect of this new broadcast paradigm is giving the consumers more than they had before. Extra camera angles, behind-the-scenes cameras, multiple additional audio choices, picture-in-picture dual feeds are all now possible to enhance the primary program they're watching. This is not new. As far back as 2002, we also did this type of multichannel coverage for three World Cups. It wasn't streaming, but it forecast what streaming might make available. Last, I wanted to add that this streaming makes interactive elements much more available. At Top Rank, long before it was common, we had social network comments viewed in weigh-in shows. It allowed live commentators such as Crystina Poncher to answer viewers questions and reference their comments live. This interactive enhancement for the viewers makes them a part of the broadcast and much more interested in staying involved. We did this in my weigh-in shows for years.

When the COVID-19 pandemic hit the U.S. in early 2020, Top Rank, like most businesses, had a forced hiatus. When we started producing fights again in June for ESPN in the United States, without an audience, at the MGM convention center in Las Vegas, the internet became indispensable. The few people who absolutely had to be in the room where the fights happened—the fighters, two corner people, a few commission supervisors, camera people, audio people, and a few staff—all had to be "in the bubble."

Everyone tested upon entering the secure area at the MGM, waited in their room ten hours for the results, spent all their time on a secure floor with a private elevator, with isolated eating, training, and dressing rooms, isolated exercise and entertainment areas, and absolutely no contact with people outside the bubble.

The production staff for ESPN was in Bristol, Connecticut, on the ESPN campus in their own isolated areas. Only one announcer was there, Joe Tessitore. Andre Ward, Tim Bradley, and Mark Kriegel all called the show from their homes using internet streaming. Feeds of the signals and replays were fed to Bristol as well. The producers and graphics people were in Bristol, too. The director was the only one in Las Vegas.

Our international show was also a surrealistic "necessity-is-the-mother-of-invention'" production, with our announcers in California, segregated in a small studio, made possible because our multidirectional transmission was on the internet. I had to feed the live video and natural sounds to California, then bring their commentary, compensating for audio delays, back to Las Vegas and combine everything into a program feed that went around the world, all on the internet. During the pandemic, we produced thirty-two shows that way, helping ESPN fill the content void created by the live sports drought.

On May 20, 2023, Bob Arum did what he had done for more than fifty years: he showed what a masterful promoter does. He came out on top in the face of adversity. Vasiliy Lomachenko had been a great champion for Top Rank. Managed by Bob's friend and associate Egis Klimas, Vasiliy from Ukraine had become one of the greatest in the sport with his skill, discipline, and positive attitude. After leaving a massive payday on the drawing board to fight for his country during the Russian attack, Vasiliy returned to the ring in 2023. He faced Devin Haney, who won the belt after defeating George Kambosos. For a variety of speculative reasons Haney prevailed over the Top Rank fighter Lomachenko. After the fight was over, it was revealed that Bob Arum had signed Haney to a contract two nights before the match.[13] A great promoter, like a good Boy Scout, prepares for the worst and hopes for the best.

12

END OF AN ERA

Big events, from Top Rank's Muhammad Ali events to Sugar Ray Leonard, Tommy Hearns, Marvin Hagler, Oscar De La Hoya spectacles, the fights of Larry Holmes, Ken Norton, Julio César Chávez, Félix Trinidad, to Tyson PPVs or the Pacquiao or Mayweather mega-events, are unlike any other boxing events. The excitement in the air, and the throngs of press and broadcasters who show up for only these extravaganzas, make it like a World Cup two or three times a year.

Since I started examining such things in my forties, I have believed that Marcus Aurelius was right: be the best you can be, courageous, with temperance, justice, and well-educated, because that is all you truly control. If you are not familiar with my favorite Roman emperor, he was a great philosopher as well. I heartily recommend his book *Meditations*, which he never intended anyone to read. (After his death, his wishes were ignored to burn his books because he had written them to himself.) Marcus was a great and good man. This was remarkable because he was the wealthiest and most powerful man in the world at the time and didn't need to be. His belief, commonly called stoicism, was that you should control what you can in your life, be accountable for yourself and your actions, and worry about little else because you can't control it. Virtue is sufficient for happiness. The only things that are truly under your control are your actions. If you are truly as good as you can be, honorable, honest, ethical, and moral, you will live the best life you can. Living this way is much more important than wealth or accolades, a truly amazing attitude for someone who could be the opposite of these principles and get away with it. Ironically, his son, Commodus, was perhaps the worst of Rome's emperors.

Bob Arum's ninetieth birthday. Marty Corwin

Don King and Bob Arum are excellent examples of one of Marcus Aurelius's creeds. If you are stopped, another path is still open. Your progress might seem to be cut off, but another path is there for you to take if you look for it. When HBO gave Don an ultimatum to take less than he wanted on a new long-term deal, he created another path by starting Showtime off in boxing. When people thought the retirement of Oscar De La Hoya would mean the end of Top Rank, Bob Arum exceeded expectations with new stars and events like Erik Morales versus Marco Antonio Barrera I, II, and III, and eventually Manny Pacquiao.

Marcus Aurelius believed it wasn't important that you fell down but vitally important how you got back up. Boxing has had its share of scandals. I acknowledge that the sport has seen incidents of regrettable behavior through the years, some perpetrated by fighters and trainers but also a few notable ones by promoters. The sport has suffered some black eyes in its 250-year history.

In 1965, Muhammad Ali scored a controversial first-round KO of Sonny Liston, prompting people to wonder if he took a bribe or was pressured to lay down. Liston's death of a heroin overdose five years later fueled the flames again.

When Benny "the Kid" Paret died in the ring at the hands of Emile Griffith, the scandal occurred in the twelfth round when the referee chose not to stop the massacre. This fight led to stricter guidelines for stopping fights after consecutive unanswered blows.

In the late 1990s, the IBF was investigated and found to have taken bribes to change rankings or give certain fighters title shots. Robert Lee, president of the IBF, and three other officials were charged. Several promoters, including Don King and Bob Arum, were cited for paying to have their fighters treated preferentially.

Shane Mosley admitted that he used EPO, an endurance enhancing drug, in his fight with Oscar De La Hoya.

Cheating is one thing, but assault in the middle of a boxing match is unusual. In the third round of his rematch with Evander Holyfield, Mike Tyson bit off a piece of Holyfield's ear. Directing the world feed for that event, I showed the replay in slow motion from every angle at least twelve times. I asked the truck engineer to open the truck door because I was getting nauseated and needed the air.

In 2009, Antonio Margarito, facing Shane Mosely, was caught putting plaster on his wraps, which would harden when his hands sweated. Mosley knocked him out after his manager made Antonio rewrap his hands three times.

Jake LaMotta is known to have taken a dive against Billy Fox, receiving a payoff and a promise of a title shot against Marcel Cerdan. The story started as spectators saw LaMotta seemingly holding up the weak-kneed Fox until the fourth round and then inexplicably letting Fox throw enough unanswered blows for the fight to be stopped.

In 1976, Don King started the United States Boxing Championships. ABC liked the idea and agreed to televise the event. The fighters included were unheralded; later, it turned out that King had falsified records and rankings by *Ring* magazine's rankings, which King had bought. Don claimed he was unaware of the subterfuge and wasn't charged. ABC backed out, however.

In 2010, Edwin Valero, an exciting super featherweight boxer with twenty-seven KOs in as many fights, eighteen in the first round, was accused of killing his wife. He was found hanged in his prison cell. His family doubts that he committed suicide.

One of boxing's biggest scandals occurred in 1983. Luis Resto and his trainer, Panama Lewis, conspired to cheat. Their criminal activity ended Billy Collins's career. Resto and Lewis removed padding from Resto's gloves and put plaster of paris on the wraps to make them harden. Both were arrested, and Resto admitted the offense. Billy Collins couldn't fight again after the bout, suffering from a torn iris and blurred vision. He began drinking after he stopped boxing and drove his car into a wall, killing himself nine months later at the age of twenty-two.

I bring these incidents up to highlight that one of the things a promoter must have is resilience. When a fighter hurts the sport, he hurts all the people who work hard to promote it. When one promoter is caught in a scandal, the public wonders whether all promoters act this way. This is more proof that Bob Arum's remarkable tenure at the top of the sport, especially, will never be repeated in my opinion.

The reason I am focusing on Arum and King, despite all the other promoters who have succeeded in boxing, besides the obvious answer that I was a department head for both, is that I believe their accomplishments are exceptional. They were unique promoters—in many ways—two of a kind. I also believe there will never be another like them.

They were both self-made men. One, Bob Arum, through scholarly pursuits, and the other, Don King, as an extension of his great skill as a street hustler. They both had the qualities that made them exceptional promoters: working 24/7; combining the skills of negotiator, lawyer, marketer, spokesperson, and business manager; having the rare resilience and determination required for overcoming adversity.

Tex Rickard was the closest example of these features in a historical figure, but many would agree there will never be another Tex Rickard either.

Promoters like Bob and Don have had so many events that their stories, difficulties, and triumphs are so voluminous as to defy recollection by one man. Bob does remember the high points and especially the events that surprised or amused him. One incident that falls into the latter category is the post-fight press conference after James Toney defeated Mike McCallum in August 1992 Toney hated McCallum and his group so much that he started a brawl. Because security was everywhere in anticipation of this, Toney went after the only unprotected member of McCallum's group, his lawyer. Bob said that still makes him laugh.[1]

Arum also recounts the story of a cut man, pronounced dead during a fight, who he saw a few weeks later working a fight. Don remembered his attempt to sign the Klitschko brothers with a little smoke and mirrors. After Wladimir won gold at the Olympics, Don King called Vitali's cell phone out of the blue. He invited them both to the United States to his house. Vitali, sitting next to Wladimir at the time, was impressed that someone as big as Don King was calling him and offering amazing financial rewards if they'd meet him and get on board with the proposal that he had for them. They decided to hear him out. After arriving in the United States and being driven to Don's house, they were very impressed with everything. Don spoke of irresistible fortunes and what he could do for them. At one point, Don sat down at his grand piano and played *Don Giovanni* by Mozart like a concert pianist. This impressed Vitali the most. He couldn't believe Don King was so talented. He was being persuaded to join with this amazing man. Unfortunately for DK, Vitali peeked behind the curtain and noticed, as he came closer, that Don's fingers were missing some keys that were going down by themselves. It was a player piano. Vitali decided they should not sign.

The reason I believe there will never be another is that boxing, and all sports promotion, has changed in a way that a new Don King or Bob Arum entering the profession wouldn't be able to do it the way that they did. Corporations and broadcasters who are owned by multibillion-dollar conglomerates are now controlling sports like never before. Agents are making TV deals, not promoters acting on their own. Broadcasters are trying to be promoters themselves. And, last, fighters who have a little bit of success are trying to be their own promoters now.

The world has changed. Promoting boxing has as well. It saddens me that figures like Jake Paul get the attention they do today. His posturing is perfect for the short-attention-span, look-at-me generation. With literally no accomplishments, he preens in public like a champion. The truth is that he calls himself a boxer, but when he finally fought a boxer, and a weak boxer at that, he lost. He does make a great deal of money by being a—gag—influencer. I understand that and give him credit for making money for nothing. But it weakens the great sport of boxing. It creates fans who care about jumping on a celebrity boxer's bandwagon rather than appreciating the skill and accomplishments of true athletes. Floyd Mayweather made a fortune inflating himself above his all-time skills, but at least he was a champion. I give him full credit. I hope the trend turns back to promotions built on real matchups between worthy combatants.

Fighters are different now than in Joe Louis's day. Whereas many fighters came into boxing to escape poverty, now many of these same athletes, and their mothers, prefer to try the NFL, where there are more openings and possibilities for financial success. In the NFL, you know you might get hurt, but you don't "expect" to get hurt. In boxing, win or lose, this might be your last fight. Punches to the head can be deadly.

Boxing broadcasting has changed. How the viewers get their fights and news about fights and fighters is completely different. Social media have made the conversation about the sport more immediate, sometimes more suspect, but always more voluminous. The change in delivery to the viewers has changed and will continue to change geometrically going forward.

DAZN is a good example of this change. The internet streaming network has made deals directly with boxers like a promoter has throughout the history of the sport. Last year they signed a deal with Anthony Joshua directly to make him leave his longtime network, Sky Sports, in the United Kingdom. His promoter of record, Eddie Hearn, hailed the signing as a good thing. He is the son of longtime promoter Barry Hearn, who was a great sportsman promoting everything from boxing to snooker, pool, darts, bowling, ping pong, and fishing in the United Kingdom. Eddie left his six-year deal with Sky Sports to take all his fights to DAZN.

When a network makes deals directly with boxers, it limits their potential bout pool considerably and diminishes the number of top fights the fans might get to see. They are not about to let their cash cow fight a contender signed with a rival network. Where it airs becomes more important than who they fight. A promoter shops for the best fights, best paydays, and biggest events regardless of where they air. This is much more favorable to the fighters and the fans. Tyson Fury, for example, fought on ESPN in the United States and BT (British Telecom) in the United Kingdom. Joshua now only fights on DAZN. Great fights are less likely now because networks sign fighters, so crossover is not allowed.

There are many new entries into the boxing promotion business. Streaming will make a much larger choice of boxing events available to the general public. A far greater number of promoters will be offering all that content, some good and some forgettable. The broadcast networks also take a greater control over the content. Many broadcasters, from Showtime to DAZN, act like promoters. They arrange the fights to meet their programming desires based on anticipated ratings. Boxing promotion is different today and will never go back to Don and Bob's style of business. It is clearly the end of an era.

The perceived feud between Bob and Don was real. Don believed that Bob Arum enlisted the friends he had in the Southern District federal court to make legal troubles for him. Bob believed Don was unethical and stole fighters from him. He believed Don stole Ali and Foreman, who both fought for Main Bouts and Top Rank, to fight for him in Zaire. Over the years they traded barbs on a regular basis. They really didn't like each other. This was not staged. The two last spoke on Arum's ninetieth birthday. King, who is three months older than Arum, called to wish him well and tell him he was hosting a dinner in his honor. They both found it funny that they—two of the last living important links to the golden age of boxing in this country, from Ali to Tyson—had lived this long.

"We communicate, but not all the time," Arum says of King. "I mean, he infuriates me now, only because of the politics. He's such a Trump guy."

Bob Arum's accomplishments are so impressive that I believe they will never be repeated. His six decades in boxing are the greatest sign of his pedigree. But Don King has his own impressive list of accomplishments and "firsts":[2]

1. Promoted more than five hundred world championship fights
2. Paid nearly one hundred boxers $1 million or more in a purse.
3. Promoted or copromoted half of the top-ten pay-per-view events of all time.
4. Promoted or copromoted ten of the top grossing events of all time.
5. First to guarantee a $10-million purse (Rumble in the Jungle)
6. First to receive $1 million for a network match (May 16, 1975—Ali versus Lyle)
7. First to receive $2 million for a network match (November 5, 1977—Norton versus Young)
8. First to generate a $6-million gate (October 2, 1980—Holmes versus Ali at Caesars)
9. First to guarantee a boxer $10 million (June 20, 1980—Leonard, when he faced Duran)
10. First to pay a Featherweight $1 million (August 21, 1981—Salvador Sanchez, when he faced Gomez)
11. First to generate an $8-million gate (June 11, 1982—Holmes versus Cooney at Caesars)
12. First, and only, promoter to stage forty-seven world championships in a single year (1994)

The last fight for Arum and King together was between José Ramírez and Amir Imam in March 2018. In March 2011, seven years earlier to the day, Top Rank's Miguel Cotto fought Don King Productions' Ricardo Mayorga for the WBA super world super welterweight championship. Yes, this was the real title of the fight and demonstrates one of the problems with the boxing associations.

This was the first time an Arum fighter had met a King fighter since the two fights that ended the decade of the nineties. In September 1999, Oscar De La Hoya lost to Félix Trinidad at the Mandalay Bay Casino, and the next year in September, Julio César Chávez Sr. faced Oscar De La Hoya at the UNLV Thomas & Mack Center in Las Vegas. At the press conference after Trinidad upset De La Hoya, King went on a long rant about his own victory over Bob Arum. "The lights are out in Arumville," King said. He went on and on with no end in sight. A Top Rank press person pulled the plug on what Bob called "bellowing." Don called it censorship and said it got him some more attention. "Bob is my best promoter," Don added.

Don did have a habit of being long-winded. After a two-hour press conference where Don spoke about everything under the sun, one of boxing's premier journalists, Kevin Iole, wrote, "We were subjected to the incoherent blathering of the long[-]winded King." I've always loved that line.

In 1996 or 1997, Jimmy Binns, a Philadelphia lawyer and mouthpiece for the WBA, introduced Don in my favorite introduction of all time. Before a packed house of hundreds of people, Jimmy said, "Unaccustomed as he is to public speaking, Don King has reluctantly agreed to say a few words." Sarcasm at its finest.

In the lead up to Cotto versus Mayorga, we were in New York on a press tour. My video crew for Top Rank was slated to interview Bob, and later, Don King in the same room. I suggested, and was told that it was impossible, that we have Bob for thirty minutes, both together for thirty minutes, and then Don alone for thirty minutes. I said I'd like to try to arrange it. I asked both men and both told me "no problem." It was to promote the fight, and both men knew instinctively the promotional value of the meeting. When they got together after Bob's initial interview, I asked some softball questions first about the event, then went for the red meat. "Everyone thinks you both hate each other; how real is that image?"

Bob answered first that, "Don and I have a long history. We both promoted competing big events, but we can do business together."

"Yes," Don chimed in, "I'll do business with anyone, even this guy," then launched into a belly laugh.

"Do you remember," Bob asked Don, "the time you tried to get into my ring at Caesars Palace at the Leonard-Hagler fight? I had to grab you and wound up ripping your jacket."

"You finally admit that," King said. "Now I can sue you."

The reason Arum grabbed Don, keeping him from the ring after Leonard-Hagler, was because in 1978 when Ali defeated Leon Spinks in a tough fifteen-round fight to become the three-time heavyweight champion, Bob was sitting ringside and watched in amazement as King went into the ring and held up Ali's arm, also getting photographed in a picture that was seen around the world. King had nothing to do with the fight.

The photo of me with Don and Bob together, on the back cover, was from that Cotto-Mayorga press day. After the interview together, I suggested to the photographer that he stand by, and I asked the men to shake hands for a photo. Bob rolled his eyes but then did it anyway. They made a big gesture of shaking hands with big smiles. The photographer said he did better with that picture, getting world-wide requests, than almost any other he had ever shot.

Now, however, in semiretirement, both men also have kind words for each other, intermingled with a few barbs embedded in the compliments. Bob has said that King was a great promoter despite promoting himself more than his fighters. He also says he worked harder because of King and made sure people knew how he took care of his fighters because he couldn't condone shorting his fighters like King did.

For his part, Don King said that Bob made him work harder, too. He said people would only know how great he was because they compared him with Arum.

"If you're an athlete and you roll over an inferior opponent, it doesn't enhance you. Don was a worthy opponent," Arum said. "There's never been a better salesman in boxing than Don King. He was my measuring stick. He was a guy who made me work so hard. I think he made me a better promoter just like I made him a better one."[3]

In an ESPN interview in 2018, Arum said, "We're like old warriors, old fighters who are reliving our old battles. My feelings for him are like two fighters who have been through wars against each other and now that the wars are over, they have shared memories of the wars. It doesn't necessarily make us friends or enemies, but it makes us people who have had shared experiences."[4] King once referred to Arum as "the master of trickeration" and "the prince of eviality."

"King was a pussycat to deal with," Arum said. "Once the deal was done, he didn't interfere."[5]

When King was asked about today's fighters, he said, "These guys are not dedicated and committed to the sport like the older guys were. They all want to read the headlines, and when you go out and extol them virtuously and say things about them, they believe the things to the extent they don't have to do nothing. They believe it's going to be like osmosis; it's going to fall from the sky."[6]

Shortly after HBO aired its docudrama on King, *Only in America*, he said, "Let me write it down for you. Muhammad Ali is a multimillionaire. Larry

Holmes a multimillionaire. Mike Tyson, he sleeps on a bed of money. HBO, I made you motherfuckers a fortune. Oh, I could go on and on. You love my black ass! You know why? Because I'm exciting. You ain't making no movie on Bob Arum, are you? It's entertainment, baby! That's all! Heroes and villains, angels and devils, shit, if you didn't have Don King you would have to invent him. And for all of you out there saying this and that, remember this: many fighters step into the ring, but only one is still King.

"I'm the best promoter in the world because I haven't taken a day off work since I left the penitentiary, and because I have read all the great philosophers like St. Thomas Aquinine (*sic*).

"Martin Luther King took us to the mountain top: I want to take us to the bank. I'm not fighting the Civil War, I'm fighting the poverty war."[7]

In 2015 after Wladimir Klitschko failed to generate a sellout at Madison Square Garden for his eighteenth title defense, Arum was asked if boxing's slow decline in the United States is due to most potential young fighters finding other avenues, like the NFL, for their talents. Bob summed it up by saying, "Boxing is often for poor people who don't have any other alternative to make their way in life. We can't get white middle-class kids into boxing. Let's be honest: No parent in their right mind is going to let them come to a gym. I wouldn't let my kid go into boxing."[8]

When I look back on my nearly thirty years in boxing, I realize what a great deal I've learned from both Don King and Bob Arum. I didn't adopt everything I learned from them, but I learned from watching them and used what I thought best suited me to grow and get better at my job and life in general. The main thing I learned is that I couldn't possibly do what they did. I'm lacking almost all the job skills necessary to be a promoter: remarkable intelligence; willingness to work around the clock; ability to negotiate with anyone regardless of their résumé; ability to work with people I detest; ability to be interviewed anywhere, anytime, with the right answers and the confidence to always appear in control of the situation; and an iron constitution that allows one to get up again when you've been knocked down and many have counted you out. Did I mention that you also need the thickest skin on the planet?

Don taught me to look at things in different ways. When he seems to be boxed in, he pivots to the side and comes at you from an angle you didn't expect. One day at the office in Deerfield Beach, Don had his twelve-cylinder Mercedes and a huge Bentley, both of which had to get up to his home in Palm Beach. He asked me to follow him in the brand-new Bentley. It was the most expensive thing I've ever driven. The car, possibly a limousine, had huge balloon tires. It drove with a very "swishy" ride because of the tires. It made me very nervous. When we arrived at his home, he asked me how I liked it. I told him the "swishy" ride from those tires made it difficult to drive. He said, "I didn't buy the damn thing to drive it!" I hadn't thought that through, of course. Don taught me to think twice before answering. He also taught me how to negotiate. The art of negotiation, like diplomacy, is letting them get your way.

Bob Arum taught me to be straight and direct with everyone. He is a no-bullshit guy who tells you exactly what he thinks of your ideas. Bob also taught me, which is the opposite of Don King, to surround yourself with good people and trust them to do their jobs. If you must be involved in everything, you can't do as much; and if you're not available, nothing gets done.

Bob was asked a few years ago if he considered retirement. "Why should I quit?" Bob answered. "As long as I can talk and get on a plane I'm going to keep working."[9] "I love what I do. We've got exciting young fighters who are already world champions or are going to be soon. I'm having a blast." And with his successor, Todd duBoef, already handling the business and absorbing many of the headaches in the promoting world, why not keep on as the face of Top Rank.

As our twenty-sixth president, Teddy Roosevelt, said, "It is not the critic who counts: not the man who points out how the strong man stumbles or where the doer of deeds could have done better. The credit belongs to the man who is actually in the arena, whose face is marred by dust and sweat and blood, who strives valiantly, who errs and comes up short again and again, because there is no effort without error or shortcoming, but who knows the great enthusiasms, the great devotions, who spends himself for a worthy cause; who, at the best, knows, in the end, the triumph of high achievement, and who, at the worst, if he fails at least he fails while daring greatly, so that this place shall never be with those cold and timid souls who knew neither victory nor defeat."

ENDNOTES

CHAPTER 1

1 Arthur Krystal, Ron Oliver, and Jeffrey Thomas Sammons, "Boxing, History, Early Years," *Encyclopedia Britannica*.

2 Tracy Callis, "James Corbett," February 18, 1933, *Cyberboxingzone.com*, 2006.

3 Barak Orbach, "Prizefighting and the Birth of Movie Censorship," June 25, 2014.

4 Parmalee, "Top Rank Boxing Debuted on ESPN 40 Years Ago," *Fightnews.com*, April 10, 2020.

5 John Maynard, "George Michael to Step Down as Sports Anchor," *Washington Post*, November 16, 2006.

6 Kevin Patra, "Superbowl XLIX's Most-Watched Show in US History," *NFL.com*, February 2, 2015.

7 Tim Dahlberg, "50 Million Could Watch Mayweather–MacGregor in U.S. Alone," Associated Press, August 22, 2017.

8 Cork Gaines, "The Mayweather–Pacquiao Fight Numbers Are In. They Shattered Expectations by Tens of Millions of Dollars," *Business Insider*, May 12, 2015.

9 Timothy Rapp, "Mayweather vs Pacquiao Reportedly Generated 600 Million in Revenue," *Bleacher Report*, June 10, 2015.

10 "Boxing Styles," *ArgosSummitBoxing.com*, July 5, 2013.

11 Gilbert Rogin, "Mister Boxing Himself," *Sports Illustrated*, August 6, 1962.

12 "A Comeback for the Sweet Science," *Forbes*, November 12, 1979.

13   Alex Reid, "Only in America," *TalkSport*, June 9, 2022.
14   Steve Farhood, "Boxing Broadcast Firsts," *New York Times*, April 24, 2015.
15   Fredrick A. Kugel, *Television*, 1965, 78.
16   Bill Lee, "Zaire's Fight Promotion Opens New Gold Mines," *Morning Herald*, November 18, 1974.
17   John Cassidy, "We Need Real Competition, Not a Cable-Internet Monopoly," *New Yorker*, February 13, 2014.

CHAPTER 2

1   Kevin Iole, "Bob Arum: How Don King Swindled 2.5 Million from Me," *Yahoo Sports*, April 1, 2016.
2   Kevin Iole, "Bob Arum Explains Infamous 'Yesterday I Was Lying Today I'm Telling the Truth' Line," *Yahoo Sports*, March 29, 2016.
3   Phil Berger, "Boxing Notebook. A Tyson HBO Deal That Wasn't," *New York Times*, December 12, 1990.
4   Alan Goldstein, "I'm No Palooka," *Baltimore Sun*, August 18, 1995.
5   J. Russell Peltz, *Thirty Dollars and a Cut Eye*, self-published, 2021.
6   Scouting, "Now a Gentleman," *New York Times*, July 22, 1987.
7   Roberto José Andrade Franco, "Top Rank's Bob Arum Is Still the Boss of All Bosses," *ESPN*, April 29, 2022.
8   Michael Katz, "Brenner Makes Imperfect Match," *New York Times*, June 3, 1980.
9   Katz, "Brenner Makes Imperfect Match."
10   Dave Anderson, "Harold Smith: Man and His Money Remain a Mystery," *New York Times*, February 8, 1981.
11   Jerrold K. Footlick with David T. Friendly, "Boxing's Biggest Scam," *Newsweek*, February 16, 1981.

CHAPTER 3

1   John Kifner, "A Boy's Death Ignites Clashes in Crown Heights," *New York Times*, August 21, 1991.
2   Kevin Iole, "How NFL Legend Jim Brown Pushed Bob Arum into Boxing," *Yahoo Sports*, March 28, 2016.
3   K. R. Keyser, "The Death of a Son," *Good Words and Works*, November 15, 2010.
4   T. J. Simers, "The Toughest Time for Arum," *Los Angeles Times*, October 23, 2010.

5 Mike Puma, "Only in America," *ESPN Sportscenter Biography*.

6 Luke Norris, "More Articles: Boxing," *Sportscasting*, December 31, 2020.

7 Jack Newfield, *Only in America: The Life and Crimes of Don King* (New York: William Morrow, 1995).

8 E. J. Kisell and W. Joseph Campbell, "Birns Is Bomb Victim," *Cleveland.com*, March 30, 1975.

9 Rick Porrello, "Kill the Irishman," *Next Hat Press*, April 11, 2011.

10 Brynley Louise, "The Truth about Don King," *News Daily*, April 30, 2020.

11 Mark Kram, "Introducing, in the Back Room, the Man with a Package," *Sports Illustrated*, January 28, 1974.

12 Ira Berkow, "Arum Is Proven Ringmaster," *New York Times*, April 7, 1987.

13 Gilbert Rogin, "The Facts about the Big Fight," *Sports Illustrated*, October 8, 1962.

14 Steve Carp, "50 Years of Boxing and Bob Arum Is Still Having Fun," *Las Vegas Review Journal*, March 26, 2016.

15 Roberto José Andrade Franco, "Top Rank's Bob Arum Is Still the Boss of All Bosses," *ESPN*, April 29, 2022.

16 Andrade Franco, "Top Rank's Bob Arum Is Still the Boss of All Bosses."

CHAPTER 4

1 Michael Woods, "Bob Arum, the Best Ever to This Point," *The Ring*, April 15, 2023.

2 David Giddens, "Ali vs Chuvalo," *CBC Sports*, March 24, 2016.

3 Giddens, "Ali vs Chuvalo."

4 Dave Skretta, "Book Smart and Street Smart. Arum at Top of Boxing," Associated Press, November 7, 2009.

5 Mark Kram, "Introducing, in the Back Room, the Man with a Package," *Sports Illustrated*, January 28, 1974.

6 Kram, "Introducing, in the Back Room, the Man with a Package."

7 Roberto José Andrade Franco, "Top Rank's Bob Arum Is Still the Boss of All Bosses," *ESPN*, April 29, 2022.

8 Kram, "Introducing, in the Back Room, the Man with a Package. 4

9 Gaston Kroub, "Three Lessons from Lawyer Bob Arum," *Above the Law*, February 26, 2019.

10 Dave Anderson, "The Marcos Thrilla," *New York Times*, March 10, 1986.

11 Anderson, "The Marcos Thrilla."

12 Anderson, "The Marcos Thrilla."

13 Dave Anderson, *In the Corner* (New York: William Morrow, 1991), 288.

14 Thomas Hauser, "The Unforgiven," *The Guardian*, September 3, 2005.

15 "Joe Frazier," *Daily Telegraph*, November 8, 2011.

16 "Karriem Allah. Black Belt," *Active Interest Media*, 35 1976.

17 "54 Facts You Probably Don't Know about Don King," *Boxing News 24*, January 14, 2008.

18 Kram, "Introducing, in the Back Room, the Man with a Package."

19 Michael Rosenthal, "Bob Arum on Leon Spinks' Upset of Muhammed Ali," *Boxing Junkie*, February 6, 2021.

20 Felix Dennis and Don Atyeo, *Muhammad Ali: The Glory Years* (New York: Miramax, 2003).

21 Peter Bonventre, "Palookaville, U.S.A.," *Newsweek*, November 5, 1979.

CHAPTER 5

1 Alex Reid, "Only in America," *TalkSport*, June 9, 2022.

2 "Muhammad Ali," Sports News, United Press International, February 3, 1981.

3 Wally Matthews, "At 86 Don King Is Semi-Retired But Still Working Every Angle," *New York Times*, November 3, 2017.

4 Kyle Dalton, "Where Is Don King Today?" *Sportscasting*, April 15, 2020.

5 Thomas Hauser, "Don King Still Longs for the Spotlight," *The Guardian*, June 14, 2023.

6 Mike Puma, "Only in America," *ESPN Sportscenter Biography*, June 8, 2011.

7 "The Only in America Man," *BoxingPosters.com*.

8 Paul Magno, "Looking Back at the Ring Magazine/Don King Scandal," *MaxBoxing.com*, January 4, 2018.

9 Roberto José Andrade Franco, "Top Rank's Bob Arum Is Still the Boss of all Bosses," *ESPN*, April 29, 2022.

10 Michael Katz, "Don King's Control Grows," *New York Times*, May 15, 1983.

11 Katz, "Don King's Control Grows."

CHAPTER 6

1 Thomas Hauser, "At 91 Don King Still Longs for the Spotlight," *The Guardian*, June 14, 2023.

2 Red Smith, "The Big Money behind Friday's Big Fight," *New York Times*, June 16, 1980.

3 Pete Axthelm, "The Matador and the Bull," *Newsweek*, June 23, 1980.

4 Declan Warrington," Roberto Duran Got under Sugar Ray's Skin," *Talk-Sport*, November 12, 2022.

5 Ray Monell, "Roberto Duran Tells the Real Story behind the 'No Mas' Bout," *New York Daily News*, August 25, 2016.

6 Steve Springer, "On the Ropes," *Los Angeles Times*, January 17, 2001.

7 Thom Greer, "Roberto Duran," *Knight-Ridder News Service*, August 4, 1982.

8 Joe Starita, "Friday Night Fever Fight," *Miami Herald*, November 12, 1982.

9 Anson Wainwright, "Best I Faced: Aaron Pryor," *The Ring*, October 10, 2016.

10 Kyle Dalton, "Where Is Don King Today?," *Sportscasting*, April 15, 2020.

11 Brynley Louise, "The Truth behind the Multiple Murders of Don King," *Film Daily*, April 30, 2020.

12 Hauser, "At 91 Don King Still Longs for the Spotlight."

13 Corina Knoll and Jeff Gottlieb, "AEG Pushed Michael Jackson to Perform," *Los Angeles Times*, April 29, 2013.

14 J. Randy Taraborrelli, *Michael Jackson: The Magic, The Madness, The Whole Story, 1958–2009* (New York: Grand Central, 2009).

15 Alex McCarthy, "The War," *TalkSport.com*, May 23, 2022.

16 Lance Pugmire,"I Had Never Seen Anything Like It," *The Athletic*, April 15, 2020.

17 Michael Katz, "Hearns Races toward Rematch with Hagler," *New York Times*, July 30, 1985.

18 Philip H. Dougherty, "Advertising: Generating Publicity for a Fight," *New York Times*, September 30, 1985.

19 Steven Crist, "Sports People, Well-Earned Bonus," *New York Times*, March 20, 1986.

20 Roberto José Andrade Franco, "Top Rank's Bob Arum Is Still Boss of All Bosses," *ESPN Magazine*, April 29, 2022.

21 Ira Berkow, "Leonard Beats Hagler for Title on Split Decision," *New York Times*, April 7, 1987.

22 Michael Katz, "Leonard Chooses Retirement after Finding Spark Is Gone," *New York Times*, May 13, 1984.

23 Dave Raffo, "Ray Leonard and Angelo Dundee, Who Have Been Together . . . ," United Press International, October 19, 1988.

24 Lee Cleveland, "The Fight Saga," *American Culture 24/7*, July 3, 2022.

25 Earl Gustkey, "Woman, 20, Is Fatally Shot in Hearns Home," *Los Angeles Times*, June 11, 1989.

CHAPTER 7

1 "Geezers at Caesars," *Orlando Sentinel*, January 9, 1990.
2 Richard O'Brian, "Douglas' Knockout of Tyson Still Resonates 20 Years Later," *Sports Illustrated*, February 11, 2010.
3 Bobby Brown and Nick Chiles, *Every Little Step: My Story* (New York: Dey Street Books, 2016).
4 Phil Berger, "Boxing Officials Could Overturn Defeat of Tyson," *New York Times*, February 12, 1990.
5 "Sports People—Trump Plans to Meet with Arum and Duva," *New York Times*, February 8, 1991.
6 Jeff Ryan, "Fat, Funny, and Forty Two, But Certainly No Fraud," *The Ring*, August 1991.
7 Luke Norris, "Why Tyson vs George Foreman Never Happened," *Sportscasting*, April 13, 2020.
8 Phil Berger, "Decision Goes to Barkley after a 12-Round Brawl," *New York Times*, March 21, 1992.
9 Pat Putnam, "Boring, Not Boxing," *Sports Illustrated*, June 29, 1992.
10 Diego Morilla, "Largest Audience for Boxing," *The Ring*, February 22, 2023.
11 Bernard Fernandez, "132,000 Plus. A Boxing Attendance Record Unlikely to Ever Be Broken," *Sweet Science*, February 17, 2020.
12 Fernandez, "132,000 Plus."
13 Graham Houston, "Chavez-Randall Upset Remembered," *Boxing Social*, May 11, 2022.
14 "Foreman Group Files Lawsuit," *New York Times*, August 16, 1994.
15 Tim Kawakami, "A Wild Week in Heavyweight Division," *Los Angeles Times*, November 7, 1994.
16 Mike Puma, "Only in America," *ESPN Sportscenter Biography*, 2016.

CHAPTER 8

1 Jay Caspian Kang, "The End and Don King," *Grantland*, April 4, 2013.
2 Michael Vitez, "De La Hoya Camp Says No Rematch," *Philadelphia Inquirer*, April 14, 1997.
3 Tom Friend, "Rematch? De La Hoya's Corner Says No," *New York Times*, April 14, 1997.

4   Wallace Matthews, "At 86 Don King is Semi-Retired But Still Working Every Angle," *New York Times*, November 3, 2017.

CHAPTER 9

1   William F. McNeil, *The Rise of Mike Tyson, Heavyweight* (Jefferson, NC: McFarland, 2014).
2   "Tyson's Sister Is Dead at 24," Associated Press, February 22, 1990.
3   Simon Hatterstone, "Mike Tyson: 'I'm Ashamed of So Many Things I've Done,'" *The Guardian*, March 21, 2009.
4   Mike Costello, "Mike Tyson Staying Clean But Still Sparring with Temptation," *BBC Sport*, December 18, 2013.
5   Mike Puma, "Sportscenter Biography: 'Iron Mike' Explosive In and Out of Ring," April 7, 2010.
6   Mike Tyson Quotes archived April 4, 2012, at the Wayback Machine.
7   Rob Tannenbaum, "Mike Tyson on Ditching Club Life and Getting Sober," *Rolling Stone*, December 4, 2013.
8   Puma, "Sportscenter Biography."
9   "Mike Tyson Net Worth," *NetWorthCity.com*, June 7, 2014.
10   Phil Berger, "Foreman and Tyson Book a Doubleheader," *New York Times*, May 1 1990.
11   "'Iron' Mike Tyson," *CyberBoxingZone.com*, April 27, 2007.
12   Joyce C. Oates, "Mike Tyson," *Life Magazine*, March 1987.
13   Samuel Pinnington, "Trevor Berbick—The Soldier of the Cross," February 4, 2007.
14   Graham Houston, "Which Fights Will Tyson Be Remembered For?"; Phil Berger, "Tyson Unifies W.B.C.-W.B.A. Titles," *New York Times*, March 8, 1987.
15   Phil Berger, "Tyson Retains Title In 7 Rounds," October 17, 1987.
16   David Christian, "Mike Tyson's Arching Uppercuts & Leaping Left Hooks Explained." *TheModernMartialArtist.com*, November 17, 2017.
17   Phil Berger, "Tyson Keeps Title With 3 Knockdowns in Fourth," *New York Times*, January 3, 1988.
18   Jake Donovan, "Crowning and Recognizing a Lineal Champion," *BoxingScene.com* February 16, 2009.
19   "Sports People: Boxing; King Accuses Cayton," *New York Times*, January 20, 1989.
20   Richmann, "What If Mike Tyson And Kevin Rooney Reunited?," *SaddoBoxing.com*, February 24, 2006.

21 "Sports People: Boxing; Tyson and Givens: Divorce Is Official," *New York Times*, June 2 1989.

22 Dan Rafael, "The Upset: Buster Melts Iron Mike,. *ESPN*, June 9, 2005.

23 Kevin Kincade, "The Moments: Mike Tyson vs Buster Douglas," *EastSide-Boxing.com*, July 12, 2005.

24 "The Top 10 Sporting Upsets." *Herald Sun*, January 13, 2021.

25 Lee Bellfield, "Buster Douglas–Mike Tyson," *SaddoBoxing.com*, February 16, 1990.

26 "Tyson's Thoughts on Loss to Douglas," *TheFightCity*.

27 Phil Berger, "Arum Testifies," *New York Times*, July 6, 1990.

28 Earl Gustkey, "Douglas Is Being Led Astray," *Los Angeles Times*, February 27, 1990.

29 Gustkey, "Douglas Is Being Led Astray."

30 Phil Berger, "Tyson Scores Round 1 Victory," *New York Times*, December 9, 1990.

31 Lee Bellfield, "March 1991—Mike Tyson vs. Razor Ruddock," *SaddoBoxing.com*, March 13, 2005.

32 Phil Berger, "Tyson Floors Ruddock Twice and Wins Rematch," *New York Times*, June 29, 1991.

33 E. R. Shipp, "Tyson Gets 6-Year Prison Term For Rape Conviction in Indiana," *New York Times*, March 27, 1992.

34 Dan Cancian, "The True Story of Mike Tyson's 1992 Rape Conviction," *Newsweek*, June 1, 2021.

35 E. R. Shipp, "Tyson Gets 6-Year Prison Term For Rape Conviction in Indiana," *New York Times*, March 27, 1992.

36 Dave Anderson, "The Tyson, Olajuwon Connection," *New York Times*, November 13, 1994.

37 David Usborne, "Tyson Gets a Hero's Welcome," *The Independent*, March 27, 1995.

38 "Record Numbers for Fight," *New York Times*, May 9, 2021.

39 Lee Bellfield, "Frank Bruno vs. Mike Tyson II," *SaddoBoxing.com*, March 19, 2005.

40 Staff and Wire Reports, "Money Gets Lewis Out of the Way for Tyson Fight," *Los Angeles Times*, May 17, 1996.

41 Frank Litsky, "Bronchitis D Stops Tyson; Seldon Fight Is Off," *New York Times*, July 4, 1996.

42 Mitra Anurag, *Sportskeeda.com*, January 31, 2021.

43 Sanjeev Shetty, "Holyfield Makes History," BBC *Sports*, December 26, 2001.

44   John Katsilometes, "Holyfield Knocks Fight Out of Tyson," *Las Vegas Review-Journal*, November 9, 1996.

45   Michael Carbert, "Tyson vs Holyfield," *TheFightCity*, November 9, 2021.

46   "Tyson Finalizes Divorce, Could Pay Ex $9 Million," *Jet*, February 3, 2003.

47   "Lane Late Replacement, Center of Action," *AP via Slam! Boxing*, June 29, 1997.

48   "Holyfield vs. Tyson—'Fight of the Times,'" *AP via Slam! Boxing*, June 29, 1997.

49   Andrew Lopez, "ESPN25: Sports Biggest Controversies," *ESPN*, May 27, 2006.

50   "Tyson DQd for Biting Holyfield," *AP via Slam! Boxing*, June 29, 1997.

51   "Tyson Banned for Life," *AP via Slam! Boxing*, July 9, 1997.

52   "Mike Tyson Timeline," *ESPN*, July 16, 2009.

53   Alex Reid, "Don King Went from Prison to Boxing's Biggest Promoter," *TalkSport*, June 9, 2022.

54   "Rusty Tyson Finds the Perfect Punch," *BBC News*, January 17, 1999.

55   "Tyson Jailed over Road Rage," *BBC News*, February 6, 1999.

56   Katherine Shaver, "Mike Tyson Gets 1 Year for Assault," *Washington Post*, February 6, 1999.

57   Royce Feour, "No-Contest; More Trouble," *Las Vegas Review Journal*, October 4, 1999.

58   Timothy W. Smith, "Tyson Is Cleared to Fight in Britain," *New York Times*, January 14, 2000.

59   "Tyson Lashes Out at Women's Group," *New York Times*, January 1, 2000.

60   "Tyson Fight Ends in Farce," *BBC Sport*, June 25, 2000.

61   Donald G. McRea, "Mike Tyson, Rags to Riches and Back to Rags." *Boxing Hype*, November 30, 2020.

62   James Slater, "Golota Stunned Onlookers," *Boxing News*, October 20, 2021.

63   John Gregg, "Iron Mike Makes Golota Quit," *BoxingTimes.com*, October 20, 2021.

64   "Tyson Tests Positive for Marijuana," Associated Press, January 1, 2001.

65   Bill Pennington, "Lots of Ifs, So Tyson Postpones June Bout," *New York Times*, May 9 2001.

66   Dan Rafael, "Tyson Angered by Alleged Remark by Nielsen," *ESPN*, October 13, 2001.

67 "Tyson Defeats Nielsen by KO in Sixth Round," *SE Missourian*, October 14, 2001,

68 Kyle Dalton, "Tyson Bit Lennox Lewis in Press Conference Brawl," *Sportscasting*, May 2, 2020.

69 "Tyson Media Circus Takes Center Stage," *ESPN.com*, January 2, 2002.

70 "Lewis Stuns Tyson for Famous Win," *BBC Sport*, June 9, 2002.

71 Thomas R. Umstead, "HBO Rings in a PPV Knockout," *Variety Group*, May 14, 2007.

72 Jake Elman, "A Cocaine Filled Night Cost Etienne His Reputation and His Freedom," *Sportscasting*, June 1, 2020.

73 "Tyson Knocks Out Etienne in 49 Seconds," *Sports Illustrated*, February 23, 2003.

74 Elman, "A Cocaine Filled Night."

75 "Tyson Files for Bankruptcy," *BBC Sport*, August 3, 2003.

76 *In re Michael G. Tyson*, Chapter 11 petition, August 1, 2003, case no. 03-41900-alg, U.S. Bankruptcy Court for the Southern District of New York.

77 Richard Sandomir, "Tyson's Bankruptcy Is a Lesson in Ways to Squander a Fortune," *New York Times*, August 5, 2003.

78 K-1 Reports Official Mike Tyson Fight, *TysonTalk.com*, April 17, 2020.

79 "Williams Shocks Tyson," *BBC*, July 31, 2004.

80 "Tyson Camp Blames Injury," *BBC Sports*, July 31, 2004.

81 "Tyson Quits Boxing after Defeat," *BBC Sports*, June 12, 2005.

82 Sammy Rozenberg, "Tyson Happy with Exhibition, Fans Are Not," *Boxing Scene*, January 2, 2013.

83 "Mike Tyson Pleads Guilty to Drug Possession," *Reuters*, September 24, 2015.

84 "Tyson Jailed on Drugs Charges," *BBC News*, May 29, 2009.

85 "Tyson's Daughter Dies after Accident, Police Say," *CNN*, May 27, 2009.

86 "Boxers Chavez, Tszyu and Tyson Elected to Int'l Boxing Hall of Fame," *Ibhof.com*, December 7, 2010.

87 Frank Scheck, "Mike Tyson: Undisputed Truth: Theater Review," August 8, 2012.

88 "Mike Tyson Cares Foundation," October 20, 2011.

89 Guilherme Cruz, "Coach Says Mike Tyson Aiming to Knock Out Roy Jones Jr. Despite Rules: 'No One Spars a Full Month for an Exhibition,'" *MMA Fighting*, January 10, 2022.

90 Guilherme Cruz, "Who Is Mike Tyson's Trainer Rafael Cordeiro?," *Sporting Excitement*, November 25, 2020.

91 "Mike Tyson's Premium Cannabis Brand Expands," Associated Press wire, July 14, 2022.

CHAPTER 10

1 Steve Springer, "Morales Brawls to Victory Over Powerful Barrera," *Los Angeles Times*, February 20, 2000.

2 "WBC Declares De La Hoya Welterweight Champion," *The Independent*, March 21, 2000.

3 Kevin Iole, "The Post Game," *Yahoo Sports*, August 13, 2001.

4 Steve Springer and Greg Krikorian, "US Drops Inquiry of Arum," *Los Angeles Times*, June 27, 2006.

5 Steve Springer and Greg Krikorian, "US Drops Inquiry of Arum," *Los Angeles Times*, June 27, 2006.

6 Mark Vester, "Manny Pacquiao Now a Top Rank Fighter," *Boxing Scene*, November 19, 2006.

7 David Berlin, "Boxing and the Law: Judah-Mayweather and Its Aftermath," *Sweet Science*, May 22, 2006.

8 Greg Bishop, "Boxing Iis Ready for a Re-birth, Again," *New York Times*, November 14, 2009.

9 Gareth Davies, "Manny Pacquiao," *Daily Telegraph*, November 16, 2009.

10 Greg Bishop, "Bob Arum Loses His Son," *New York Times*, November 11, 2010.

11 Dan Rafael, "Antonio Margarito to Have Surgery," *ESPN.com*, November 14, 2010.

12 Michael Katz, "Scouting," *New York Times*, April 5, 1985.

CHAPTER 11

1 Steve Carp, "50 Years of Boxing and Bob Arum Is Still Having Fun," *Las Vegas Review-Journal*, March 29, 2016.

2 Ron Borges, "Boxing Picture Is Fading Out on Network TV," *Boston Globe*, March 20, 1991.

3 Gaston Kroub, "Three Lessons from Bob Arum," *Above the Law*, February 26, 2019.

4 Tim Smith, "Seeking Headlines; Bob Arum Fights to Get Boxing in Newspapers," *Daily News*, June 13, 2009.

5 Dave Skretta, "Bob Arum," Associated Press, November 7, 2009.

6 Michael Rosenthal, "Arum's New Strategy," *The Ring*, March 10, 2010.

7 Richard Sandomir, "Pugilistic Throwback," *New York Times*, June 7, 1996.

8   Wallace Matthews, "At 86 Don King Is Semi-Retired but Still Working Every Angle," *New York Times*, November 3, 2017.

9   Alan Dawson, "Bob Arum, 88, Says He Might Die Before His Prospects Become Champions," *Business Insider*, January 8, 2020.

10   Matthews, "At 86 Don King Is Semi-Retired but Still Working Every Angle."

11   Carp, "50 Years of Boxing and Bob Arum Is Still Having Fun."

12   Dan Rafael, "ESPN and Top Rank Announce Historic Agreement," *ESPN*, August 2, 2018.

13   Robert Segal, "Bob Arum on Lomachenko," *Boxing News 24*, May 22, 2023.

CHAPTER 12

1   Roberto José Andrade Franco, "Top Rank's Bob Arum Is Still the Boss of All Bosses," *ESPN Magazine*, April 29, 2022.

2   "Bob Arum's Accomplishments," *Boxing News*, January 14, 2008.

3   Dan Rafael, "Bob Arum and Don King Go Head to Head Once Again," *ESPN*, March 16, 2018.

4   Rafael, "Bob Arum and Don King Go Head to Head Once Again."

5   Steve Carp, "50 Years of Boxing and Bob Arum Is Still Having Fun," *Las Vegas Review-Journal*, March 29, 2016.

6   Kyle Dalton, "Where Is Don King Today," *Sportscasting*, May 7, 2020.

7   From a live interview.

8   Joe Drape, "Boxing Struggles But It Has a Culture in Its Corner," *New York Times*, April 28, 2015.

9   Carp, "50 Years of Boxing and Bob Arum Is Still Having Fun."

BIBLIOGRAPHY

"54 Facts You Probably Don't Know about Don King." *Boxing News 24*, January 14, 2008.

"A Comeback for the Sweet Science." *Forbes*, November 12, 1979.

"Bob Arum's Accomplishments." *Boxing News*, January 14, 2008.

"Boxers Chavez, Tszyu and Tyson Elected to Int'l Boxing Hall of Fame." *Ibhof.com*, December 7, 2010.

"Boxing Styles." *ArgosSummitBoxing.com*, July 5, 2013.

"Foreman Group Files Lawsuit." *New York Times*, August 16, 1994.

"Geezers at Caesars." *Orlando Sentinel*, January 9, 1990.

"Holyfield vs. Tyson—'Fight of the Times.'" *AP via Slam! Boxing*.

"'Iron' Mike Tyson." *CyberBoxingZone.com*, April 27, 2007.

"Joe Frazier." *Daily Telegraph*, November 8, 2011.

"Karriem Allah. Black Belt." *Active Interest Media*, 351976.

"King Accuses Cayton." *New York Times*, January 20, 1989.

"Lane Late Replacement, Center of Action." *AP via Slam! Boxing*.

"Lewis Stuns Tyson for Famous Win." *BBC Sport*, June 9, 2002.

"Mike Tyson Cares Foundation." October 20, 2011.

"Mike Tyson Net Worth." *NetWorthCity.com*, June 7, 2014.

"Mike Tyson Pleads Guilty to Drug Possession." *Reuters*, September 24, 2015.

"Mike Tyson Timeline." *ESPN*, July 16, 2009.

"Mike Tyson's Premium Cannabis Brand Expands." Associated Press wire, July 14, 2022.

"Money Gets Lewis Out of the Way for Tyson Fight." *Los Angeles Times*, May 17, 1996.

"Muhammad Ali." *United Press International*, February 3, 1981.

"The Only in America Man." *BoxingPosters.com*.

"Record Numbers for Fight." *New York Times*, May 9, 2021.

"Rusty Tyson Finds the Perfect Punch." *BBC News*, January 17, 1999.

"Sports People—Trump Plans to Meet with Arum and Duva." *New York Times*, February 8, 1991.

"The Top 10 Sporting Upsets." *Herald Sun*.

"Tyson and Givens: Divorce Is Official." *New York Times*, June 2, 1989.

"Tyson Banned for Life." *AP via Slam! Boxing*, July 9, 1997.

"Tyson Camp Blames Injury." *BBC Sports*, July 31, 2004.

"Tyson Defeats Nielsen by KO in Sixth Round." *SE Missourian*, October 14, 2001.

"Tyson DQd for Biting Holyfield." *AP via Slam! Boxing*, June 29, 1997.

"Tyson Fight Ends in Farce." *BBC Sport*, June 25, 2000.

"Tyson Files for Bankruptcy." *BBC Sport*, August 3, 2003.

"Tyson Finalizes Divorce, Could Pay Ex $9 Million." *Jet*, 2003.

"Tyson Jailed on Drugs Charges." *BBC News*, May 29, 2009.

"Tyson Jailed over Road Rage." *BBC News*, February 6, 1999.

"Tyson Knocks Out Etienne in 49 Seconds." *Sports Illustrated*, February 23, 2003.

"Tyson Lashes Out at Women's Group." *New York Times*, January 1, 2000.

"Tyson Media Circus Takes Center Stage." *ESPN.com*, January 2, 2002.

"Tyson Quits Boxing after Defeat." *BBC Sport*, June 12, 2005.

"Tyson Tests Positive for Marijuana." Associated Press, January 1, 2001.

"Tyson's Daughter Dies after Accident, Police Say." *CNN*, May 27, 2009.

"Tyson's Sister Is Dead at 24." Associated Press, February 22, 1990.

"WBC Declares De La Hoya Welterweight Champion." *The Independent*, March 21, 2000.

"Williams Shocks Tyson." *BBC*, July 31, 2004.

Anderson, Dave. "Harold Smith: Man and His Money Remain a Mystery." *New York Times*, February 8, 1981.

———. *In the Corner* (New York: William Morrow, 1991), 288.

———. "The Marcos Thrilla." *New York Times*, March 10, 1986.

———. "The Tyson, Olajuwon Connection." *New York Times*, November 13, 1994.

Andrade Franco, Roberto José. "Top Rank's Bob Arum Is Still the Boss of All Bosses." *ESPN*, April 29, 2022.

Anurag, Mitra. *Sportskeeda.com*, January 31, 2021.

Axthelm, Pete. "The Matador and the Bull." *Newsweek*, June 23, 1980.

Bellfield, Lee. "Buster Douglas—Mike Tyson." *SaddoBoxing.com*, 1990.

———. "March 1991—Mike Tyson vs. Razor Ruddock." *SaddoBoxing.com*, March 13, 2005.

Berger, Phil. "Arum Testifies." *New York Times*, July 6, 1990.

———. "Boxing Notebook. A Tyson HBO Deal That Wasn't." *New York Times*, December 12, 1990.

———. "Boxing Officials Could Overturn Defeat of Tyson." *New York Times*, February 12, 1990.

———. "Decision Goes to Barkley after a 12-Round Brawl." *New York Times*, March 21, 1992.

———. "Foreman and Tyson Book a Doubleheader." *New York Times*, May 1, 1990.

———. "Tyson Floors Ruddock Twice and Wins Rematch." *New York Times*, June 29, 1991.

———. "Tyson Keeps Title With 3 Knockdowns in Fourth." *New York Times*, January 3, 1988.

———. "Tyson Retains Title in 7 Rounds." *New York Times*, 1987.

———. "Tyson Scores Round 1 Victory." *New York Times*, 1990.

———. "Tyson Unifies W.B.C.-W.B.A. Titles." *New York Times*, 1987.

Berkow, Ira. "Arum Is Proven Ringmaster." *New York Times*, April 7, 1987.

———. "Leonard Beats Hagler for Title on Split Decision." *New York Times*, April 7, 1987.

Berlin, David. "Boxing and the Law: Judah-Mayweather and Its Aftermath." *Sweet Science*, May 22, 2006.

Bishop, Greg. "Bob Arum Loses His Son." *New York Times*, November 11, 2010.

———. "Boxing Is Ready for a Re-birth, Again." *New York Times*, November 14, 2009.

Bonventre, Peter. "Palookaville, U.S.A." *Newsweek*, November 5, 1979.

Borges, Ron. "Boxing Picture Is Fading Out on Network TV." *Boston Globe*, March 20, 1991.

Brown, Bobby, and Nick Chiles. *Every Little Step: My Story* (New York: Dey Street Books, 2016).

Callis, Tracy. 2006. "James Corbett." *CyberBoxingZone.com*. From *Corbett*, February 18, 1933.

Cancian, Dan. "The True Story of Mike Tyson's 1992 Rape Conviction." *Newsweek*, June 1, 2021.

Carbert, Michael. "Tyson vs. Holyfield." *Fight City*, November 9, 2021.

Carp, Steve. "50 Years of Boxing and Bob Arum Is Still Having Fun." *Las Vegas Review Journal*, March 26, 2016.

Cassidy, John. "We Need Real Competition, Not a Cable-Internet Monopoly." *New Yorker*, February 13, 2014.

Christian, David. "Mike Tyson's Arching Uppercuts & Leaping Left Hooks Explained." *TheModernMartialArtist.com*, November 17, 2017.

Cleveland, Lee. "The Fight Saga." *American Culture 24/7*, July 3, 2022.

Costello, Mike. "Mike Tyson Staying Clean But Still Sparring with Temptation." *BBC Sport*, December 18, 2013.

Crist, Steven. "Sports People, Well-Earned Bonus." *New York Times*, March 20, 1986.

Cruz, Guilherme. "Coach Says Mike Tyson Aiming to Knock Out Roy Jones Jr. Despite Rules: 'No One Spars a Full Month for an Exhibition.'" *MMA Fighting*, January 10, 2022.

———. "Who Is Mike Tyson's Trainer Rafael Cordeiro?" *Sporting Excitement*, November 25, 2020.

Dahlberg, Tim. "50 Million Could Watch Mayweather–MacGregor in US Alone." Associated Press, August 22, 2017.

Dalton, Kyle. "Tyson Bit Lennox Lewis in Press Conference Brawl." *Sportscasting*, May 2, 2020.

———. "Where Is Don King Today?" *Sportscasting*, April 15, 2020.

———. "Where Is Don King Today?" *Sportscasting*, May 7, 2020.

Davies, Gareth. "Manny Pacquiao." *Daily Telegraph*, November 16, 2009.

Dawson, Alan. "Bob Arum, 88, Says He Might Die before His Prospects Become Champions." *Business Insider*, January 8, 2020.

Dennis, Felix, and Don Atyeo. *Muhammad Ali: The Glory Years*. (New York: Miramax, 2003).

Donovan, Jake. "Crowning and Recognizing a Lineal Champion." *BoxingScene.com*, February 16, 2009.

Dougherty, Philip H. "Advertising: Generating Publicity for a Fight." *New York Times*, September 30, 1985.

Drape, Joe. "Boxing Struggles But It Has a Culture in Its Corner." *New York Times*, April 28, 2015.

Elman, Jake. "A Cocaine Filled Night Cost Etienne His Reputation and His Freedom." June 1, 2020.

Farhood, Steve. "Boxing Broadcast Firsts." *New York Times*, April 24, 2015.

Feour, Royce. "No-Contest; More Trouble." October 4, 1999.

Fernandez, Bernard. "132,000 Plus. A Boxing Attendance Record Unlikely to Ever Be Broken." *Sweet Science*, February 17, 2020.

Footlick, Jerrold K., with David T. Friendly. "Boxing's Biggest Scam." *Newsweek*, February 16, 1981.

Friend, Tom. "Rematch? De La Hoya's Corner Says No." *New York Times*, April 14, 1997.

Gaines, Cork. "The Mayweather-Pacquiao Fight Numbers Are in. They Shattered Expectations by Tens of Millions of Dollars." *Business Insider*, May 12, 2015.

Giddens, David. "Ali vs Chuvalo." *CBC Sports*, March 24, 2016.

Goldstein, Alan. "I'm No Palooka." *Baltimore Sun*, August 18, 1995.

Greer, Thom. "Roberto Duran." *Knight-Ridder News Service*, August 4, 1982.

Gregg, John. "Iron Mike Makes Golota Quit." *BoxingTimes.com*, October 20, 2021.

Gustkey, Earl. "Douglas Is Being Led Astray." *Los Angeles Times*, February 27, 1990.

———. "Woman, 20, Is Fatally Shot in Hearns Home." *Los Angeles Times*, June 11, 1989.

Hatterstone, Simon. "Mike Tyson: 'I'm Ashamed of So Many Things I've Done.'" *The Guardian*, March 21, 2009.

Hauser, Thomas. "At 91 Don King Still Longs for the Spotlight." *The Guardian*, June 14, 2023.

———. "The Unforgiven." *The Guardian*, September 3, 2005.

Houston, Graham. "Chavez-Randall Upset Remembered." *Boxing Social*, May 11, 2022.

———. "Which Fights Will Tyson Be Remembered for?" *ESPN*, October 23, 2008.

In re Michael G. Tyson, Chapter 11 petition, August 1, 2003, case no. 03-41900-alg, U.S. Bankruptcy Court for the Southern District of New York.

Iole, Kevin. "Bob Arum Explains Infamous 'Yesterday I Was Lying Today I'm Telling the Truth Line.'" *Yahoo Sports*, March 29, 2016.

———. "Bob Arum: How Don King Swindled 2.5 Million from Me." *Yahoo Sports*, April 1, 2016.

———. "How NFL Legend Jim Brown Pushed Bob Arum into Boxing." *Yahoo Sports*, March 28, 2016.

———. "The Post Game." *Yahoo Sports*, August 13, 2001.

K-1 Reports Official Mike Tyson Fight. *TysonTalk.com.*

Kang, Jay Caspian. "The End and Don King." *Grantland*, April 4, 2013.

Katsilometes, John. "Holyfield Knocks Fight out of Tyson." *Las Vegas Review-Journal*, November 9, 1996.

Katz, Michael. "Brenner Makes Imperfect Match." *New York Times*, June 3, 1980.

———. "Don King's Control Grows." *New York Times*, May 15, 1983.

———. "Hearns Races toward Rematch with Hagler." *New York Times*, July 30, 1985.

———. "Leonard Chooses Retirement after Finding Spark Is Gone." *New York Times*, May 13, 1984.

———. "Scouting." *New York Times*, April 5, 1985.

Kawakami, Tim. "A Wild Week in Heavyweight Division." *Los Angeles Times*, November 7, 1994.

Keyser, K. R. "The Death of a Son." *Good Words and Works*, November 15, 2010.

Kifner, John. "A Boy's Death Ignites Clashes in Crown Heights." *New York Times*, August 21, 1991.

Kincade, Kevin. "The Moments: Mike Tyson vs. Buster Douglas." *EastSideBoxing.com.*

Kisell, E. J., and W. Joseph Campbell. "Birns Is Bomb Victim." *Cleveland.com*, March 30, 1975.

Knoll, Corina, and Jeff Gottlieb. "AEG Pushed Michael Jackson to Perform." *Los Angeles Times*, April 29, 2013.

Kram, Mark. "Introducing, in the Back Room, The Man with a Package." *Sports Illustrated*, January 28, 1974.

Kroub, Gaston. "Three Lessons from Lawyer Bob Arum." *Above the Law*, February 26, 2019.

Krystal, Arthur, Ron Oliver, and Jeffrey Thomas Sammons. "Boxing, History, Early Years." *Encyclopedia Britannica*, www.britannica.com/sports/boxing.

Kugel, Fredrick A. *Television* (1965), 78.

Lee, Bill. "Zaire's Fight Promotion Opens New Gold Mines." *Morning Herald*, November 18, 1974.

Litsky, Frank. "Bronchitis D Stops Tyson; Seldon Fight Is Off." *New York Times*, July 4, 1996.

Lopez, Andrew. "ESPN25: Sports Biggest Controversies." *ESPN*, May 27, 2006.

Louise, Brynley. "The Truth about Don King." *News Daily*, April 30, 2020.

———. "The Truth behind the Multiple Murders of Don King." *Film Daily*, April 30, 2020.

Magno, Paul. "Looking Back at the Ring Magazine/Don King Scandal." *MaxBoxing .com*, January 4, 2018.

Matthews, Wally. "At 86 Don King Is Semi-Retired but Still Working Every Angle." *New York Times*, November 3, 2017.

Maynard, John. "George Michael to Step Down as Sports Anchor." *Washington Post*, November 16, 2006.

McCarthy, Alex. "The War." *TalkSport.com*, May 23, 2022.

McCormick, Eliott. "The Legacy of Douglas vs. Tyson." *TheFightCity*, February 12, 2024.

McNeil, William F. *The Rise of Mike Tyson, Heavyweight* (Jefferson, NC: McFarland, 2014).

McRea, Donald G. "Mike Tyson, Rags to Riches and Back to Rags." *Boxing Hype*, November 30, 2020.

Mike Tyson Quotes archived April 4, 2012, at the Wayback Machine.

Monell, Ray. "Roberto Duran Tells the Real Story behind the 'No Mas' Bout." *New York Daily News*, August 25, 2016.

Morilla, Diego. "Largest Audience for Boxing." *The Ring*, February 22, 2023.

Newfield, Jack. *Only in America: The Life and Crimes of Don King* (New York: William Morrow, 1995).

Norris, Luke. "More Articles: Boxing." *Sportscasting*, December 31, 2020.

———. "Why Tyson vs George Foreman Never Happened." *Sportscasting*, April 13, 2020.

O'Brian, Richard. "Douglas' Knockout of Tyson Still Resonates 20 Years Later." *Sports Illustrated*, February 11, 2010.

Oates, Joyce C. "Mike Tyson." *Life Magazine*, March 1987.

Orbach, Barak. "Prizefighting and the Birth of Movie Censorship." *Yale Journal of Law & the Humanities*, June 25, 2014.

Parmalee. "Top Rank Boxing Debuted on ESPN 40 Years Ago." *FightNews.com*, April 10, 2020.

Patra, Kevin. "Superbowl XLIX's Most-Watched Show in US History." *NFL.com*, February 2, 2015.

Peltz, J. Russell. *Thirty Dollars and a Cut Eye*. Self-published, 2021.

Pennington, Bill. "Lots of Ifs, So Tyson Postpones June Bout." *New York Times*, May 9, 2001.

Pinnington, Samuel. "Trevor Berbick—The Soldier of the Cross." February 4, 2007.

Porrello, Rick. "Kill the Irishman," *Next Hat Press*, April 11, 2011.

Pugmire, Lance. "I Had Never Seen Anything Like It." *The Athletic*, April 15, 2020.

Puma, Mike. "Only in America." *ESPN Sportscenter Biography*, June 8, 2011.

———. "Sportscenter Biography: 'Iron Mike' Explosive In and Out of Ring." April 7, 2010.

Putnam, Pat. "Boring, Not Boxing." *Sports Illustrated*, June 29, 1992.

Rafael, Dan. "Antonio Margarito to Have Surgery." *ESPN.com*, November 14, 2010.

———. "Bob Arum and Don King Go Head to Head—Once Again." *ESPN*, March 16, 2018.

———. "ESPN and Top Rank Announce Historic Agreement." *ESPN*, August 2, 2018.

———. "Tyson Angered by Alleged Remark by Nielsen." *ESPN*, October 13, 2001.

———. "The Upset: Buster Melts Iron Mike." *ESPN*, June 9, 2005.

Raffo, Dave. "Ray Leonard and Angelo Dundee, Who Have Been Together . . ." United Press International, October 19, 1988.

Rapp, Timothy. "Mayweather vs Pacquiao Reportedly Generated 600 Million in Revenue." *Bleacher Report*, June 10, 2015.

Reid, Alex. "Don King Went from Prison to Boxing's Biggest Promoter." *TalkSport*, June 9, 2022.

———. "Only in America." *TalkSport*, June 9, 2022.

Richmann. "What If Mike Tyson and Kevin Rooney Reunited?" *SaddoBoxing.com*, February 24, 2006.

Rogin, Gilbert. "The Facts about the Big Fight." *Sports Illustrated*, October 8, 1962.

———. "Mister Boxing Himself." *Sports Illustrated*, August 6, 1962.

Rosenthal, Michael. "Arum's New Strategy." *The Ring*, March 10, 2010.

———. "Bob Arum on Leon Spinks' Upset of Muhammed Ali." *Boxing Junkie*, February 6, 2021.

Rozenberg, Sammy. "Tyson Happy with Exhibition, Fans Are Not." *Boxing Scene*, January 2, 2013.

Ryan, Jeff. "Fat, Funny, and Forty Two, But Certainly No Fraud." *The Ring*, August 1991.

Sandomir, Richard. "Pugilistic Throwback." *New York Times*, June 7, 1996.

———. "Tyson's Bankruptcy Is a Lesson in Ways to Squander a Fortune." *New York Times*, August 5, 2003.

Scheck, Frank. "Mike Tyson: Undisputed Truth: Theater Review." August 8, 2012.

Scouting, "Now a Gentleman." *New York Times*, July 22, 1987.

Segal, Robert. "Bob Arum on Lomachenko." *Boxing News 24*, May 22, 2023.

Shaver, Katherine. "Mike Tyson Gets 1 Year for Assault." *Washington Post*, February 6, 1999.

Shetty, Sanjeev. "Holyfield Makes History." *BBC Sports*.

Shipp, E. R. "Tyson Gets 6-Year Prison Term for Rape Conviction in Indiana." *New York Times*, March 27, 1992.

Simers, T. J. "The Toughest Time for Arum." *Los Angeles Times*, October 23, 2010.

Skretta, Dave. "Bob Arum." Associated Press, November 7, 2009.

———. "Book Smart and Street Smart. Arum at Top of Boxing." Associated Press, November 7, 2009.

Slater, James. "Golota Stunned Onlookers." *Boxing News*, October 20, 2021.

Smith, Red. "The Big Money behind Friday's Big Fight." *New York Times*, June 16, 1980.

Smith, Tim. "Seeking Headlines; Bob Arum Fights to Get Boxing in Newspapers." *Daily News*, June 13, 2009.

Smith, Timothy W. "Tyson Is Cleared to Fight in Britain." *New York Times*, January 14, 2000.

Springer, Steve. "Morales Brawls to Victory over Powerful Barrera." *Los Angeles Times*, February 20, 2000.

———. "On the Ropes." *Los Angeles Times*, January 17, 2001.

Springer, Steve, and Greg Krikorian. "US Drops Inquiry of Arum." *Los Angeles Times*, June 27, 2006.

Starita, Joe. "Friday Night Fever Fight." *Miami Herald*, November 12, 1982.

Tannenbaum, Rob. "Mike Tyson on Ditching Club Life and Getting Sober." *Rolling Stone*, December 4, 2013.

Taraborrelli, J. Randy. *Michael Jackson: The Magic, The Madness, The Whole Story, 1958–2009* (New York: Grand Central, 2009).

Umstead, Thomas R. "HBO Rings in a PPV Knockout." *Variety Group*, May 14, 2007.

Usborne, David. "Tyson Gets a Hero's Welcome." *The Independent*, March 27, 1995.

Vester, Mark. "Manny Pacquiao Now a Top Rank Fighter." *Boxing Scene*, November 19, 2006.

Vitez, Michael. "De La Hoya Camp Says No Rematch." *Philadelphia Inquirer*, April 14, 1997.

Wainwright, Anson. "Best I Faced: Aaron Pryor." *The Ring*, October 10, 2016.

Warrington, Declan. "Roberto Duran Got under Sugar Ray's Skin." *TalkSport*, November 12, 2022.

Woods, Michael. "Bob Arum, The Best Ever to This Point." *The Ring*, April 15, 2023.

INDEX

FIGHT INDEX

ABOUT THE AUTHOR

Marty Corwin is a television producer and director who has covered live televised sports for more than forty-five years. After a decade covering NBA, NHL, and MLB for Viacom/Paramount, Marty has been covering boxing since 1993, first as vice president of television for Don King and for the past twenty-five years as director of television production for Top Rank.

www.ingramcontent.com/pod-product-compliance
Lightning Source LLC
Chambersburg PA
CBHW030305100426
42812CB00002B/571